HONG KONG & CHINA GAS CHINESE COOKBOOK

HONG KONG & CHINA GAS CHINESE COOKBOOK

Special Editorial Consultant

T. C. Lai

Editorial Consultant

Jane Ram

Edited By

David W. Perkins

Designed By

Peter C. Cook

Published for The Hong Kong & China Gas Co., Limited by
Pat Printer Associates Limited
Hong Kong, 1978

This book was designed and published for The Hong Kong &
China Gas Co., Limited by Pat Printer Associates Limited, 69
Wyndham Street, Hong Kong.

Printed by Paramount Printing Co., Ltd., 499 King's Road,
North Point, Hong Kong.

Colour separations by Tenon & Polert, Hong Kong, and Dai-
Ichi Seihan Co., (Hong Kong) Ltd.

Filmsetting in Garamond by Phototype Limited, Hong Kong.

Photographs by Raymond Wong, Benno Gross and Leong Ka
Tai, especially commissioned for this book.

Printed in Hong Kong.

Contents

Photo: Hugh Van Es

"The art of Chinese cooking," according to my venerated Chinese gourmet-mentor, Master James Wei (whom I seem to meet wherever the best Chinese food is served), "is to make the meat taste like vegetables and the vegetables taste like meat, without either the meat or the vegetables losing their original texture."

The Master will read this book, I know, with respect and admiration — but perhaps with that occasional specialist dissent which French wine-tasters display in their earnest and personalised sampling of new and old grape varieties ("east or west side of the vineyard, would you say?")

For example, he would insist, I suspect, that Honan should still be separated from the northern (Peking-Shantung) region as a fifth major school of regional Chinese cooking, because, in his and other classicists' opinion, Honan's Yellow River carp is uniquely localised and should not be incorporated with Shantung's steamed bread and dumplings and Peking duck and barbecued meat. (That is the sort of argument which delights if bemuses foreign-devil gluttons at perfect Chinese banquets, especially if the explosive *Kaoliang*

liqueur has followed the warm, encouraging *Shaohsing* wine.)

Anyway, this study will help to stifle some of those adhesive and spurious myths about Chinese food. There is, for example, the tedious myth: "One hour after a Chinese meal you want another Chinese meal." Perhaps a Western gourmand who customarily on cheeseburgers feeds, and drinks the milk of Bass, will feel unbloated after the manifold variety of a *dim-sum* lunch. But anyone who has been treated to a normal Chinese dinner, built around, say, Szechwan smoked duck and steamed bread, and later complained of premature hunger would be an abominably valiant trencherman. The Chinese do not stuff their bellies today for tomorrow's ache, but they know the best stuffing and flavours for most bellies — today and tomorrow.

Most of the myths, of course, raise venerable but hopeful heads above the mirages of virility and seduction. These we may skirt with heightened colour and averted eye, noting only that the viands and sauces of reputed restoration or stimulation are, happily, always a delight to the palate, on the short run; even if, unhappily, they disappoint the libido, on the long stand. The mythical elixirs include not only rhinoceros horn, bird's nest soup, monkey's brains and "gold-and-silver flowers" — those esoteric standbys and stand-ups — but also such familiar staples as "drunken shrimps", snapping turtle, eels-and-garlic, snake-blood and of course aconite, that sturdy, long-brown plant-friend.

Hong Kong boasts the widest-varied selection of Chinese dishes anywhere — in excellent restaurants easily accessible from all central hotels (most of which also have their own first-class Chinese dining-rooms). The food can be expensive or most reasonable. (Foreign-devil visitors to Peking, Shanghai and Canton, it should be added, always get preferential booking and service in restaurants there.)

Uniquely in the world, Japanese travel agencies are organising group tours in Hong Kong which give eating priority over sightseeing and/or shopping. Over two days, four "imperial banquets" are included in the overall cost of the tour: two lunches and two dinners. These correlated "imperial banquets" follow the guidelines laid down by Emperor Sung Tai Tzu seven centuries ago: first, the Jade Hall Feast (to which the Emperor invited noble visitors); second, the Dragon Door Feast (originally for his leading government officials); third, the Golden Flower Feast (for successful government scholars); and fourth, the Belling Deer Feast (for aristocrats and army chiefs).

Hong Kong has an advantage over other world Chinatowns because rare Chinese dishes and ingredients are imported from the mainland. Bear's paw and elephant's trunk are some of the strange delicacies available.

I still cherish notes of one of my first banquets as the guest of The Master, James Wei. He summoned seven other guests — all Han, mature and discerning diners of "unbounded stomach" — but, to his chagrin, could organise only four master cooks, at two days' notice, to prepare his nine courses. He made it clear that he adhered to the Erasmus table roll-call: no more than nine.

He contested, politely but firmly, my suggestion that the old Shanghai which I humbly remembered in 1940 could have been classified as a number one zone of regional Chinese cuisine.

"Shanghai had many acceptable restaurants like the Sun Ya on Nanking Road," he conceded, amidst a murmur of approval from his Han guests. "But food or dishes of its own — none, pah, none! The one common and unique claim for each of the five regional food schools which I have listed is that any respectable restaurant in each zone can — rather, could — offer its patrons on demand on any night more than 100 different courses prepared from local products." He brooded, then added: "I would say, more precisely, at least 108 different courses."

Master Wei, essentially a fair and reasonable man, proceeded: "I would praise Shanghai because the best *Shaohsing* wine once came from spring water on a hill on the outskirts of Shanghai. You must drink *Shaohsing* at blood temperature. When cold, reject. Drink with full heart and open throat. Remember that over-indulgence brings neither headache nor thirst in the morning. Remember, also, that while Confucius, a diner of moderation, argued that the meat a man ate should not be enough to make his breath smell of meat more than rice, he imposed no limit on wine consumption — so long as the diner 'did not become disorderly'."

The company drank to Confucius.

Meanwhile, our four admirable cold *hors d'oeuvres* — "drunken chicken", pig's kidney, mutton and tiny clams — had been plucked by nine pairs of chopsticks, and the delicate Shantung fish with wine had been followed by Szechwan hot-peppered chicken, the magnificent Hunan *tou fu* or curd (frozen for eight hours, cooked for twelve), the dazzling, jewel-like Hupeh meatballs, the roast Cantonese suckling-pig (of which, of course, only the skin was eaten), the Lanchow steamed dumplings, the Foochow fish soup, and the lotus-root sweet.

"We could have had Szechwan smoked duck," Master Wei, ever the unsatisfied perfectionist, brooded. "Or Honan sweet-and-sour carp. Or Peking duck. Or monkey-head — we are having difficulty in getting supplies of monkey-head, which as you well know, is a special kind of mushroom, tastier, I believe, than French truffles."

An elderly general from Peking hailed Master Wei's reference to Honan sweet-and-sour carp and, amidst general applause, saluted our host for his insistence that Honan cooking should not be merged with the Peking-Shantung school.

He then recited a celebrated poem in honour of Honan's Yellow River carp.

Out in the garden in the moonlight,

Our servant is scraping a golden carp with so much vigour

The scales fly everywhere —

Perhaps they go as high as heaven;

The beautiful stars up there might be the scales of our fish.

We drank to the carp. And then to the stars.

"Which special dish did you prefer tonight, sir?" I asked the oldest diner at our table, a gentle professor whose life lies behind him in Peking University.

"May I echo the excellent riposte of your Master Thoreau to that question?" he replied, with a bow and out-thrust chopsticks. "The dish I liked, and like, the best here is, as Thoreau said, the nearest."

Our party toasted Thoreau.

The four cooks were paraded and, bowing, joined in a common toast. The pretty girl waitresses were summoned and, bowing, accepted another toast.

"I must apologise," Master Wei told us, formally and conventionally, "for a most indifferent meal."

It could happen only at a Chinese Dinner.

Richard Hughes was a World War II correspondent in the Middle East and some-time editor of the Sydney Sunday Telegraph before he took to the Far East in 1946 as a correspondent representing the Sunday Times, the Economist and several Australian newspapers. Since then he has travelled extensively in China (although he first saw that country in 1940, on a visit to Shanghai). He is the author of 'The Chinese Communes' and 'Hong Kong: Borrowed Place — Borrowed Time', a book that provides a remarkable insight into the relationships of Hong Kong with her northern neighbour.

Mr Hughes finally established Hong Kong as his base in 1956, bringing him as close as possible to China. Still a prolific contributor to newspapers and magazines in many parts of the world, he nevertheless manages on the slightest pretext to make time to enjoy one of the greatest passions that he shares with his Chinese wife: the continuing exploration of the inexhaustible world of Chinese food.

Wanchai Showroom circa 1910.

The soft glow of gaslight first illuminated Hong Kong's streets and buildings in 1862, the year after a Mr William Glen obtained a concession to supply gas to the City of Victoria from Hong Kong's then governor, Sir Hercules Robinson. The company responsible was The Hong Kong & China Gas Company, Limited which was formed in London on May 31, 1862 to take up the concession. It was Hong Kong's first public utility company, and its formation marked the beginning of a new and exciting era.

Hong Kong progressed rapidly over the years, taking on the unique international character which typifies it today.

The Gas Company has developed and grown with Hong Kong. While it no longer lights Hong Kong's streets and buildings, it provides efficient water-heating and cooking facilities to a major section of the population; and, in particular, gas has come to be accepted as the ideal medium for the cooking of Chinese food.

Through this development and expansion, the company has become very much involved with the community. Many housewives in Hong Kong today were given their first cooking lesson at one of the Gas Company's special courses; and there are many bachelors, even, who credit the company with providing them with their culinary skills.

The company's latest Towngas Centre, opened in 1977, is continuing this tradition. Featuring a magnificent classroom equipped to accommodate practical cooking classes, and an ultra-modern theatre used for cooking demonstrations, the centre is staffed by a team of professional home economists.

It was therefore a natural progression of ideas that led to the Gas Company's decision to share even more of its knowledge and expertise by compiling its own Chinese cookbook.

Many months of painstaking research by experts in the field culminated in an outstanding collection of cultural and culinary facts.

Several writers contributed material for the text which encompasses such far-ranging subjects as food's 'Yin and Yang duality' and the unusual foods served at Imperial Banquets.

Practical Classroom in the Towngas Centre, 1977.

A team of photographers produced the beautiful colour photographs that appear throughout the book — mouth-watering visual impressions of the delicious results of the many recipes.

All of the dishes featured were selected by Chinese cooking experts in consultation with some of Hong Kong's leading chefs, each of whom is a specialist in a particular style or cuisine. The recipes cover the whole delightful spectrum of Chinese food, from everyday items to elaborate banquets. They are all authentic and thoroughly tried and tested.

This Hongkong & China Gas Chinese Cookbook is the result.

It is a book that is intended to give the reader a comprehensive introduction to Chinese food: its history; the uniquely Chinese philosophies of eating; the remarkable range of ingredients; the methods of preparation; the styles and methods of cooking; and the approach of the Chinese people to eating at home and dining out.

Above all, it is a book that is intended to provide a view of Chinese food that is as diverse and entertaining as the food itself.

Acknowledgements

Photographs of China: Richard & Sally Greenhill, London.

Additional photographs of Hong Kong: The Hong Kong Tourist Association.

Map of China used for the end papers is reproduced with kind permission of the Librarian, University of Hong Kong.

Particular thanks are due to Miss Carolina Barros, Mrs Mary Jackson, Miss Kat Wong, Miss C. Ching, Mrs Margaret Wong and Mrs Salina Yu for their assistance in the organisation and testing of the recipes; to Miss Marina Silva for her many hours of typing and compilation; and to the staff at the Towngas Centre for their assistance in testing the dishes and in producing the final recipes.

Our thanks are also due to: Miss Annie Wu, the Jade Garden Group of Restaurants and the World Trade Centre Club for considerable assistance, advice and the use of their premises on many occasions; the management of the Lee Gardens Hotel for assistance in the preparation of the banquet dishes; The Mandarin Hotel for kind permission to reproduce excerpts from its 'Imperial Banquet' menu; the Miramar Hotel, the Nathan Hotel, the Village Restaurant, the Jade Garden Restaurant, the Hoover Restaurant, the Riverside Restaurant, Lok Yu Teahouse and Mr Ho Chun Wai of Lamma Island for the use of their facilities for the taking of some of the photographs; Shaw Brothers Studios for assistance with the loan of props for photographs; and to the many people who have given freely of their advice and assistance in so many ways.

The Editorial Team

T. C. Lai — Special Editorial Consultant
T.C. Lai is Director of the Department of Extramural Studies of the Chinese University of Hong Kong and is responsible for the organisation of the extensive educational programme that the department runs for the general public. His work is reflected in his hobby: the introduction of Chinese culture to English language readers via his books, of which 25 have been published to date. They include 'Chinese Food for Thought', 'Chinese Calligraphy', 'Chinese Painting', 'Chinese Seals', 'A Book of Chinese Friendship' and an introduction to the work of the well-known 20th century Chinese painter, Ch'i Pai Shih.

Jane Ram — Editorial Consultant
Jane Ram developed an early interest in Chinese culture, going on to study Chinese Language and Chinese History at Durham University where she graduated with honours. She has lived in Hong Kong for some 15 years, during which time she has travelled extensively throughout Asia and to China, and has established a reputation as a writer on a wide range of subjects, from cooking to the Arts. She is the editor of several magazines and a regular contributor to newspapers and magazines in the region.

Lucy Lo — Recipes Consultant
Lucy Lo is one of the most popular personalities in the field of Chinese cooking in Hong Kong. She is the author of 'Chinese Cooking with Lucy Lo', and she has also worked on many other cookbooks, including the Hong Kong Philharmonic's fund-raising publication, 'The Taste of Music'. Mrs Lo learned her craft during a stay of several years in Canton, returning to Hong Kong as a true expert. She has been a Chinese cooking instructor with the Gas Company and the Y.W.C.A. for over ten years, and for the last seven years she has been a judge in the Towngas Annual Inter-School Cooking Competition (Chinese Section).

Jacki Passmore — Recipes Editor
As well as being a student of the London Cordon Bleu Cookery School, Australian-born Jacki Passmore has studied cooking in many Asian countries. She now lives in Hong Kong where she pursues a busy career as a cookery writer and editor. She is the author of several cookbooks — including 'All Asian Cookbook', 'Indian Cookery' and 'Chinese Cooking for Health and Beauty' — and the co-author of '5,000 Years of Tea'. Her articles, recipes and food presentations have appeared in a number of international magazines.

The Photographers

Benno Gross
Born in Denmark and starting his career with magazines in Copenhagen, he came to Hong Kong in 1964. Since then, he has travelled throughout Asia, Europe and South America on photographic missions. He has specialised in elaborate studio subjects, producing the studies of ingredients, utensils and crockery, and the noodle maker series for this book. With his Chinese wife and Chinese staff, he is no stranger to Chinese food.

Leong Ka Tai
Leong Ka Tai is well-known in Hong Kong as a fashion photographer and has held several exhibitions of his work in Hong Kong. Born in Taiwan, he came to Hong Kong in 1976, where he set up his own studio, Camera 22. Mr. Leong was commissioned to produce a series of photographs for this book to illustrate the way in which food relates to the everyday life of people in Hong Kong.

Raymond Wong Yan Che and Philip Kwok Lup Hi
Raymond Wong was born in Hong Kong and has worked with leading photographers since 1972. Now operating his own studio, he has won many awards in design competitions for his photographs. He has exhibited his work in local arts shows and teaches photography at the First Institute of Art & Design, and the Hong Kong Polytechnic.

Philip Kwok, also born in Hong Kong, was trained as an illustrator and designer and has exhibited his work in art and design shows in Hong Kong. Now a partner in Illustration Workshop, he has worked with Raymond Wong as Art Director on the food photographs for this book, where his passion for, and knowledge of, Chinese food has contributed to the 'authentic flavour' of the photographs.

The Chefs

黎泰 (Lai Tai) — Southern Region Chef
Now assistant executive chef of the Jade Garden Group of Restaurants, Lai Tai was apprenticed in Macau at age 14. Coming to Hong Kong at age 17 he worked first on *dim sum* dishes, then on roasted and barbecued dishes at the famous Luk Kwok Hotel of 'World of Suzie Wong' fame. After working at various Hong Kong restaurants, and a two-year period back in Macau, he joined the Jade Garden Restaurant and since has represented Hong Kong in Chinese cooking promotions in Kuala Lumpur, Japan and Thailand.

鄒立思 (Tsou Li Szu) — Northern Region Chef
Born in Shantung, China, Tsou Li Szu worked in restaurants first in Peking, then in Shanghai, before coming to Hong Kong in 1952. He has worked in some of the best-known Northern restaurants in Hong Kong, including the Princess Garden Restaurant, and worked in Singapore in a specialist Northern-style restaurant. He is now the chief chef at the Hoover Restaurant where he specialises in dishes adapted from traditional recipes of his native Shantung province.

張泉甫 (Cheung Chuen Po) — Eastern Region Chef
Apprenticed at age 15 to the master chef Tai Poon Chue in Shanghai, Cheung Chuen Po stayed in his job in that city for ten years before coming to Hong Kong in 1951. He worked in a number of well-known Shanghai-style restaurants, eventually joining the Great Shanghai Restaurant in 1967, where he is now a partner and controls a staff of 30.

陳啟德 (Chan Kai Tak) — Western Region Chef
Born in Hong Kong and apprenticed to his father — himself a master chef at the Hotel Miramar — Chan Kai Tak has specialised in the Szechwan-style cuisine. With training in some of Hong Kong's best-known restaurants, he joined the World Trade Centre Club in 1976, where he is in charge of all dishes prepared in the Western regional style. In 1978 he won the 'Food World Magazine' competition with a specially-created Szechwan-style dish.

梁傑 (Leung Kit) — Formal Dinner Chef
Leung Kit, as executive chief chef of the Lee Gardens Hotel's Rainbow Restaurant, prepared the dishes presented in the banquet section of this book. Born in Nam Hoi, China (near Canton), he came to Hong Kong and at age 14 was apprenticed in the Cafe de Chine. After World War II he worked in several Cantonese-style restaurants before joining the Lee Gardens Hotel in 1972, where he personally oversees the preparation of the dishes for special dinners and banquets.

黃年壽 (Wong Nin Siu) — Buns and Pastries Chef
Born in China, Wong Nin Siu came to Hong Kong in 1962, joining the Yuet Bun Lau Restaurant in Kowloon as a Pastry Chef. After ten years he moved to the Great Shanghai Restaurant where he has continued to specialise in the buns and pastries popular in all four of the Chinese regional cuisines.

Chapter 1

Background

A brief introduction to the history of Chinese cuisine ... its development, region by region ... and the establishment of a 'health food' cult that is the oldest in the world.

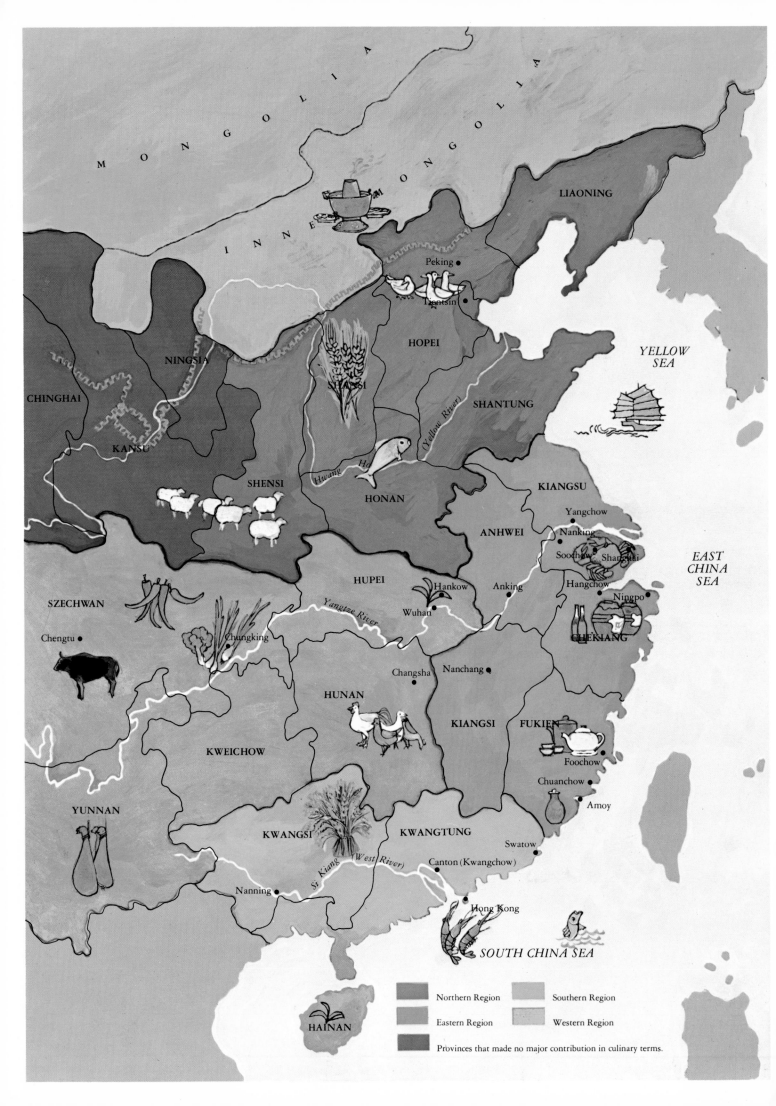

MONGOLIA

INNER MONGOLIA

LIAONING

Peking •

Tientsin •

HOPEI

*YELLOW
SEA*

CHINGHAI

NINGSIA

SHANSI

SHANTUNG

KANSU

KIANGSU

SHENSI

Hwang   Ho

HONAN

(*Yellow River*)

Yangchow •
Nanking •
Soochow •   Shanghai •
Hangchow •

ANHWEI

*EAST
CHINA
SEA*

SZECHWAN

HUPEI

Hankow •
Wuhan •

Anking •

Ningpo •

CHEKIANG

Chengtu •

Yangtze River

Chungking •

Changsha •   Nanchang •

HUNAN

KWEICHOW

KIANGSI   FUKIEN

Foochow •

Chuanchow •

YUNNAN

KWANGSI

Si Kiang   (West River)

KWANGTUNG

Amoy •

Swatow •

Canton (Kwangchow) •

Nanning •

Hong Kong •

SOUTH CHINA SEA

	Northern Region		Southern Region
	Eastern Region		Western Region

Provinces that made no major contribution in culinary terms.

HAINAN

Chinese food is justly famous. Initiates cannot help but marvel at the rich range of styles and the unlimited wealth of dishes; and even the most dedicated devotee never loses this initial sense of wonder. Because, with its treasury of simple and elaborate fare from one of the most varied continents of the world, Chinese food provides a lifetime of discovery with something for everyone, every time.

Geography determined the great contrasts in conditions in China, from sub-arctic in the north to sub-tropical in the south. Rugged mountains, deserts, fertile plains, lakes, rivers, and the seas that bound the country from north-east to south-west created varying lifestyles and, as a result, varying eating habits. A glance at the map shows how many regions were isolated from others for thousands of years by insuperable natural barriers.

Again, the peoples of China originated in many different cultures, and each brought a unique legacy to the development of Chinese civilisation in all its aspects. History tells us how some regions remained politically independent for centuries, and how each province interacted with its neighbours and with the central authority in the capital.

In more recent times, transport has steadily improved, facilitating the movement of people, and of foodstuffs, from one part of China to another. However, purely local cooking survived in each region — sometimes enriched by ideas from outside, but usually with imported ideas and ingredients being used for new creations. Consequently, the repertoire of the Chinese chef and the Chinese home cook alike has been constantly enlarged.

Consider the size of China as compared with that of the continent of Europe; then consider the remarkable variations throughout Europe in geography, climate, culture and cuisine. In this way, it is possible to appreciate more readily how, even today, Chinese cooking can still be classified into separate groups, according to region.

The most basic, and traditional, division is between the cooking of the rice eaters of the central provinces and the south and that of the northerners, eaters more of wheat and other grains. At the same time, further classification is desirable; so we have adopted the convenient method of dividing Chinese cooking into four main regional groups, referring to them by the four cardinal points of the compass. These regional groups and the most important provinces in each, in terms of their contribution to the cooking of their region, are: Northern (Hopei, Shantung and Honan), Southern (Kwangtung), Eastern (mainly Fukien, but including Kiangsu) and Western (Szechwan and Yunnan).

Such a method of classification is, we admit, rather simplistic as there are people who would argue, for example, that the province of Honan (河南) — not to be confused with the province of Hunan (湖南) — has a cuisine that is so individualistic that it should be treated separately ... as should the cuisines of Peking, Canton and Shanghai, because of their really very considerable importance.

These arguments cannot be denied. But to accept them without qualification would be to have to acknowledge the countless culinary subtleties from every individual province, city, town and, even, village that is famous for a particular main course or vegetable dish, perhaps, or for a secret recipe for festival desserts. Accordingly, in treating a country that covers an area of some 4,000,000 miles and has a history going back more than 5,000 years, divisions have to be drawn somewhere!

Waste not, want not

While China's bustling cities and industrial centres tend to dominate news about the country, the majority of the population is in the countryside, as it has been for centuries. Farming in China has always been intensive, and it is estimated that eight out of every ten people spend their lives working on the sorely limited cultivable land available, in the struggle to produce vital food.

17

Clearly, a region's primary crop largely determines what goes into the cooking pots; but there is more to the story than whether or not the local climate supports the cultivation of rice or wheat.

Nothing goes to waste in a Chinese farming community, and every animal must earn its keep. This accounts for the ever-present chickens and pigs which dispose of kitchen scraps and leftovers and are otherwise able to forage for themselves. So eggs, chicken and pork supplement what the soil produces directly, at virtually no cost.

The recurring miseries of drought and flooding in many regions made famine more than a spectre for the people. By sheer force of circumstance, 'waste not, want not' became the order of life. It applied in good times as well as in bad — with results in the kitchen that hold more than a few surprises for the Westerner.

Frugality has been turned to advantage by

generations of ingenious Chinese cooks.

In many parts of the world, for example, duck webs and chicken feet are simply discarded, denying people the discovery of how delicious such things can taste when properly prepared. Yet prodigal European poultry farmers now export them in bulk to Hong Kong.

Some cultures rather grandly reject what they call 'offal'. But, even more so than their French counter-parts, Chinese chefs can turn almost every part of almost any creature into a meal; and chicken's blood, bone marrow and a host of unclassifiable organs are among the more mysterious ingredients of many delectable dishes that emerge from Chinese kitchens.

Live to eat, or eat to live

The continual threat of shortage is the key to the complex subject of Chinese food. For just as it led to experimentation, by necessity, with the use of 'unusual' ingredients, it also helped to shape both the pattern of the Chinese family meal and the whole Chinese philosophy of eating.

For the poorest Chinese family, a meal may comprise only cooked rice (or, less typically, noodles) with whatever can be afforded in the way of meat, fish, vegetables or even just sauce to add flavour and, hopefully, extra nutriment. The better off the family, the more varied the selection of additional dishes will be. But, hearing testimony to the Chinese heritage, it is still the rice (at least in the southern provinces) that forms the basis of the meal; and the additional dishes are almost incidental to it in a way that has no real equivalent in Western cuisine.

By the same token, concern with the quality of food is a universal Chinese characteristic. Mindful of the past, they are less inclined to take things for granted. Indeed, most Chinese find the legendary Anglo-Saxon indifference to the look and taste of food quite incomprehensible.

Living in a country that has never enjoyed unbroken years of predictable harvests, the Chinese have, often enough, found it hard to eat to live. Perhaps this is why they acquired a preoccupation with eating, and inclined, when times were easier, to live to eat.

Whatever is the case, it is only the outcome that matters: namely, the development of the most exciting and diverse cuisine of any country in the world.

By Imperial Command

It is not easy to define the boundaries of northern style cooking. Arguments can perhaps best be avoided, though, by concentrating on the Yellow River basin and, more specifically, on the two provinces of Shantung and Hopei. These provinces can lay claim to a singular place in Chinese history. Shantung was the homeland of two of China's greatest philosophers, Confucius and Mencius. Hopei is where we find Peking, the national capital throughout a great deal of the country's recorded history. In fact, the two provinces are so closely linked that they can, to all intents and purposes, be regarded as one — forming what has been called 'the cradle of Chinese civilisation'.

Shantung was probably the major source of the indigenous cooking of Northern China, although Honan most certainly made some contribution. Hopei — or, more accurately, the city of Peking — acted, on the other hand, as a sort of melting pot, bringing together both regional and 'imported' cooking styles and methods.

The Chinese Dynasties

	BC	AD
Hsia*	2205 - 1767	
Shang (or Yin)*	1766 - 1123	
Chou*	1122 - 256	
Ch'in*	255 - 207	
Han	206 -	219
Three Kingdoms		220 - 264
Six Dynasties		265 - 588
Sui		589 - 617
T'ang		618 - 906
Five Dynasties		907 - 959
Liao (Tartar)		907 - 1123
Sung		960 - 1279
Chin (Tartar)		1115 - 1234
Yuan (Mongol)		1280 - 1367
Ming		1368 - 1643

Hung Wu	1368 - 1398
Chien Wen	1399 - 1402
Yung Lo	1403 - 1424
Hung Hsi	1425
Hsuan Te	1426 - 1435
Cheng T'ung	1436 - 1449
Ching T'ai	1450 - 1456
T'ien Shun	1457 - 1464
Ch'eng Hua	1465 - 1487
Hung Chih	1488 - 1505
Cheng Te	1506 - 1521
Chia Ching	1522 - 1566
Lung Ch'ing	1567 - 1572
Wan Li	1573 - 1620
T'ai Ch'ang	1620
T'ien Ch'i	1621 - 1627
Ch'ung Cheng	1628 - 1643

Ch'ing (Manchu)   1644 - 1911

Shun Chih	1644 - 1661
K'ang Hsi	1662 - 1722
Yung Cheng	1723 - 1735
Ch'ien Lung	1736 - 1795
Chia Ch'ing	1796 - 1820
Tao Kuang	1821 - 1850
Hsien Feng	1851 - 1861
T'ung Chih	1862 - 1874
Kuang Hsu	1875 - 1908
Hsuan T'ung	1908 - 1911

*Note: The dates shown here are according to the 'orthodox' chronology, as opposed to those shown in the ancient 'Bamboo Annals'. Additionally, Chinese Tables prefer to show as the beginning of the Ch'in Dynasty the year 246 BC, when Cheng Wang ascended the throne — although it was not until 221 BC that he finally proclaimed himself 'First August Emperor'.

Considerable outside influence came from Mongolia. For centuries, people from this region filtered south into China. Later, Mongolia supplied several successions of China's rulers. So, in one way and another, many of the region's native dishes were adopted by the Northern Chinese as their own.

Other major influences came, of course, from the Imperial Palace. As was so clearly evidenced during the Mongol rule, the types of dish that were served at court tended to find their way in due course onto humbler tables — albeit adapted sometimes to cater to less exalted tastes ... and pockets.

The greatest artists and artisans were regularly summoned to Peking from the distant provinces of the country to entertain, to ply their crafts and — it goes without saying — to cook, by Imperial command. During each succeeding dynasty, the court became the focal point of more, and increasingly sophisticated, skills. The resources at the Emperor's disposal grew richer in variety. Whatever the

background of each new conqueror who came to power, it was not long before he and his descendants fell in with the lifestyle of the capital. Luxury and elegance were powerful forces in the wooing of even the most barbaric; and the products of the Imperial kitchens predictably contributed to the wooing process.

The 'non-rice lands'

The weather in Northern China is too cold for the cultivation of rice. However, the alluvial plain of the Yellow River and the wind-blown yellow earth of the Shensi, Shansi, Ninghsia and Kansu loess lands have for millenia proved fertile ground for raising wheat, millet, barley, *kaoliang* and other grain crops. Thus, the use of flour as a staple dominates the kitchen skills required in the region.

Sweet potatoes and many kinds of bean flourish. Again, Chinese cabbage, Tientsin cabbage and numerous related green vegetables do particularly well. It is an unusual meal at which cabbage is not served in some shape or form. Which accounts for the countless carvings, in jade and other stones, with such vegetables as their subject — a very real indication of their popularity, and of their importance.

Beyond the Great Wall

When considering what is often referred to now simply as 'Peking food' (a convenient, though rather inaccurate, description), it helps to remember how close Peking is to the northernmost boundaries of China. Indeed, the city is barely 40 miles away from the nearest point of the Great Wall; and, from there, the border of Inner Mongolia is not much more than 100 miles away.

Built during the Ch'in Dynasty (255 BC to 207 BC) as a barrier against full-scale invasion by Tartar hordes, the wall served its purpose for centuries. Yet it represented as much a challenge as a deterrent — and the challenge was finally overcome, although it took no less a warrior than the legendary Genghis Khan to do so. From AD 1206, the Mongols held sway in Northern China. Their armies moved into the rest of the country and, in 1280, Kublai Khan ascended the throne as undisputed

Emperor of the whole of China.

The tribes of Northern China were mainly nomadic, rarely settling for long enough to cultivate any crop, and with only a number of sheep and goats to accompany them on their wanderings. Mutton and goat's meat (usually despised in other regions because of their distinctive smell) thus became a feature of the northern flavour — as did the game caught by hunters in the great forests of the north.

Freshwater fish, crabs and shrimps came from the Yellow River. The Gulf of Chihli provided the salt-water equivalents. However, these were by no means everyday foods for the majority of the people.

In particular, it has to be borne in mind that many of the invaders and their followers were Moslems, so pork and all pig 'by-products' were forbidden to them. While mutton features prominently, then, in any listing of authentic Northern Chinese dishes, pork is something of an oddity.

Beating the cold

As well as restricting the types of ingredient that are locally available, the cold winters of the north have traditionally dictated the methods of preparing food.

Sesame oil and other oils are used rather lavishly, to help to combat the rigours of the climate. (Many people find that this makes northern food less palatable than other regional foods, especially in warmer weather.) Vinegar and extra salt dominate flavouring, cutting the oil; and garlic and scallions are used to absorb some of the oily excess.

All manner of dumplings are popular — sometimes steamed, and sometimes fried for added richness. By the same token, thick pancakes, steamed 'silk thread' bread, hefty noodles and pastry 'spectacle cases' filled with stir-fried vegetables and minced meat are all typical of the hearty fare on which the Northern Chinese thrive.

Apart from methods of cooking in the kitchen, methods of cooking at the table, too, were ingeniously designed to beat the cold by raising the temperature.

Today's modest table-top griddle, on which diners at a Mongolian Barbecue cook their own food (thin slices of meat that are dipped, when they are ready, into a bowl of beaten egg and /or into bowls of various piquant sauces), is no more than a poor relation of yesterday's vast, charcoal-heated stove tops.

Similarly, the variations on the Chinese fire kettle theme — the best known of which is the always-popular Mongolian Hot Pot — were all intended originally to warm as they fed.

The Manchu influence

The last, and long-lasting, period of Imperial rule in China was during the Ch'ing Dynasty (1644 to 1911) which followed the ousting of the native Chinese house of Ming by the invading Manchus.

Unlike the Mongols, the Manchus could boast no cuisine of their own. However, as they established their hold over the country, and added Mongolia, Sinkiang and Tibet to the Manchu-Chinese Empire, they gradually turned from war-like pursuits to the pursuit of pleasure. One result of this process was the creation or development, in the second half of the Ch'ing Dynasty, of exquisitely-refined dishes — for Imperial consumption.

The cooking of other regions (especially that of Southern China) became increasingly popular in the Palace ... and in Peking itself. Possibly because of this, purists argue that there is now no true style of northern cooking, but that the Northern Chinese have, as another writer has put it, "simply adopted the best of the rest of China as their own." To which we would reply: "And the results leave no room for complaint!"

The Southern Flavour

Outside China, in whatever countries Chinese restaurants are to be found, the chances are that people are most familiar with the distinctive taste and texture of cooking from the provinces of Kwangtung and, to a lesser extent, Kwangsi — often described simply as 'Cantonese food'.

Rice is the staple of this region, with the sub-tropical climate making it possible to produce three crops a year, even though the earth is not over-hospitable in the main. Sugar-cane and citrus trees flourish, along with a host of other fruit and vegetables. Almost anything the ambitious cook could desire to use can be raised. For the region is kind to its farmers. They have always had a predictable life, for the most part. The mild winters do little harm to crops or trees, and even the monsoon rains seldom cause disastrous flooding of the fields.

Since the earliest days, the coastal people of Southern China have happily made the sea their life and their source of livelihood, with generation after generation of families building or manning the boats that harvest the surrounding waters. Not surprisingly, seafood of all kinds dominates the food markets, usually still alive and swimming or twitching. Dried and salted fish and shrimps also form an important element of the southern flavour, sometimes in the form of pungent sauces. Pork, of course, is by far and away the most important meat, though chicken, too, can be high on the shopping lists. Beef, on the other hand, is not greatly prized, and mutton is seldom eaten.

The Emperor first sent pensioned-off soldiers to colonise the restless southern provinces during the Ch'in Dynasty (255 BC to 207 BC); but they remained relatively isolated for long periods from Imperial authority. Political independence was translated in many ways; a separate dialect was retained and so, of course, was a unique culinary tradition.

In contrast with the sporadic influence from the north and the central provinces, foreign influence was strong in Canton and the other parts of the south coast. Arab traders came in large numbers as early as AD 400, forming their own settlements where they operated for hundreds of years as middlemen in commerce with the West. The first Europeans, the Portuguese, arrived before the end of the 15th century, and they were soon followed by other Western merchants.

By the middle of the last century, many Cantonese families involved in the foreign trade had made great fortunes. Their new-found wealth was spent on every conceivable luxury, including the finest food. The chefs of Canton were encouraged to develop a vast selection of elaborate dishes, using none but the rarest and most expensive ingredients. Even today, good Cantonese food is costly, as everything must be fresh and perfect before the cook will consent to use it. Furthermore, the Cantonese have mastered the art of producing the two most extravagant of all Chinese dishes — shark's fin and bird's nest soups — to a degree of finesse that can be rivalled only by another southern people, the Ch'ao Chow (or, as they are called in the Cantonese dialect, the Chiu Chow).

The fame of the Cantonese chefs spread far and wide. Their creations were regular favourites on the tables of the Emperor, almost 2,000 miles away. And when the Manchu Court left the capital on its royal tours of the country, Kwangtung was a favoured destination as the Imperial household could relish the exquisite food of the region in its place of origin, where the cook had everything to hand.

Eat in Kwangchow

There is a Chinese saying that advises one to be born in Soochow, renowned for its beautiful women; to eat in Kwangchow, renowned for its fine cooking; to dress in Hangchow, where the finest silks are made; and to die in Liuchow, where the best coffin wood is found.

It may not be possible today to test the validity of this advice as it relates to birth,

clothing and death. Fortunately, however, eating is another matter; and as anyone who has been privileged to enjoy really first quality Cantonese food will agree, the advice in this regard is hardly open to question.

Tint, taste and fragrance

With so many foreigners being a part of the scene in Cantonese cities, chefs became adept at preparing food for the 'red-haired devil' palate. Purists claim that the sweet and sour 'school' developed as a part of this process of compromise — although the author Yuan Mei (1716 — 1797) included in his cookery book a pork recipe with vinegar as the dominant ingredient. Be that as it may, sweet

and sour should be approached with caution. If nothing else, it can dominate casual acquaintance with Cantonese food to the exclusion of the truer and more subtle delights.

The emphasis in Cantonese cooking is always on enhancing the tint, taste and fragrance of the main ingredients. The cook uses ginger, for example, to highlight a flavour, not to obscure it. Fast cooking is used to retain the natural colour of food, and to give it a crisp texture. Cantonese cooking is definitely the least oily of the regional styles and is noted for its stir-fried, roasted and steamed dishes. In particular, the region offers a bewildering range of *dim sum* dishes — almost all of them steamed, and all of them deservedly famous for their delicate texture as they 'touch the heart', to give one literal translation of the characters (點心) that form the name.

Going round

The chrysanthemum garden;

Toasted rice cake,

Glutinous rice dumpling,

Mother told me to go and see the dragon boat,

I didn't go,

Went to tend the chickens instead.

When they grew big enough,

They were taken to be sold.

How much did I get?

I got three hundred 'tsin',

With a gold waistband

And a silver waistband,

I ask Granny to come out to receive my salutations.

Anon

Chop suey

The main reason for Cantonese food's being so universally well known is that emigration from China's south coast has been almost continuous for the past 100 years and more. Sons, and even whole families, have travelled to virtually every part of the world in search of their fortune. A remarkable number of them have ended up by running highly successful restaurants overseas.

During the middle of the 19th century, the Chinese were encouraged to immigrate into America to work on the construction of the new network of railways in that country. Local food appealed not at all to the homesick labourers, and they inevitably appointed one of their number as cook. Occasionally, as a particular stretch of track was completed, a cook would stay on to cater for the people of one of the towns that had sprung up along the line ... and the cycle would then be repeated.

The story has it that such a cook found himself faced one day with an army of hungry patrons, but without the authentic ingredients that he needed. Accordingly, he desperately cooked up a mixture of makeshift ingredients, concealed the result with a sauce, and served it to his customers. At that point, he was probably about to flee the scene; but, to his amazement, he heard cries of pleasure on all sides. He was saved ... and he had invented *chop suey* into the bargain.

Undoubtedly, the story is apocryphal. But its moral is that *chop suey* — whatever the origins — is a dish that will never be found in any self-respecting Chinese restaurant.

South of the Yangtze

The eastern provinces of China are often grouped together as forming the rice heartland of the country. The large majority of the region falls south of the Yangtze, with the Grand Canal and other waterways linking even the northernmost areas with the great river system. The coastal provinces of Kiangsu, Chekiang and Fukien and the inland provinces of Anhwei and Kiangsi between them cover such varied terrain that it is all but impossible to generalise about almost any feature.

The climate is basically sub-tropical, with warm and wet summers. Yet the winters are severe in the areas around Shanghai and, at their height, snow is quite regularly seen on the palm trees. Thanks to the range of climate, Eastern China produces wheat and barley in the north to supplement the rich rice harvests further south. The Yangtze delta and thousands of miles of canals ensure that most of the region is well irrigated. Vegetables of all kinds flourish, with 17 varieties of bean alone. Peanuts thrive along with bamboo shoots and water chestnuts. Peaches, plums and many kinds of citrus and other fruits are as abundant as the vegetables. The mountains of the warmer southern provinces are ideal for tea plantations. In fact, Fukien is perhaps the best known of China's tea-growing provinces, and it was from its ports that graceful tea clippers sailed in the early 19th century to carry the precious leaves to Europe.

Such trade brought prosperity to the residents of the many coastal cities of Eastern China. As in Canton, in later years, the leisured class were able to cultivate a fine taste in all the refinements of life, including the best food.

There was no lack of good ingredients to inspire the cooks. Pork was the most common meat; but donkey's meat and venison were only two of the more exotic items that could be found in the markets of the bigger towns. From the long coast-line came a wealth of seafood; and the inland waterways and lakes supplied all manner of freshwater delicacies (such as the still popular Shanghai hairy crab),

as well as proving excellent breeding grounds for a host of birds, from geese to teal.

The lifestyles of the major cities of Eastern China were shaped by different influences. Before 1949, for example, Shanghai was an international centre, numbering some of the world's wealthiest businessmen among its residents. They came from all over China, and from Europe and the USA, bringing a cosmopolitan touch to life— and to food — in Shanghai.

Hangchow, described by Marco Polo as "the noblest city in the world", was the refuge chosen by the Mongol court during its exile in the 13th century, and there is no doubt that some of the Imperial ways rubbed off onto the cooks of this beautiful city. Nanking, too, was the seat of government for long spells, and several rulers imposed their gourmet tastes on the capital-in-exile.

It is difficult to particularise about this region of China. Nevertheless, some of the specialities of certain cities must be singled out.

Nanking was long famous for its pressed duck. Yangchow was responsible for the development of quite the most superb recipes for rice and noodles with vegetables, still regarded as the perfect ending to a formal banquet; and China's sizzling rice dishes had their origin there too. Shaohsing produced the 'wine' (actually a rice spirit) that contributes its pungent flavour to much of the region's food and is still one of China's key exports where overseas Chinese gourmets and restaurant owners are concerned. Amoy soy sauce was considered to be the best in China (today's major soy sauce manufacturing company in Hong Kong had its beginnings in Amoy). Soochow was renowned for *dim sum* as delicate and desirable as its women. Hangchow, with its lakes, was where the ultimate in beautifully prepared freshwater fish was to be found.

At the same time, two eastern provinces exerted a lasting influence over the eating habits not only of most of China, but of

Europe as well. Chekiang was the source of vinegars that were unmatched in quality and range; and Kiangsi had huge deposits of *kaolin,* the raw material for a flourishing industry that produced exquisite porcelain tableware, highly prized by Chinese and Westerner alike.

Shanghai taste buds

Shanghai was for so long an international city that it might seem to be something of a contradiction in terms to talk of a Shanghai tradition of cooking. Yet while all types of food were certainly available in the city during its heyday, distinctive local flavours remained.

The winters were so cold that a typical meal would include heavier wheat-based breads and dumplings, with robust noodles; and as in Northern China, additional oil would be used in an attempt to counteract the effects

of the weather. During the enervatingly hot summers, foods changed and took on a distinctly lighter texture and taste. As a result, an elaborate tradition of cooking in this style evolved, making good use of the soya bean

products available in the region, and of the preserved mushrooms and vegetables for which Shanghai was famed. Indeed, the preserving of foods was brought to a fine art in Shanghai and its environs, and preserved fish and shrimps, as well as the rather controversial '100-day-old egg', rated highly among the products that were associated with the city.

Probably striving to rejuvenate jaded taste buds, the cooks of Shanghai also introduced several distinctive flavouring tricks, one of the more unusual of these being the addition of a little raw sugar to certain meat and fish dishes, to offset the salt used in the basic seasoning.

Three blades — 100 dialects

The people of Fukien have been dubbed *san pa tao* (三把刀), meaning literally that they are good for three blade-wielding crafts: barbering, tailoring and, more especially, cooking. This province was regarded by outsiders with unremitting caution, and for good reason. It was one of the last provinces to submit to The Son of Heaven's mandate, and its inhabitants retained a singular independence. Their non-conformity went far beyond the area of politics. The terrain was so rugged that villages inland were almost totally isolated from each other to the extent that it is said that there were some 100 different dialects, many of which were mutually incomprehensible.

Not surprisingly, the existence of some 100 dialects is reflected in a not dissimilar number of styles of Fukienese cooking. Typical of them all, however, is an enjoyment of the original flavour of a food, with no disguising and the addition of no more than the occasional highlight. Cooking methods are usually simple in themselves, although the process of preparation can demand many patient hours of shredding and chopping of ingredients.

Pig's blood and chicken's blood — steamed until they reach a custard-like

consistency — are used for quite a number of famous Fukienese recipes. In fact, soft food is something of a feature of the cooking of this province, with the regular occurrence of dishes that can best be described as 'semi-soups'. *Congee* or *chu* (粥) is popular, and the great selection of soups seems to be a logical solution to the problem of linking the other mainly plain steamed and boiled food. These soups — most of which are clear — will constitute at least a quarter of the dishes at any Fukienese meal, and a popular Fukienese saying is that if your host serves you only one soup at a meal, he does not regard you as a friend.

'Crystal cooking' is the apt description of the method of stir-frying that is so popular with the Fukienese; and 'red cooking' is equally popular — using a modicum of soy sauce in slow stewing or braising. The distinctive flavour of many other Fukienese dishes comes from the use of *hung chiao* paste, made from the lees of red wine, which imparts a musky note to the food. Sometimes the fruits that abound in the province are used to enhance a dish (lemon or orange peel can turn a plain meat or fish dish into something bordering on the poetic); and water chestnut may be called on to add its own interestingly crunchy texture.

Hoklo

No description of the range of eastern flavours would be complete without at least a mention of the Hoklo people, whose deep fried food — usually featuring the use of lard — dominates so much Chinese cooking in places like Singapore. The Hoklos were among the numerous tribes of sea gypsies that were so prevalent in Eastern China, and many of them chose to emigrate to other parts of Southeast Asia.

Hakka

The food of the Hakka people is humble in contrast with that of the other foods of the region. So much so that the Cantonese regard it as rather coarse, not to say pedestrian. But its redeeming grace is that it relies heavily on carefully-contrasted natural flavours for its appeal. For example, heated rock salt is used for cooking chicken, with the whole bird being placed in a large *wok* and buried in the salt to produce a crisp-skinned, delicately-flavoured result.

Altogether, a thrifty approach runs right through the range of Hakka food, with anything and everything that is remotely edible being pressed into service in the cooking process.

There is still contention as to where the Hakkas should be placed in geographical terms. It is known that they originated in Northern China (hence their name, given to them by the southerners and conveying the meaning of 'guest family'); but they have since come to be associated almost exclusively with China's southern and southeastern provinces — notably Kwangtung and Fukien. With its simplicity and economy, then, Hakka cooking must be said to have more in common with the Fukienese school than with the more extravagant traditions of the Cantonese.

Western China remained politically independent for many centuries, and it was not until 1252 that Kublai Khan became the first emperor to make any impact in the area. Central influence over the western provinces increased during the 17th century AD, but the former feudal states retained their own rulers. Life changed only marginally, and the parallel development of palace and peasant styles of cooking was one of the stranger results of the resistance to change.

Eventually, the Sino-Japanese war saw Chungking established as the capital-in-exile and, for the first time, the province of Szechwan attracted international notice. Many cooks emigrated from Szechwan to the USA at that time, founding a strong tradition of Szechwan cooking in New York and other cities; but few people outside China know much about the other western provinces to this day.

The food of the western region is unique in Chinese cooking. Characterised by strong yet ingenious spicing, it causes most people to cough and gasp for air on first acquaintance ... only to come back for more in due course.

There is regular comment on the similarities between Szechwan food and the foods of Thailand, Burma and, to an even greater extent, India. The fierce spicing certainly has its roots in Indian cooking — a simple explanation being that many Buddhist missionaries were active in China from the first century AD onwards, making their way into the rest of the country through Yunnan and then Szechwan. In fact, the Burma Road of World War II was simply a retracing of the Way of the Buddha, trodden out some 2,000 years earlier.

The Buddhists, and the traders who followed in their footsteps, carried foreign spices and herbs — and the knowledge of their use in medicine and in cooking. Subsequently, the new varieties of plant must have grown as abundantly as all the others to which farmers turned their hands in the fertile soil of Szechwan's Red Basin.

Irrigation systems were constructed over 2,000 years ago to supplement the water from the four rivers that literally (in Chinese characters, 四川) give the province its name. Intensive cultivation ensures three crops a year of rice, the staple; and maize, millet, *Kaoliang*, potatoes, beans, peas and other vegetables, and sugar cane thrive — as does a wide variety of fruit. From the dense bamboo forests of the northern area comes not only the panda, but also various game animals, including deer. Thanks to the bounty of the land, fodder is plentiful. Chickens and pigs are raised in prodigious numbers; and hams from Szechwan — and still more so from the neighbouring Yunnan province — have a well-earned reputation for their unrivalled quality. Beef is relatively common as there is intensive breeding of oxen, primarily as draught animals for the salt mines of Szechwan. Waterways and flooded paddy fields are used for freshwater fish cultivation and, more usually, as 'farms' for the ducks that feature prominently in the cooking of the region.

The ready supplies of salt made its liberal use a main feature of Szechwan cooking, but it soon pales into insignificance as the master cook turns to the most powerful weapon in his armoury: the chilli.

The chilli peppers of Szechwan are light years away from the comparatively insipid capsicums or even the medium-firepower larger chillies used in most other parts of the world. Indeed, these Szechwan specials have few rivals. Enthusiasts claim merely that they awaken the palate. Other people find them to be indescribably, and often unbearably, hot. In any event, they are traditionally fried to bring out the maximum flavour — an indication of their strength being that the oil in which they are fried takes on the ability to pep up other dishes.

A prevailing philosophy of many self-styled Szechwan restaurants seems to be: "Add plenty of chilli and you are in business."

Yet the Szechwan flavour by no means begins and ends with that much-maligned spice, for an equally important contribution is made by the small brown peppercorns (also known as Szechwan pepper or fagara) that are hotter than the more universally recognized black peppercorns, while having a distinctive hint of anise in their flavour, too.

Garlic is important, as are ginger and the common or garden Western onion. Tangerine peel is dried and grated, then added to meat dishes in particular to give them an unusual citrus tang. Another favourite is the facetiously-named 'fish sauce' — actually made from black beans among other things, and with not an element of fish in it. Mixed flavours are prevalent, combining not the ubiquitous sweet and sour, but sour, hot, salt and sweet together — arguably experienced at its best in the well-known sour-hot soup that is an essential part of anyone's introduction to Szechwan food.

Rice ribbons

Nature worked on a grand scale in shaping the western provinces of China, giving them mountains rising to the clouds and rivers running swiftly through steep-sided gorges. In the densely-populated province of Szechwan, man shaped the landscape in his own way, winding rows of rice terraces like ribbons around the foothills, to take full advantage of the rich earth and the 11-month growing season.

Generally, Szechwan cooks reject the use of sauces, so the variety of texture in any given dish is a factor of real importance. Thus walnuts or cashew nuts are combined with chicken breast; or mushrooms and various

33

types of fungus are used to provide crisp, rubbery or feathery contrasts. There are dishes — based on beancurd or chicken, for example — that are cooked to be as smooth as silk. Beef may be finely shredded, and yet cooked so that it emerges as decidedly chewy. Pickles, a side-product of the local salt industry, are often served as a separate appetizer, adding still more variety.

As in other regions, stir-frying features large in Szechwan cooking, though it takes on an added significance as it is meant to achieve a deliberate effect: namely, the reduction of gravy or juice to the extent that the finished dish acquires the 'fluffiness' that the cook is looking for. Simmering and steaming are common cooking methods (in one type of Szechwan speciality, tiny steamers are used to cook chicken, pork or beef that has been rolled into broken rice and spices). Spit roasting and splash frying are also used; and to complete the spectrum, as it were, both chicken and duck are often smoked — with tea leaves and, perhaps, camphor wood adding their flavour to the smoking process.

South of the clouds

The provinces of Hupeh and Hunan have long been famous for the fighting spirit of their people, and it is Hunan, of course, that can claim the honour of being the home province of no less a Chinese than Mao Tse-tung.

These land-locked areas have a great deal in common with Szechwan, at least as far as food is concerned. Hunan is known for its excellent glutinous rice and for its air-cured meats and fermented beancurd.

Yunnan — the Chinese name for which (雲南) translates as 'south of the clouds' — is a mountainous region that has never proved hospitable to farmers. The inhabitants count themselves fortunate if they can grow a little wheat and rice to supplement wild fruit and vegetables. Yet livestock manage to survive to provide meat and — as was pointed out earlier — the ham from this province is of the best. Indeed, Yunnan has a culinary heritage that ranges from the cooking of the hundreds of thousands of Moslems, who were brought in by Kublai Khan's administration to colonise the area, to that of its southern neighbours: Vietnam, Laos, Burma and, indirectly, India. That Yunnanese food is seldom encountered outside China, then, is one of the few disappointments in store for those who set out really to explore the world of Chinese cooking.

The Yin-Yang Duality

Every aspect of life in China is governed by the balance between the complementary elements of *Yin* and *Yang*. Since the Chou Dynasty, if not earlier, the *Yin* has represented the female negative, dark, cold, wet facets of the world and everything in it; and the *Yang* has represented the contrasting male, positive, bright, hot, dry qualities. It is only to be expected that these dual principles influence what people eat and drink.

Every individual is nominated by one of the two elements. According to the nature of his constitution, a man should eat and drink chiefly those things which will help to retain his normal balance.

Chinese folk medicine depends largely on the interpretation of the balance of the *Yin* and *Yang*. If this is disturbed, illness results. The traditional herbalist will feel the main pulses of the body to decide which element currently has the upper hand and how matters should be corrected through what he prescribes.

Categories are broadly divided into the cooling *Yin* foods, which are bland, thin and low-calorie and the heating *Yang* foods which are rich and oily. Interestingly enough, brandy is considered to be 'hot': whisky and beer ('foreigner's herb tea') are 'cool'. A more traditional cooling beverage is sugar cane juice.

The nature of the food can be intensified, and even to some extent changed, by the way

in which it is cooked. The methods of cooking are broadly classified from coolest to hottest, ranging from cold-water infusion to deep-frying. Boiling is regarded as cool, but stir-frying is already medium-heating. The length of cooking time is also considered when the nature of the method is defined. The food becomes increasingly heating when a long period of deep-frying is involved, but prolonged boiling intensifies the cooling effect.

Food as Preventive Medicine

Country people all over the world use leaves, seeds, tree bark and plant roots in their cooking as a matter of course. Flavour and variety are matched by real, or imaginary, benefits to the health. Naturally, the Chinese, too, discovered the valuable medicinal and restorative properties of many everyday plants

---

"Apart from foods which are poisonous in themselves, there are many which should not be eaten together as they do not harmonize and are apt to cause great discomfort and inconvenience."

Imperial Cookery Book of the Mongol Dynasty — *Yin Shan Cheng Yao*

---

and shrubs, as well as readily available animal products. The Taoists and the Buddhists introduced more systematic use of what had previously been tried largely by instinct. And perhaps more than 2,000 years ago, an extensive pharmacopoeia began to be established.

Many traditional medicines to this day are produced in the form of leafy soups or infusion of roots. The herbalist and the medicine shop have a vast range of plant products and animal products, and minerals, from which to draw. The beneficial effects of ginseng are today generally acknowledged, and even cautiously endorsed, by those trained in Western medicine. But this is only one of many substances used as a tonic since time immemorial. Ginger has long been reputed to have a similar effect on the constitution.

Again, chicken soup scarcely needs justification as a restorative, even if few people would go along with the traditional Chinese belief that duck soup is sufficiently powerful to bring about a reconciliation between estranged husband and wife.

In Han times, theorists were aware of the need for a balanced and complete diet. One of the medical treatise of the period is cited by Dr. Joseph Needham in his comments on Hygiene and Preventive Medicine. The treatise is 'The Huang Ti Nei Ching', in which Su Wen says: "Taking the five cereals as nutriment, the five fruits as assistants, the five meats as chief benefactors and the five vegetables as supplements, and combining together the *ch'i* and the *wei* (tastes) in the diet; this blending is what benefits the mind and body".

Dr. Needham also makes a conclusive case for the Chinese dieticians of the 14th century who had clear understanding of the importance of vitamins in the prevention of many deficiency diseases. Many of the early works on nutrition concentrated on prohibitions: avoiding leeks with honey, for example, or fish with milk. Others simply tabulated the current popular knowledge about food and theories on the interaction of the *Yin* and *Yang* with the five elements.

The Imperial Dietician, Hu Ssu-hui, during his term of office from 1315-1330, wrote a work on the principles of correct diet which can be considered something of a turning point. "Many diseases can be cured by diet alone," he states, citing beri-beri and other deficiency diseases as examples.

Dr. Needham quotes Ch'en Chih on the subject of the elderly, who are usually reluctant to take medicine; Ch'en Chih pointed out that it is far more satisfactory to treat them with proper food than with drugs. Nutritional therapy should always be tried before resorting to drugs. "Experts at curing diseases are inferior to specialists who warn against diseases. Experts in the use of medicines are inferior to those who recommend proper diet."

"Sympathetic Magic"

Dr. Gerald Choa, a former director of the Hong Kong Government's Medical and Health Department, has described as 'sympathetic magic', many of the traditional beliefs about food and drink that do not have a clear therapeutic value. In an address to the Royal Asiatic Society in October 1966, he commented: "The Chinese also practise organotherapy — and it is here particularly, that we run into ideas of sympathetic magic. When people have a weakness or supposed weakness in a certain organ, or when they want to improve its functioning or power, they eat the corresponding organ of an animal.

"We have, therefore, to congratulate the Chinese people on their happy confusion of medicine and food. This makes their medicine less of a medicine, but makes their food more of a food. There seems to be a symbolic significance in the fact that the God of Gluttony appeared even in our semi-historical period, the god of *T'ao T'ieh* (饕餮) being found today as a favourite motif among our earliest bronze and stone sculptures. The spirit of *T'ao T'ieh* is in us. It makes our pharmacopoeias resemble our cook books and our cook books resemble a pharmacopoeia, and it makes the rise of botany and zoology as branches of the natural sciences impossible, for the Chinese scientists are thinking all the time of how a snake, a monkey, or a crocodile's flesh or a camel's hump would taste.

True scientific curiosity in China is a gastronomic curiosity".

"Ladies at dinner parties often go for fish-eyes and fish bones. The more adventurous folk are said to try monkey brains and eat the 'unmentionable' parts of animals. But many items which are taken do indeed have therapeutic value. The Chinese have liver therapy for anaemia, as did Western medicine, until it was superseded largely by vitamin B12. They also realise the benefits of green vegetables such as spinach, which have a good iron content, and use them for the treatment of another form of anaemia.

"Western medicine uses an extract of pancreas — insulin — for the treatment of diabetes. The Chinese eat pig's pancreas for this disease — not fully efficient, in fact, but they have another cure for diabetes, in the hairy roots of sweet-corn. Eating peanuts and soya beans when the feet become swollen is a practice the Chinese have adopted since ancient times and it is still used today. Their value in cases of beri-beri are of course recognised in Western medicine."

Less easily proven are the powers of the fringe foods, many of which come into the category of exotica, or extremely expensive foods at best. Gelatinous substances like shark's fin, green turtle (and its eggs) and bird's nest are believed to be good general tonic foods and of special value in ensuring a perfect complexion. In most cases such foods are cooked with nutritious and first-class chicken stock, which is certainly highly beneficial.

Extracted from Lin Yu Tang's 'Enjoyment of Living'.

Chapter 2
Ingredients

*An examination of the attitudes
of the Chinese to their food ... and
of the 'make the most of everything'
philosophy that dictates what
goes into it.*

Everything but the Feathers

With any style of cooking, what emerges from the kitchen to be set before the diners will be only as good as what went into the kitchen. As the English proverb has it: "You can't make a silk purse from a sow's ear."

Chinese epicureans would be the first to agree with this sentiment; but, at the same time, they would be dismayed by so light a dismissal of a sow's ear. For, like almost every part of almost every creature, it constitutes in their minds a possible candidate for the cooking pot — as long as it is fresh.

The Chinese attitude to what goes into their kitchens was colourfully illustrated in an interview with Michael Chow, the owner of widely patronised Chinese restaurants in London and Beverly Hills, that was published in Newsweek magazine in 1977. Referring to an approach to food that is nothing if not adventurous, he commented: "If you give a chicken to a Chinese, he'll eat everything but the feathers. If the Chinese don't eat the feathers, nobody can."

He was not exaggerating.

Amazing ingenuity, born of the traditional thriftiness of the Chinese, is as much a part of the philosophy of Chinese cooking as the striving for diversity, true flavour and visual appeal. Virtually nothing is too humble to be considered as a potential ingredient. And whether the diners are expecting something worthy of an Imperial Banquet or merely a snack, the Chinese cook always feels the challenge to do the greatest possible justice to whatever is available. In short, Chinese cooking involves more than knowing how to use ingredients.

Equally importantly, it also involves knowing how to choose them.

In this regard, freshness is by far the most important criterion. Granted that the majority of Chinese are obliged to cut some corners — having neither the money to spend on much more than staple ingredients, nor the time to spend on what should, ideally, be twice-daily (morning and afternoon) trips to the market.

But freshness is something on which they refuse to compromise. So much so that refrigeration is regarded with suspicion. Because refrigeration is thought to be a compromise and, as such, it must lead to some loss of quality.

No chicken, for example, survives the freezing process completely unchanged. The same can be said of pork and other meats. And seafood invariably loses something if it is refrigerated anywhere along its way from the sea to the stove. All of which is not to say that the Chinese are averse to preserved foods. On the contrary, several ingenious preservation methods — very different from refrigeration — are commonly used. But, once again, nothing will be preserved that is not absolutely fresh to begin with.

Shopping around

Few Chinese cooks set out for the market with fixed ideas as to what they are going to buy. A change in the weather means changes in market prices; so the shopper will know what represents the best value for money only after seeing what the market folk have for sale.

In many households there is still likely to be a copy of an old almanac that gives the 24 key points of the year and sets out elaborate instructions as to what food should be a good buy at any given time. Today, however, it would seldom be referred to, instead, a cook prefers to decide what is in season on the evidence of his, or her, own eyes. And it would be an unimaginative — and extravagant — cook who tried to do otherwise.

"Never use for food meat which falls on the ground and does not leave a wet patch or which is found to be warm after having been left overnight."

Imperial Cookery Book of the Mongol Dynasty — *Yin Shan Cheng Yao*

41

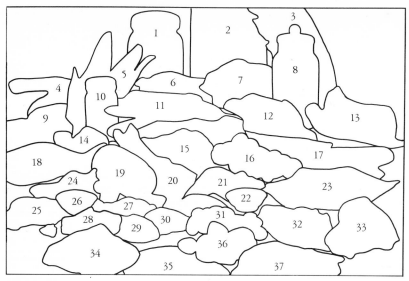

1. Red Dates
2. Dried Mushrooms
3. Dried Fish-Lips
4. Agar-Agar
5. Shark's Fin
6. Pickled Cabbage
7. Bird's Nest
8. Cloud Ear Fungus
9. Dried Squid
10. Preserved Beancurd
11. Chinese Sausages
12. Jelly Fish
13. Dried Fish
14. Honeyed-Date
15. Lily Flowers
16. Dried Longan
17. Sea Laver
18. Dried Duck's Kidney
19. Brown Peppercorns (Fagara)
20. Melon Seeds
21. Cinnamon Bark
22. Monosodium Glutamate
23. Salted Black Beans
24. Dried Tangerine Peel
25. Melon Seeds (black)
26. "Five-Spices" Powder
27. Dried Lotus Seeds
28. Star Anise
29. Sesame Seeds (black)
30. Cloves
31. Ovoid Cardamom
32. Lily Bud
33. Rock Crystal Sugar
34. Walnuts
35. Sesame Seeds (white)
36. Conpoy
37. Dried Shrimps

Pork

China has an umatched range of climatic and geographical conditions, providing a seemingly endless wealth of raw materials on which any cook can draw. Indeed, variety is one of the Chinese cook's greatest preoccupations. Different tastes, tints and textures must complement each other. No single ingredient should be allowed to overpower the others.

A blank canvas

Many of the most treasured Chinese foods have little real substance in themselves. Bird's nest and shark's fin, for example, resemble nothing more than rather flavourless gelatine until the alchemy of the kitchen imparts some delicious added taste during the final stages of their preparation.

On a humbler level, the concern that the cook should determine the final texture and flavour of each dish could explain the overwhelming devotion of the Chinese to pork.

People are sometimes surprised to learn that pork features in probably as many as seven out of ten Chinese meat dish recipes. But there are several good reasons for this. Not only are low production costs and near-universal availability strong arguments for its

acceptance by all except the Moslem minority in China, it also has the perfect qualities demanded by the Chinese cook: it has virtually no distinctive smell; its texture is smooth, rather than fibrous; and it responds to almost any kind of treatment. So, like a painter facing a blank canvas, a cook can do with pork whatever imagination may dictate.

Pork marries with any vegetable or flavouring agent. It submits almost equally well to all cooking methods. It can be minced, shredded, sliced or cubed. It can be served in large chunks ... or even as a whole pig or piglet.

Other meats are described literally by the animal from which they come, so that mutton, for example, is called 'sheep meat' (羊肉). Perhaps the ultimate indication of pork's popularity, then, is that it is often spoken of simply as 'meat' (肉).

Happy is the man, woman or child whose religion does not prohibit the enjoyment of the meat of the pig, prepared by a cook with the whole palate of kitchen colour to command. Not for nothing is the Chinese character for home (家) made up from the radical for roof (宀) over the character for pig (豕).

Beef

Beef cattle have never been raised in China. Consequently, no 'steak cult' has developed there, even among the wealthiest of gourmets. Instead, such beef as there is comes, more often than not, from the ox and the buffalo.

Long used by the Chinese as draught animals — to pull ploughs; to power vast millstones to crush sugar cane, rock salt and grain; and to haul buckets to raise water from the wells — oxen and buffaloes came to be regarded as faithful servants and friends. Nevertheless, few owners could afford sentiment to persuade them to pension off an ox or a buffalo that had outlived its usefulness. So, provided that it was not sick, the faithful servant and friend usually ended its days in the

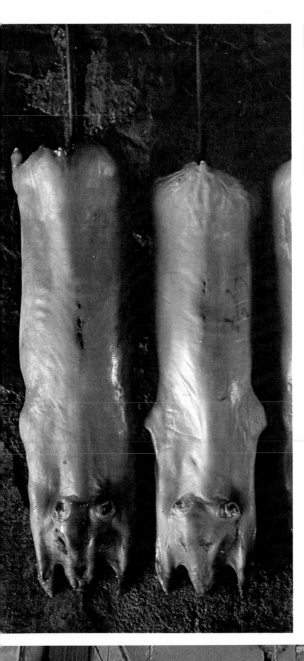

cooking pot.

Perhaps it is because an ox or a buffalo would not be killed before it was well past its prime, or perhaps it is because of the revulsion of most Chinese from the sight and smell of red meat; but, whatever the reason, the number of Chinese beef dish recipes is relatively small. And the majority of them originated in the Moslem-influenced regions of China's north and west.

As oxen and buffaloes were kept for anything but the production of meat, the Chinese have devised several ways of overcoming the lack of tenderness of their beef, and of actually taking advantage of its characteristics.

Generally, the meat is shredded, or sliced finely, always against the grain, so that the fibres are not unduly long. (Several recipes require shredded beef to be deep-fried to produce a crisp, yet chewy, effect that can be delectable; and one of the recipes that make

the best use of finely-sliced beef is for so-called Cantonese Fillet, with the meat being marinated to the ultimate degree of tenderness prior to quick stir-frying). Another method of preparing beef is mincing — especially popular in Northern China — to make rich dumplings, judiciously flavoured with ginger and a little Chinese parsley or scallion. Again, no brief description of beef as an element of Chinese food would be complete without a mention of the delicious dried beef (牛肉乾) — cured with spices — that is sold, wherever Chinese people are found, as a tasty, albeit expensive, snack.

Finally, it is worth noting that the rather fibrous texture of beef is not the meat's only drawback where the Chinese cook is concerned. Beef also has a too pronounced taste for the Chinese palate and needs to be disguised by the use of fairly strong flavourings.

Lamb, Mutton and Goat's Meat

There was a time when lamb, mutton and goat's meat were contemptuously dismissed by most Chinese as no more than barbarian meats — fit only for the Mongols who had introduced them into the country. What is more, while there have been changes in this attitude, they have had no great effect on Chinese eating habits overall. So just as sheep and goats are not a common sight in China's country-side, their meat is not a common sight on its dinner tables.

Mutton dressed as lamb

To discuss sheep and goats in the Chinese language is to invite confusion. Both animals share the same Chinese character (羊) — although the goat may be more accurately described as 'mountain sheep' (山羊). And distinguishing between the young and old of either species can be complicated enough to render epigrams about mutton dressed as lamb (or, for that matter, goat dressed as kid) well-nigh untranslatable.

Linguistics aside, though, it is true to say that goat's meat can be discounted here and, furthermore, that mutton still finds acceptance among remarkably few Chinese other than those in Northern China and those, mainly in the north and the west, who adhere to Moslem beliefs. Thus, mutton is far from readily available in Southern China, for example, where only the largest food markets will have a stall at which it can be bought.

The reason for the meat's unpopularity is, simply, its strong smell. And even mutton devotees appear to feel the need to mask its character to some degree as in most mutton dishes the meat is sliced or shredded and then

braised with plenty of powerful scallions and other fierce disguises.

One can only assume that the nomads who kept herds of sheep and goats in the northern border regions of China must have discovered how good their meat can taste when simply roasted or barbecued. But, despite several authors' having left accounts of attending such meals, no recipes have come down to us.

All the same, we have those nomads' descendants to thank for today's Mongolian hot pots and barbecues to which finely-sliced mutton can make quite the most tasty contribution.

Other Meats

Animals of all kinds must once have thrived in the dense forests of Northern China and in the remotest regions of the rest of the country. But the rabbits and hares and the many kinds of game, about which one reads in literature on China, seem to have been hunted down mainly to provide the ingredients for special dishes to be set before the royal and the rich, rather than on humbler tables.

Venison was (and continues to be) considered as a delicacy — though it could be argued that it has always been a rather unimportant by-product of the deer in comparison with the antlers, with their supposed rejuvenating properties. Less understandably to the Westerner, bear's paw was also highly prized — as, indeed, it still is by some Chinese, along with a number of similarly exotic items.

However, such foods have never had a place in everyday Chinese cooking. And if rabbits and hares and other more commonplace creatures ended up in the domestic cooking pot — as, surely, they must have done — there seem to be no records of the ways in which they were prepared.

Chicken

In Chinese terms, the chicken could well be called 'the pig of the poultry world'. For, like the pig, it can fend largely for itself on farmyard pickings and domestic left-overs; its flesh has no real smell or particular texture; and, within certain obvious physical limitations, it is so versatile that few cooks are not happy to work with it. Furthermore, unlike the pig, the chicken provides a meat that is acceptable to all religions.

In common with many people, the Chinese regard chicken as easy to digest and extremely nutritious. In fact, one suspects that, if constant demand did not make fresh chicken a relatively expensive buy, the majority of Chinese would proably eat it almost every day. (Remember that frozen chicken is seen to be a rather poor substitute.) As it is, chicken is so highly esteemed that it regularly forms a part of the festive offerings made by the Chinese to their ancestors; and restaurant menus often honour it with the name of the legendary bird that is the 'hero' of so much Chinese folk-lore; the phoenix.

Recipes for chicken dishes are numerous, and they cover all manner of foods as the flesh combines happily with vegetables, nuts and noodles alike.

A whole chicken can simply be boiled in a mixture of soy sauce and spices to produce the famous dish, Soya Chicken (油雞), that has made the reputation of many Cantonese restaurants in particular. Or it may be used for soup, in which case it will be cooked until it is so soft that the diners can separate the flesh from the bones with a mere push of a chopstick. Again, a whole chicken can be roasted in any one of a variety of ways. Whereupon, however, it will not be carved at the table — an idea quite foreign to the Chinese. Instead, the cook chops it into easily manageable pieces before it leaves the kitchen, arranging the pieces on the serving plate to approximate the original shape of the bird.

Some people are disconcerted to find that the Chinese may serve chicken that is a little rare by Western standards, with blood remaining on the bones in some dishes, such as White-cut Chicken. At other times, inexperienced diners will have difficulty in separating pieces of chicken from each other, or in removing splinters of bone from the flesh — operations that the Chinese cook is not expected to perform beforehand.

As we have already said, every part of a chicken can be put to good use by the Chinese cook — except the feathers. And even the toughest bird can be turned into the wonderful chicken stock which forms the base for so many of the cook's best sauces and soups.

Duck and Goose

Compared with the chicken, the duck is a rather less tractable creature in the kitchen. Its flesh has a quite determined smell and a distinct texture, quite apart from carrying a good deal of fat; and it tends to combine less well than chicken with other food.

The birds are almost as cheap to raise as chickens, though. So the smallest Chinese hamlet appears to have its own duck pond, with flooded paddy, streams, lakes and waterways rarely very far away. However, there is some dissention over the place of the duck in Chinese cooking. It is certainly less economical than the chicken, as it produces less meat; and its 'Parson's Nose' is unduly large and thought by many Chinese to have an offensive odour. Yet it does have an interesting flavour and a certain appeal, not being an everyday food by any means.

No matter which argument is to be preferred, the fact remains that there are several classic duck dishes that have become famous outside China, one of which in particular — namely Peking Duck — has achieved near-universal renown.

Various other duck dishes — especially from the north and east of China — tend to be eclipsed by the fame of the Peking speciality. Many of these regional specialities feature duck cooked in a soup or a stew, with spices or other strongly-flavoured ingredients that complement the taste of the meat. Again, Nanking is known for its seasoned, dried duck; and the

Cantonese have their own version of this which is as highly prized as Chin Hua ham (金華火腿).

The goose features still further down the scale of popularity, as it were — carrying even more fat than the duck and being anything but a 'good mixer'. It cannot go without mention, though, if only because of its appeal to the *Ch'ao Chow* people who particularly relish their Ch'ao Chow Goose, a dish in which the liver and the blood of the goose are steamed and served together with the whole bird.

Pigeon and Turkey

Pigeons are no great respecters of persons wherever they occur, and in China, as in many Western countries, they have long flown wild in the cities and the countryside, arousing the ire of the inhabitants. Over the years, and around the world, revenge has been wreaked on them in the cooking pot, and the Chinese now breed them especially for that purpose. And although even these 'battery pigeons' have relatively little flesh on them, Chinese cooks have developed a number of delicacies — using minced pigeon breasts, for example — that are a tribute to such flesh as there is.

Gourmet dishes aside, the best introduction to pigeon, Chinese style, would probably be in the form of pigeon deep-fried, braised in soy sauce or boiled in a typical soup.

At the other extreme where size is concerned, the turkey plays some part in Chinese cooking; but, given the Chinese philosophy of eating, it is altogether too large a bird to be popular — too large to be prepared as a single dish, and too large to provide meat of a sufficiently subtle flavour.

At which point, some readers are probably asking themselves how it is that anyone can treat pigeon and turkey as remotely similar subjects for discussion.

The answer is simple: bearing in mind the difference in size between chicken and pigeon on the one hand and between chicken and turkey on the other, a number of chicken dish recipes can be readily and rewardingly

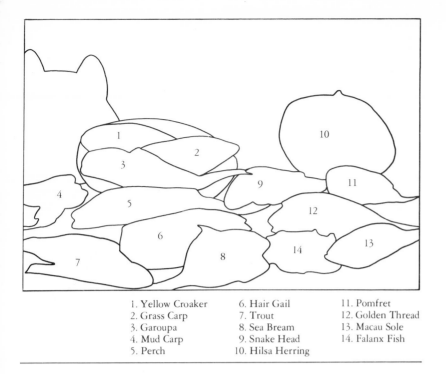

1. Yellow Croaker
2. Grass Carp
3. Garoupa
4. Mud Carp
5. Perch
6. Hair Gail
7. Trout
8. Sea Bream
9. Snake Head
10. Hilsa Herring
11. Pomfret
12. Golden Thread
13. Macau Sole
14. Falanx Fish

'translated' to allow either of the other two birds to be used.

Rice-Birds and Other Birds

The tiny rice-birds (a species also known as the paddy bird or Java sparrow) are netted in their thousands from the rice fields at harvest time. They are cooked whole, usually either in soy sauce or a similar spiced mixture, or fried. They are also eaten whole, with the small bones making a crunchy contrast to the minute covering of tasty skin and flesh.

Almost anything that flies, like anything that walks or swims, can be cooked. From quail to owl, the Chinese cook will deal happily with them all, turning them into something of an individual creation every time.

Entrails and Suchlike

The 'waste not, want not' philosophy of the Chinese has given Chinese cooks, throughout hundreds of years, the strongest possible incentive to make the most of everything. Thus, the Chinese have a vast selection of dishes using the liver, kidneys, blood or even the feet or heads of various animals and birds. What cannot be served in its own right, or combined with other ingredients, will rarely go to waste, either. Instead, it will almost certainly go into the soup pot that is an indispensable part of every Chinese cook's stock-in-trade.

Not surprisingly, the best dishes of this kind are to be found in the area of traditional home cooking, where the need for economy tends to outweigh other considerations. But gourmets, too, put enjoyment before appearances, and a fair number of recipes have been adopted by restaurant chefs, 'by popular demand'. A variety of techniques are used, often in combination, to make a delectable morsel out of quite unlikely raw materials.

Goose feet braised with abalone, for example, is a highly prized (and highly-priced) dish — as are stir-fried duck's tongues, bone marrow stewed with duck's feet, and stir-fried frog's bladders.

Fish

The Chinese character for fish (魚) transliterates as *yu* — a homonym for another *yu* (餘), meaning abundance or prosperity.

The carp is still the most prized. Not only is it a great delicacy, it is also commonly used in Chinese literature to represent the diligent and ambitious young scholar, competing for a place in the Mandarin hierarchy, who requires great courage and determination — like the carp of Chinese legend, swimming upstream in an attempt to become a dragon.

Fish are favourite decorative motives on buildings and brocades alike: they are believed to swim faithfully in pairs and thus often symbolise the ideal state of married bliss.

Clearly fish have always been important to the Chinese. The catching of fish is reputed to date back almost 5,000 years, and they have long been a vital element in the diet of commoner and ruler alike. The varied and long — 3,000-mile — coastline harbours abundant fish of many varieties for vast regions of China. Even land-locked provinces have lakes, canals or rivers where freshwater fish multiply. Fish breeding ponds have been in use for centuries. Consequently almost everyone has a nearby source of this valuable food.

Indeed, it would be almost impossible to list all the fish to be found on the Chinese dining table. In addition to the carp, some of the more popular are garoupa, pomfret, sole, bream and mullet. But almost everything from the smallest white bait to the largest sturgeon has a place in the kitchen. And one of the most prized delicacies also comes from the sea: the shark's fin, so vital to any banquet, and such a challenge to any cook.

Fish is another of the foods that owe their popularity with the Chinese to the fact that they can be cooked in any one of many different ways, whether as a main dish in themselves, or as ingredients of other dishes.

The Chinese like to buy their fish from the market not just fresh but, wherever possible, actually still alive and swimming in a water-filled 'carrier bag'. By the same token, many restaurants make a feature of inviting their patrons to indicate the fish of their choice from among those swimming around in the establishment's 'aquaria'.

Newcomers to Chinese food often find that they enjoy the fish dishes more than those of other cuisines that they are acquainted with. The reason for this is probably that the Chinese cook is singularly adept at bringing out the best in just about every fish: so that it still tastes like fish and yet has lost any aggressive 'fishiness', so to speak.

Salted Fish

When salted fish is being cooked, no-one remains in ignorance for very long. Kitchen doors and windows would have to be all but hermetically sealed to contain the choking fumes (and the choking cook) and the smell of the frying fish which is a tribute to its powerful taste. However, the flavour of one species of salted fish in particular — the white herring (鰽白) makes the suffering well worthwhile.

The technique is to cook the fish until even the bones become crunchy and nutty, rather than spiny and inedible. And as you eat salted fish, with plain boiled rice or congee, you seem to taste not one fish but all the fish that ever swam in the sea, seemingly concentrated in each and every bite.

Shrimps, Prawns, Crabs and Lobsters

The variety of fish available to the Chinese, from the sea or from inland waters, is closely matched by the variety of other seafood and of crustaceans of all kinds from the same bountiful sources. So the Chinese are extremely partial to shrimps and prawns — both of which are usually referred to simply as *hsia* (蝦) since they are similar in all respects except their size. Crabs, too are very popular; but lobsters are comparatively rare and, on the occasions when they are cooked, they tend to be treated in much the same way as a large sea-water crab would be.

Shrimps and prawns — and, to a lesser extent, crabs — provide further evidence of the all-important qualification for serious acceptance in Chinese cooking: namely the ability to be 'a good mixer'.

"Don't eat crabs before August."

Imperial Cookery Book of the Mongol Dynasty — *Yin Shan Cheng Yao*

Oysters

The prospect of eating raw oysters would be largely unthinkable to many Chinese, who are convinced — probably with a fair amount of justification — that any coastline is too prone to contamination for its products to be eaten without their having been thoroughly cooked beforehand. Another consideration, of course, is that oysters do not travel well; so, with China being so vast a country, they were hardly likely to remain fresh during trips to food markets at all remote from the sea. Preserved oysters could survive such journeys, though, and did — to find their way into several styles of cooking.

Abalone

Abalone in its fresh form is usually imported into China from Australia, Japan or Africa. Intrepid divers work hard to detach the pearly shell from the rocks and corals to which it clings some 30 metres or more below the

surface. Most dried abalone comes from Japan. Tinned abalone comes from Australia, Mexico and the USA. Whatever form one elects to use, however, abalone is anything but easy to prepare.

A skillful cook can stir-fry slices of fresh abalone and produce wondrously tender results; but a minute's overcooking will make it irrecoverably tough.

On the other hand, it takes many hours of boiling to render dried abalone tender enough to eat, though the trouble is well worthwhile, as its tasty tang can liven up many a Chinese soup or mixed meat dish; and when delicately-cooked dried abalone is served on a special occasion, the diners can be sure that their host is paying them a rather expensive compliment.

Consequently, canned abalone is one of the few 'convenience foods' that Chinese cooks do not blush to use, albeit the motto remains: "Handle with care."

Clams, Scallops and Conpoys

Clams respond well to almost any treatment in the kitchen and can take on new shades of meaning in the hands of a versatile Chinese cook.

1. Clams	5. Scallops	9. Lobster
2. Shrimps	6. Oysters	10. Crabs
3. Squid	7. Crabs	11. Crabs
4. Scallops	8. Prawns	12. Prawns

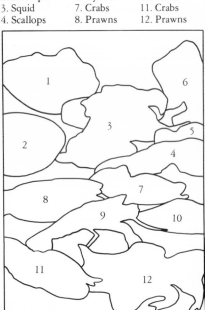

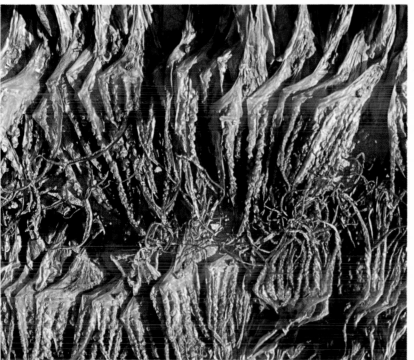

Scallops are often treated in the same ways as clams; and dried scallop — although much less popular — can be added to soups and congee, or shredded for use as a flavouring ingredient. It usually consists only of disc-shaped pieces cut from the creature's root muscle, and its preparation is a tedious process.

The conpoy — often confused with its cousin, the scallop — is rarely encountered except in its dried form.

Sea Cucumber

Sometimes called beche-de-mer (literally 'sea slug'), the sea cucumber puzzles many people on first encounter. Its unprepossessing appearance, gelatinous texture and almost total lack of aroma and flavour make it one of those ingredients in Chinese cooking that rely on the presence of other ingredients for palatability. This is not to say that it is never served on its own, but it is certainly more pleasant on first acquaintance if it is mixed with goosefeet, say, or abalone.

These strange creatures are usually available in food markets only in their dried form, although there are some shops where they are sold soaked in water, ready for the kitchen.

Jelly-Fish

While Westerners regard the gelatinous oceanic jelly-fish with nothing less than suspicion, if not outright distaste, the infinitely more pragmatic Chinese simply accept it as another god-sent ingredient. In fact, it constitutes a main ingredient of various dishes, being welcomed for its interestingly chewy texture and its bland flavour, which is 'counter-pointed' by other tastier ingredients.

Cuttlefish

Cuttlefish (or squid) is not regarded by the Chinese as one of the classier seafoods; but most people seem to enjoy it well enough when they eat it. It is readily available, inexpensive and easily cooked; and, when dried, it is popular as what could be called the Chinese version of chewing gum.

Shark's Fin

Shark's fin comes from India, Japan, Korea, Mexico and Norway as well as from the Philippines — the source of the best and by far the most expensive variety which is known as Manila Yellow. It is always sold dried, and is graded according to its size, degree of perfection and other features demanded by the gourmet. It is also one of the least approachable of materials: almost papery in appearance, but as hard as the horn that it resembles. The Chinese cook has to work long and hard, then, on soaking it to produce the requisite gelatinous texture.

Nowadays shark's fin soups tend to arrive at the table with the fins split into shreds. Only if the smallest kind of fin is used — or in the most expensive shark's fin soups, for the most special occasions — will the fins be served intact.

Shark's fin soup is among the most highly prized of all Chinese banquet dishes. So much so that it is considered a gross breach of etiquette to leave any of the soup uneaten; and stories are told of Chinese cooks who were so insulted to see their cherished creation spurned that they promptly resigned from their posts.

Bird's Nest

It is difficult to classify bird's nest (perhaps it could be called vegetable-like, though this would be to stretch a point). However, it can certainly be classified as an exotic and highly-prized a food as shark's fin: hence its inclusion at this point.

The unitiated are often astonished to learn that bird's nest really is bird's nest — albeit a very special kind. In fact, the papery-looking cups come from the outer layer of the nests built by the salangane (a type of swallow or swift) on the cliffs of the islands of Borneo and the coast of Southern Thailand and Indo-China. The birds secrete an alkaline saliva which hardens as it dries, and they use it to cement together the seaweed and other vegetation that are the raw materials for their nests, and to anchor the nests to their precarious building sites. With long and careful cleaning and preparation, these structures can be reconstituted for the benefit of gourmet diners.

The near-inaccessible location of the nests makes their collection an extremely hazardous and time-consuming operation, which explains their high price in shops and restaurants alike.

Whole bird's nests — which arrive at the table looking for all the world like opaque, creamy porcelain bowls — are the ultimate delicacy. The chips from broken nests (known as *lung nga* or, literally, dragon's teeth) are less expensive but, at the same time, considered as something of an 'also ran'.

Vegetables

Vegetable cultivation follows the general pattern of intensive farming in China, with every available patch of land, however small, being devoted to food production. Rice or wheat may be the staple crop of a particular region; but every farmer has always used his

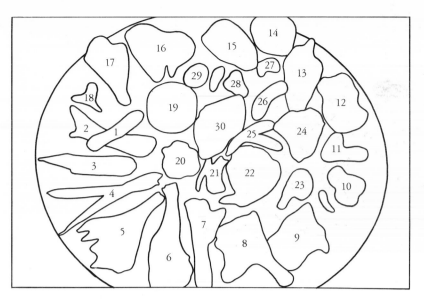

1. Chive Shoots
2. Chives (Flowering)
3. Chives
4. Angled Luffa
5. String Beans (White)
6. String Beans
7. Celery
8. Flowering White Chinese Cabbage
9. Chinese Broccoli
10. Red and Green Chillies, and Capsicum
11. Bitter Melon
12. Chinese Spinach
13. Matrimony Vine
14. White Cabbage
15. Tientsin Cabbage
16. Leaf Mustard
17. Scallions
18. Chinese Parsley
19. Winter Melon
20. Fresh Straw Mushrooms
21. Green Beans
22. Water Spinach
23. Broccoli
24. Chinese White Cabbage
25. Egg Plant
26. Chinese Marrow
27. Ginger
28. Taro
29. Yam Bean
30. Chinese Lettuce

fields at the end of a season — or between crops, if he has more than one a year — for what can best be described as 'table gardening', the forerunner of the market gardening of today.

"Mustard plants in October sprout buds".

Ancient Chinese Proverb

Thanks to the ready availability of fertilisers (including night soil, before the introduction of commercial compounds) and the ingenuity of the country's irrigation systems, fresh vegetables can be obtained almost year-round everywhere in China. What is more, the Chinese farmer seems to have been aware since the earliest days that certain vegetables — such as legumes — provide nutrition not only for human beings but also for the soil.

There again, by no means all vegetables take up precious space in the ground. Vines, bearing a variety of gourds, melons or other produce, can be trained to cover the humblest building and flourish in the sunlight on the roof. Bean sprouts need very little light and can do well indoors, on a damp cloth. Bamboo shoots grow wild. Edible seaweed is there for anyone who takes the trouble to 'harvest' it. And fish ponds and duck ponds can be used for the cultivation of lotus and water chestnut plants.

Greens for green's sake

Even before the current near-universal vogue for Chinese food, the Chinese cook's supremacy in the area of vegetable preparation was widely acknowledged; and the writers of Western vegetarian cookbooks have long extolled the virtues of the Chinese cook's way with green vegetables in particular.

It was not only the thrifty 'make the most of everything' philosophy of the Chinese that accounted for the strength of the national vegetarian cooking tradition. The Buddhists had a significant formative influence in this respect; and as long ago as the 10th century, Buddhist missionaries had won over a great number of converts. The Buddhists developed their own 'Palace' style of cooking; and, while their political power waned in later centuries, enthusiasm for their cuisine did not.

Root vegetables

Although land-hungry root vegetables are restricted to certain areas of China, they are generally valued as sources of starch and, in some cases, for their unusual colour and texture. For example, turnips are often made into a sort of white relish; and yams have various uses — as when they are grated and cooked to make crisp coatings on deep-fried sweets or savouries.

On the final analysis, it would be all but impossible to list the name of every vegetable with a place in Chinese cooking (after all, in Eastern China there are 17 varieties of bean alone!). However, the names of the vegetables that appear in the Recipes chapter of this book are listed in the glossary of ingredients, together with the names of Western vegetables that can be substituted for them if necessary.

"When eating bamboo shoots, remember the men who planted them."

Ancient Chinese Proverb

1. Chives
2. Bamboo Shoots
3. Chives (Flowering)
4. Leek
5. Scallions
6. Chinese Parsley
7. Scallions
8. Red and Green Chillies
9. Chive Shoots
10. Onions
11. Capsicums
12. Ginger
13. Shallots
14. Garlic

Bamboo

The amenable bamboo deserves a special mention. For its wood has long been one of nature's greatest gifts to the Chinese, providing a valuable raw material in building and construction, and in the manufacture of an incredibly wide range of products, from opium pipes to furniture. And it is also a valuable source of food.

The shoots of new trees, gathered as they emerge from the soil each spring, are a great delicacy when fresh; and we are fortunate that they survive drying or canning unspoiled. Less familiar are the green tips of the bamboo's branches, picked before they unfurl and used in special soup and congee. Like many other foods, these young leaves are believed by the Chinese to be highly beneficial to the health.

Preserved vegetables

Centuries before refrigeration and canning became available as ways of preserving food, the Chinese used pickling, salting and drying to store surplus vegetables and other produce 'against a rainy day'. There are several different methods of pickling. Some are calculated to keep vegetables crisp and crunchy, but for a relatively short period; others cause the vegetables to become softer, but give them a much longer life in the process. Vinegar is the usual preservative.

In regions where salt is abundant, various salting techniques were developed. Simple salting involves washing the vegetables and cutting them into bite-size pieces which are sprinkled with dry salt, left in the sun for half a day and then packed into jars — possibly after the addition of powdered chilli or other spices. It makes an attractive appetizer out of, for example, young ginger, turnip or almost any kind of cabbage. For longer storage, the prepared vegetables are scalded and then packed in layers in a sterilised jar, interspersed with layers of salt. The jar is topped up with cooled boiled water, and garlic, chilli and raw shallots can be added to provide extra taste.

Almost any kind of vegetable — like almost any kind of fish, seafood or meat — can be dried simply by hanging it in the sun. The dehydrated vegetables are reconstituted and added to soup, stew, congee or savoury dishes. However, properly reconstituting and using dried vegetables is a laborious process, so they tend to appeal far more to the Chinese housewife than to the Chinese restaurant cook.

Mushrooms

Dried mushrooms are a subject in themselves. They can be found in any market, in a bewildering array of shapes and sizes; and they are very widely used in Chinese cooking.

In fact there are very few Chinese mushrooms which are used more regularly in their fresh form — perhaps the best known of these being *ts'ao ku* (草菇) (literally straw mushrooms).

Tung ku (冬菇) (literally 'winter mushrooms') are probably the most prized variety, and the finest quality *tung ku* (pinch them to feel which are the thickest) can be very expensive indeed. They last almost indefinitely and, reconstituted, they can be used as an ingredient in many dishes, or as a dish in their own right.

Hua ku (花菇) (literally 'flower mushrooms') are thicker, but rather smaller, than *tung ku*. They are equally versatile, though, and just as easy to use.

By contrast with *tung ku* — savoury and succulent when properly prepared — other types of fungus are popular with the Chinese for their blandness and crunchy nature, which add texture to a dish, rather than flavour. *Yun erh* (雲耳) (literally 'cloud ears') are perhaps the best known examples of this type. In their dried state they resemble scraps of charred paper. When soaked and cooked they turn into perfectly shaped 'double ears'.

Soya Beans

The soya bean has often been described as 'the cow of China' because of the many valuable foods, many of them extremely high in protein content, that can be made from it.

The soya bean is the raw material for the delicious sauce that accompanies every Chinese meal, and that has most likely been used in the cooking of one or more of the dishes served.

"Bean curd, if good, is better than bird's nest.

And better than sea slugs, if these are not

first rate, is a dish of bamboo shoots."

The soya bean is also the source of bean curd, or *tou fu* (豆腐), that most versatile of foods in the hands of any cook with any degree of imagination. Unlike soy sauce, it can easily be made on a small scale: the soya beans are pre-soaked and then ground to a powder which is mixed with water to form a puree; this is strained through a cloth (a process similar to the manufacture of cottage cheese), and the resultant liquid is heated before being mixed with a little gypsum and poured into a mould to set and drain. Clearly the quality of the local water has a bearing on the bean curd's final flavour — which is why certain places, such as Sha Tin in the New Territories of Hong Kong, were once renowned for their particular *tou fu*.

Again, soya bean 'milk' is a well-liked and particularly nourishing drink, said to have kept alive many children, especially, during times of privation — as, in recent years, during World War II.

"According to the 'expenses' section of the Imperial Banqueting Court of the early 18th Century, bean curd was the cheapest of all vegetable products at six copper cash per *chin* (approximately one half-kilogram) — the most expensive being white honey, at 150 copper cash per *chin*."

One only has to go to Buddhist cooking to discover that bean curd can be made to assume almost any texture. It is most familiar in the form of a soft cake, with a consistency like cream cheese. If the entire cake is to be preserved intact during cooking, it has to be handled carefully if diners are not to be confronted by a heap of tasty, but shapeless, bits and pieces.

Dried bean curd is more tolerant of handling in the kitchen, as is frozen bean curd which, incidentally, takes on a rather different and interesting texture during the freezing process, becoming *crepe*-like and porous, rather than soft and unresisting. Freezing also seems to give bean curd a slightly smoky flavour that can add character to simple soups ... or elaborate hot pots.

Beans assume many guises in Chinese cooking and, whatever its colour or size, each variety has its special part to play. For example, broad beans and their more modest cousins, *mao tou*, make a delicious *hors d'oeuvre* when prepared Shanghainese-style.

Chinese desserts, too, can incorporate beans and peas. Yellow beans (or lentils) can be used to make several types of dish that resemble Western jelly; or they can be boiled whole, in sugar and water, and eaten hot or chilled. Another example is red beans, which are ground and sweetened to form stuffing for a number of dishes.

Exotica

Shark's fin, snow fungus, bird's nest and other ingredients, which may appear to be exotic to newcomers to Chinese food, pale into insignificance beside some of the dishes reputed to have been included in the most ostentatious banquets in the China of old.

According to certain Western authors writing on the more unusual aspects of Chinese cuisine, some of the most 'imaginative' creations were as follows: peacocks were served, stewed or dried to produce the best flavour; parakeets appeared in various dishes, as did almost all kinds of song bird (believed to be especially valuable for male potency); new-born mice were stuffed with honey to be picked up and eaten at the diners' pleasure; tiny fresh-water shrimps were served live in vinegar and soy sauce; and taro or bamboo shoots were boiled in a pot until almost cooked — at which point live frogs were thrown into the soup to be served, clutching desperately to the vegetables.

Sadly, as far as lovers of the bizarre are concerned, most Chinese authorities insist that very few of these stories are anything more than apocryphal. However, there is reason to believe that pythons were served as a delicacy, pickled in vinegar — perhaps the forerunner of the snake meat-eating cult that has a great number of followers to this day. Furthermore reindeer and ox phallus are still eaten; and one occasionally hears of people who indulge in the eating of monkey brain, while the animal is still alive — although, like the furtive dog meat-eaters who most certainly exist, these 'gourmets' are rarely encountered at first hand.

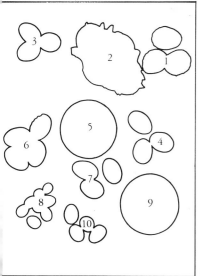

1. Preserved Eggs
   ('100-day-old')
2. Preserved Eggs served
   with pickled ginger
3. Hen Eggs
4. Red-dyed Eggs
5. Tea-Leaf (marbled)
   boiled eggs
6. Preserved Eggs
   (salted)
7. Duck Eggs
8. Quail Eggs
9. Spiced Boiled Eggs
10. Pigeon Eggs

Eggs

Unlike many peoples in the West, the Chinese are not given to eating eggs, simply boiled or fried, for their own sake. Which is not to say, though, that eggs are not regarded as an important food. They are — whether hen eggs, duck eggs or the eggs of some less domestic bird, such as the pigeon or the quail.

Hen eggs are valued in Chinese cooking for a variety of reasons other than their indisputable nourishing properties. A beaten egg, added to a soup or congee, enhances the dish's appearance as well as its goodness. A fine egg pancake, shaped to resemble a flower or something equally fanciful, is sometimes found in banquet hors d'ouevres. Egg is invaluable as a binding agent: so egg white is added to coconut pudding, for example; and egg yolk is used to seal Spring Rolls.

Hard-boiled eggs can be shelled and cooked in a soy sauce-based liquid to produce a popular snack; or their shells are lightly cracked all over (but not removed) and they are steeped in tea to give the white an attractive 'marbled' appearance.

Almost unthinkable to people who have never tried them are the strange '100-year-old eggs' (or '1,000-year-old eggs' as those of an even more imaginative turn of phrase have it). People who have tried these jelly-like objects — duck eggs that may be 100 days old — do not attempt to describe them. They simply reach for the raw ginger and vinegar dip so that they can enjoy yet another segment.

Duck eggs are not as hardy as hen eggs, so preservation is a logical way of ensuring that they do not spoil and go to waste. Lime is the usual preservative; and limey mud — or a mixture of lime, ash or chaff and salt — is where the eggs lie buried for between two and four months. In the 'curing' process the lime works on the eggs to create their unusual texture and unique flavour, which will be enhanced in the case of 'de luxe' eggs by the addition of tea, or some other flavouring agent, to the preserving mixture.

Again, duck eggs may be pickled in brine; or their yolks may be dried in the sun (until they look like apricots) and used as a filling for festive Moon cakes.

Rice

Rice is the staple of China, grown throughout most of the country and still available in regions where the climate dictates that wheat and other grains should be cultivated in its place. Morning, noon and night, it forms the most important single element in almost every meal.

Unadorned, fluffy and fragrant, boiled rice is sometimes described as being so essential to the Chinese that other foods are almost incidental: meat, fish and vegetable dishes — referred to under the collective term, *ts'ai* (菜) — are there merely to help the rice down! While this is something of an overstatement, one has to admit that rice has to be regarded as the single unifying link in a Chinese meal. Furthermore, it provides a 'cushion' for richer foods, and it complements lighter ones. But, when all is said and done, no Chinese needs a reason or an excuse for eating rice: it is simply a fact of life.

Bumping into a friend or an acquaintance, a Chinese might ask: "Have you had your food yet?" It is a rhetorical question (as when an Englishman asks: "How do you do?") ... but what is more to the point is that the Chinese word for food in such a context is the word rice. Because rice has been fundamental to the Chinese for thousands of years. In fact, legend dates its first cultivation back to the fourth millenium BC — and legend is probably underestimating for once, as archeologists now suggest that rice was well established in China a good deal earlier.

Nutritionists are dismayed at the vast quantities of white rice consumed in China — and, indeed, in other Asian countries. But the custom of polishing the grain, to remove the germ, is an ancient one — witness the fact that Confucius, writing almost 2,500 years ago, specified that his rice must be white and pure in appearance. Today, mechanical removal of the husk destroys even more protein and vitamins than did the old method of haphazard pounding in a mortar. But, being so easily digested, white rice — like the much maligned Western white bread — is unarguably 'here to stay'.

7,000 varieties. 100 recipes

The Chinese say that they have 7,000 varieties of rice, and although there is probably an element of exaggeration here — as in most popular sayings of this type — it is certainly true to say that the varieties of rice available on the market are legion. A visit to the rice wholesalers' quarter of Hong Kong, for example, is something of an eye-opener in this respect, with many hundreds of bins on show, each containing a rice of a different variety. In fact rice is probably most closely analagous to grapes as, in a sense, every crop

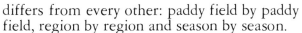

differs from every other: paddy field by paddy field, region by region and season by season.

By the same token, it is claimed that there are at least 100 methods of boiling rice, all of which are calculated to produce 'perfect' results. In this case, the figure could be an underestimation, as every Chinese cook is only too happy to extol the virtues of his or her 'Special' method. Finer points of argument aside, however, the method given in the Recipes chapter of this book is one that has been well tried over the years, and we recommend it as being simple and reliable.

Plain boiled rice is intended to be fluffy, with the conscientious cook rinsing the grains carefully before cooking. Some rices, on the other hand, are intended to be sticky, so that glutinous rice is a special variety, with its short, round grains used for many sweets that are far removed from the Western concept of a rice pudding. The grains may also be ground to produce rice flour, for desserts and other foods — and even as face powder.

Noodles

In parts of China remote from the rice-producing regions, wheat and other grains are used, for reasons of economy and convenience, as the alternative to rice to provide starch in the everyday diet; and they are used in other parts of the country, too — simply as a change. Leavened and unleavened breads of many kinds are common in Chinese food, then; but even more common are the varied and versatile members of the noodle family.

Introduce a Chinese gourmet to an Italian gourmet, and the chances are that an argument will break out before long as to whether it was in China or in Italy that pasta-type dishes were first developed. Certainly there are clear similarities between the old-fashioned noodle-making machines that can be found in villages in China and Italy alike, Again, cooks making egg noodles will employ basically the same technique, whether they are Chinese or Italian. So the argument will probably never be resolved; and — as there is basically only one way in which to make noodles and related products, and both countries have a long history of such delights — the truth could well be that the Chinese and the Italians arrived at the discovery independently.

Chinese noodles may take the form of anything from wispy, vermicelli-like strands to thick, broad 'ribbons'. They may be made with egg; and the flour that is used is a wheat flour — though there are 'bean noodles' and rice noodles' for special occasions.

Most types of Chinese noodle are

disconcertingly long, a feature that is traditionally taken, in the northern region in particular, as a symbol of longevity or an unbroken life — hence the popularity of noddles as a key dish at a birthday dinner. To make them easier to handle, these noodles will often be cut into shorter lengths; but superstition dictates that this should be done only after they have been presented at the table.

Noodles can be eaten as a snack, or selected as the basis of a main meal. At the end of a formal banquet, diners are offered the choice between de luxe noodles and special fried rice. Noodles in soup, or the ravioli-like *yun tan* (雲吞) in soup, make a warming dish on a cold day. Fried noodles, or *ch'ao mien* (炒麪), are often served with an elaborate mixture of vegetables and meat comprising the 'sauce'; and while it is hardly the 'correct' procedure, someone dining alone in a good Chinese restaurant could order a large serving of fried noodles and eat and enjoy it as a meal in itself.

Plain boiled noodles need spicy and rich sauces as accompaniment. Cold noodle dishes are served liked a salad, mixed, for example, with shredded cucumber and chicken and served with mustard and sesame paste, to produce a delicious appetiser or a dish in its own right. There are even 'instant noodles' which have come to the rescue of many a desperately rushed cook, and which are another of the very few acceptable Chinese 'convenience foods'.

In fact all that seems to be lacking is a sweet noodle dish, served as a dessert!

Young lady, if you want to eat noodles,
We will go to find old Tuan for you,
Who has flat noodles, and thin noodles
And "curtain-sticks" noodles heigh ho.

Anon

Flour is also put to excellent use in the

making of dumplings (almost a story in themselves) which range from the delicate Cantonese *dim sum* — or, in the national language romanization *tien hsin* (點心) — to the substantial *ta pao* (a big minced meat and vegetable bun) of the north. Obviously the colder climate of the north dictates the heaviness of its typical dumplings, designed to help to insulate the eater against the rigours of winter, and often fried as well as steamed to make them more filling. But even the Cantonese have their famous pork bun, *char siu bau* — or, in the national language romanization, *cha shao pao* (叉燒飽) that is guaranteed to bring a touch of warmth to the most fiercely air-conditioned restaurant.

Pancakes are regular adjuncts to other dishes, and sometimes served on their own. Peking Duck would be incomplete without

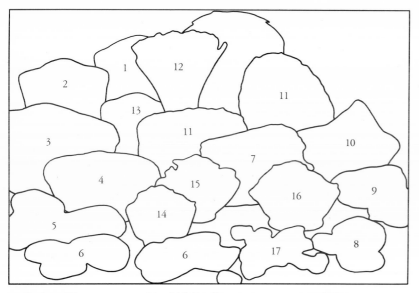

1. Glutinous Rice
2. Shanghai Rice
3. Ssu-Miao Rice
4. Yu Chien Rice
5. Noodle (dried)
6. Egg-based Noodle
7. Rice Stick Noodles
8. Noodle with shrimp-roe
9. Shanghai Noodle (slender)
10. Rice Sheet Noodles
11. Yi Noodle (fried noodle)
12. Flat Noodle (dried)
13. Red Rice
14. Silver-Needle Macaroni
15. Shanghai Noodle
16. Oiled Noodle
17. Bean Thread Vermicelli

the unleavened pancakes of which it forms the filling; and many other dishes are presented in much the same 'do it yourself' way. Spring Rolls, too, are another form of 'stuffed pancake' — although they are served ready made.

Plain steamed bread and twisted 'bread rolls' are also popular accompaniments to dishes which produce a gravy that is rich enough to be soaked up and savoured to the last drop. Also, in Northern China, a popular snack prepared at road-side foodstalls comprises nothing more than a large cartwheel of light, fresh bread — sometimes flavoured with scallions — that is cut into wedges to be eaten with small servings of spicy vegetables and meat ... a mouth-watering proposition for addicts of the smaller onion cakes that are probably their closest substitute in terms of restaurant fare.

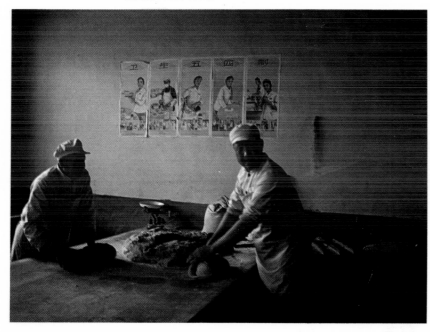

Fruit

China's abundant fruit crops match the country's vegetables and other natural products in their variety. Almost every kind of fruit grows there, in one region or another; and certain of them only really flourish in their native Chinese soil.

You need to look no further than the myriad shops and stalls of Hong Kong, piled high with fruit of every description, to realize how much is available ... and how much it is appreciated by the Chinese. After all, few things are better than a piece of water-melon or a glass of freshly-pressed orange juice as a refresher between meals; and as the final course of a banquet, fruit helps to cleanse the palate and rouse even the most torpid and well-fed diner for the journey home.

Every village in the south of China seems to have its lychee or *li chi* (荔枝) trees, producing a bountiful harvest of fruit for its devotees — a devotee of the lychee arguably being anyone who has ever tried it! The lychee season is all too short, running only from May or June to August — although there is one variety of lychee (三月紅 — literally "third moon red") that ripens earlier. At that time, people flock around the market-folks' baskets and barrows which overflow with bunches of lychees, still on their stalks. The wine-red shells, with their pearly lining, are scattered everywhere, along with the shiny dark-brown stones; and the fragrance of the fruit recalls the spring, when the honey-sweet flowers of the lychee trees perfumed the air for miles around.

A distant cousin of the lychee, the whiskery rambutan (most familiar in Malaysia) is something of a rarity in China. But another cousin, the *lung an* (literally 'dragon's eye'), follows the lychee in season and almost equals it in popularity. Much smaller than the lychee, and with a yellowish shell, the *lung an* has less flesh and a less sweet, slightly resinous, taste.

The lychee and the *lung an* are sometimes tinned, but in this form they bear little resemblance to the fresh fruit — probably because of the syrup in which they are preserved. Dried lychees, on the other hand, can be most pleasant to eat, especially when the craving for a lychee strikes you at the wrong time of the year.

Chinese peaches come in many forms; some of them flat and quite unlike the picture of the fruit that comes to the Western mind. Mountain peaches ripen in the sun — smaller than their lowland counterparts, but still distilling all manner of happy memories inside their warm skins. And in almost every region of the country there will be at least one 'local' peach to bring pleasure to the people.

Chinese artists have long been fascinated by the symmetry of the peach, and it is a favourite subject for still-life paintings, symbolizing long life. It also provides one of the most regularly recurring themes of Chinese folk art, being depicted on everything from Chinese New Year pictures and 'lucky money' packets to embroidered robes and carved wooden furniture.

The varieties of peach are second only to the varieties of the Chinese citrus fruit often referred to, more conveniently than accurately, as Mandarin oranges or tangerines. In fact these varieties range from the majestic King orange or *kan* (a hybrid of orange and tangerine) to the tiny, sweet-skinned tangerine-like kumquat.

Like the peach, the kumquat features large in Chinese superstition; and at Chinese New Year, pots of trees bearing the golden fruit brighten every home with the promise of prosperity in the year to come.

Another Chinese citrus fruit is the massive pomelo, which has been described as being like "a large woody grapefruit" ... and which clings to its tree only with the help of a friendly string bag, tied to a supporting stake.

Most Chinese citrus fruits are as good to eat as they are to look at. The few bitter ones do not go to waste, being turned into medicines or candied to produce tangy sweetmeats for special occasions. Citrus fruit

peel is dried to be used in cooking and to disguise the taste of less palatable herbal remedies — and thrifty hawkers accordingly try to sell the fruit without the peel, which they can sell in its own right!

Turning to other types of fruit, the list of names appears to be all but endless: persimmons, 'wampees', plums, cherries, seedless white grapes, loquats, star fruit (or the 'foreign peach'), apricots, 'oriental flowering apricots' (related to, but quite unlike, the plum!), bananas, pineapples, apples, pears, guavas and papayas.

Olives, too, grow well in many provinces. They are sometimes eaten green, but more often they appear as spiced sweetmeats, valued for their soothing effect on dusty throats and as a stimulant to the salivary glands and the digestive juices.

Again almost every fruit that grows in China can be found in dried form — and often in crystallized and spiced forms as well. Red dates, for example, are valued as a natural sweetener for many desserts, and are also used in many savoury stews and soups.

Nuts and Seeds

All manner of nuts — from the coconut to the gingko nut — flourish along with the other fruits of nature that thrive throughout the length and breadth of China.

Some of them provide precious oil for cooking. Peanut oil, in particular, is ideal in this respect. Its neutral flavour does nothing to detract from the subtleties of a dish; it is cheap to produce (at home, simply pound roasted peanuts in a mortar and strain the resultant oil); and nutritionists are agreed that it does little to harm the health.

Peanuts are popular snacks, too — either fried or toasted with salt, or in the winter months, warm and steaming on the street hawkers' barrows.

More elegant nuts, such as the cashew and the walnut, are usually reserved for serving in fancier meat and poultry dishes — providing an excellent accompaniment to pork and chicken especially.

Almonds are more commonly used for sweets and puddings, though walnuts feature

1. Brow Beans
2. Red Beans
3. Olive Beans
4. Red Beans (small)
5. Fox Nuts
6. Almonds
7. Peanuts
8. Dried Chestnuts
9. Sesame Seeds (black)
10. Sesame Seeds (white)
11. Black Beans
12. Walnuts
13. Gingko Nuts
14. Lotus Seeds
15. Cashew Nuts
16. Green Beans

12.	13.	14.	15.	16.
6.	7.	8.	9.	10.	11.
1.	2.	3.	4.	5.

in recipes in this category as well.

Again certain seeds — sesame, rape and sunflower, for example — provide cooking oil; and melon seeds can be preserved in all manner of ways (usually involving salting and toasting) to provide a tasty snack — notwithstanding the fact that cracking their coats open between one's front teeth, in the accepted manner, is an extremely trying operation for beginners!

Seasonings and Oils

A flavouring agent that is used to varying degress in every regional cuisine of China is the famous Five Spices or *Wu hsiang* (五香). This can be purchased ready-mixed in powder form or by the ingredient, to be blended by the cook. In the latter case, the purchaser will receive equal portions of Chinese cinnamon (*Cinnamomum cassia* — stronger in flavour and coarser in texture than other cinnamon barks), cloves, fagara (brown peppercorns), fennel and star anise. When fagara and fennel are not available, they may be replaced by black peppercorns and aniseed respectively.

A pinch of the powder is added to a dish when strong seasoning is required. The whole spices are more likely to be used in making something longer-lasting, such as *lu shui* master stock.

The mysterious MSG (Monosodium glutamate) is a ubiquitous 'instant flavouring'; but more dishes have been spoiled by the addition of too much MSG rather than by the addition of too little. So it is best to use it with caution for it can draw attention to the presence of an inferior ingredient, instead of compensating for it.

Bicarbonate of soda — capable of heightening the colour of green vegetables — is something else that should be used sparingly. With care, the greenest greens can be produced without its help — although few professional cooks will deny using a few grains of it to tenderize recalcitrant meat, in particular, and to ensure the crispest of batters in deep-frying.

Salt is important in Chinese cooking, but thanks to soy sauce and other highly-concentrated sauces, it is not quite as essential *per se* as one might think. More commonly, it is provided, spiced, as a dip to accompany deep-fried dishes (heavy salting in their cooking tends to make the batter soggy).

In some regions, white or brown sugar is used to 'cut' the flavour of the salt in a dish; brown sugar or maltose is used to glaze meats that are being barbecued; and all of these sweeteners can be mixed judiciously into certain sauces.

Another flavouring agent that no self-respecting Chinese cook will dispense with is ginger. In early summer, the ginger is cream and pink — sprouting delicate green leaves. This is when the root is at its best for pickling and preserving in vinegar, to be served in due course as an appetizer or as a side dish.

The tough, rough grey skin of older ginger roots indicates the strongest flavour. The texture may be fibrous, but cross slicing with a sharp cleaver will cut through the toughest root to release its full value. Meat, fish and vegetables respond equally well to ginger; and often a piece of ginger will be fried in cooking oil before the oil is used — no empty ritual, but a process that sweetens the oil to give it an indefinable something that lifts even the most basic dish out of the ordinary.

Garlic is almost equally indispensable, though it must be fresh because if the cloves are too old, they contribute only an unpleasant mustiness to both the food and the kitchen.

Onions, too, are important — but usually not the round Western type. China grows several varieties of scallions and shallots, some more pungent than others; and it is these that are used, mostly in modest quantities, to provide contrapuntal detail for ginger and garlic. However, they can be a great deal more intrusive, particularly in some dishes from the northern provinces.

Chilli eaters fall into two basic categories: those who say that nothing is too fierce for the human palate, and those who assert that enough is enough. Suffice it to say that the fields of China cater to both groups, supplying everything from tiny firebrands, to be used for sauces or chilli oil, to the capsicum peppers that are used more to add colour and texture to food.

In another area, Chinese parsley — more correctly called coriander — has little in common with Western parsley. What similarity there may be stops at their appearance, for the Chinese parsley makes an infinitely more determined contribution to every food it touches: very much an acquired taste.

Citrus peels and similar 'highlights' can be home-cured, or bought from specialist stores or herbalists; and also on the fringe between food and medicine is *Pai Ho* 百合 — literally '100 unities') which comes from the bulb of a certain type of lily. It is seldom used in ordinary dishes, but it has its special place in the sweet soup served at a wedding banquet because of the auspicious connotations of its name.

Vinegars are widely used. Unlike Western vinegars, but like many Chinese wines, they are usually rice-based, and they can be red, amber or very dark brown in colour. As they contain more sweet elements than Western vinegars, they lend themselves well to many dishes: in particular, the sweet-and-sour dishes that are so notorious for their appeal to the newcomer to Chinese food.

Dark vinegars — including one really sweet type of dark vinegar — are a vital ingredient in most braised and stewed dishes; and they can also be combined with dark soy sauce to make something akin to commercial Worcestershire Sauce. Red or amber vinegars combine well with shredded raw ginger as a dip to counteract the oily taste of fried dumplings, for example, and other rich foods.

Shaohsing spirit is another faithful friend of the Chinese cook. A few drops are added to almost every sauce, and the final glazing of

1. Rice Vinegar	11. Dark Soy Sauce
2. Shrimp Paste	12. Light Soy Sauce
3. Hoisin Sauce	13. Oyster Sauce
4. Chilli Sauce	14. Plum Sauce
5. Mustard	15. Pepper Salt Dip
6. Red Vinegar	16. Worcester Sauce
7. Hot Bean Paste	17. Monosodium Glutamate
8. Spicy Salt Dip	
9. Black Vinegar	
10. Chilli Oil	

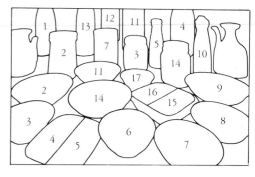

vegetables will usually include a sprinkling of Shaohsing to bring out the colour and taste to perfection.

A Continental European philosopher, Marquis Caraccidi, once said: "There are in England 60 different religious sects, but only one sauce."

The Chinese, on the other hand, have a bewildering number of sauces — either home-made or commercially-bottled — for all tastes and for all occasions.

Many commercial sauces are produced in modest quantities by factories that operate on little more than an open stretch of pavement or waste ground on the outskirts of a fishing village or rural town. Others are mass-produced in modern laboratory conditions. Thoughtfully employed, they are all equally valuable to the Chinese cook.

Soy sauce rules the kitchen as undisputed emperor. Basically a fermented extract of the soya bean, with salt added, it is available in three main types: heavy or 'black'; dark, containing caramel as colouring; and light (both in colour and flavour). The finest, and most expensive grade, represents what could be called the first infusion of the fermented beans, and is the most concentrated. Each succeeding batch of liquid is progressively less concentrated, and therefore progressively cheaper.

Also available are soy sauces flavoured with mushrooms or shrimp roe, for example, to give them an added interest.

Black bean sauce is a near relative of soy sauce, being made from salted, fermented black soya beans. Again, mention must be made of the three main types of soya bean pastes: hot (with chillies), sweet (with flour, sugar and spices) and yellow, which is very salty indeed in flavour.

Plum sauce is an indispensable accompaniment to Peking Duck and certain other rich foods, as is *Hai Hsien* sauce (海鮮醬) which combines garlic, chilli, beans and ginger with other elements.

Shrimp paste and oyster sauce are each strongly redolent of their main ingredient which, in each case, is taken fresh and subjected to a full flavour-producing fermentation process. Mustard sauce is a familiar favourite as a dip, with its regular companion, red chilli sauce; and both the latter and sesame sauce provide the Westerner, at least, with more novel taste sensations.

Thickening agents in Chinese sauces include cornstarch and lotus root powder, which is used in much the same way as arrowroot for clearer sauces.

Nothing must detract from the taste of food and the deliberately added flavouring agents; which means that natural vegetable oils are preferred in Chinese cooking. In addition to being bland and colourless, these oils can be heated to high temperatures to seal fried food, rather than permeating it and leaving it soggy and over-oily. So much so that even cold fried food does not become unappetizing if vegetable oil has been used in the cooking process.

Each region has its own preferred oil, usually determined by what the local soil produces. Peanut oil is probably the most commonly used, though maize oil is the accepted medium in some parts of the country.

Lard is rarely used for the cooking of main dishes, except when a richer result is required (as in Hoklo cuisine) as food fried with lard must be eaten while it is still piping hot — before the grease coagulates. However, Chinese pastry cooks usually work with lard, rather than with other fats, to produce their confections.

Sesame oil is more of a flavouring agent than a cooking oil; and chilli oil (made by frying chillies in a neutral vegetable oil) falls into the same category.

Chapter 3

The Chinese Kitchen

*A description of the
implements and utensils used
in the preparation and cooking
of food by the well-equipped
Chinese cook.*

Utensils

The armoury of equipment which constitutes the complete kitchen for the Western cook has no place in the Chinese food kitchen. This is literally, as well as figuratively, true. Most Chinese kitchens are small by Western standards and what space there is goes only to the vital activities and utensils. Clearly, what goes inside the kitchen must be as versatile as possible, to keep equipment to the minimum.

In the villages of old the central courtyard served as an auxilliary kitchen for residents. Today, for many people, the city pavement has taken over where the courtyard left off. You will see every stage of preparing food — rinsing rice; plucking chickens, hanging them and roasting them, too; chopping meat, or dissecting a sizeable carcass — and even the washing of dishes, all proceeding in handy lanes behind some of the grandest restaurants.

But for those who live far from open

space, all activity must be carried on within the kitchen. The stove is, naturally, the focus of activities. The old style was to build in a brick one, like an altar, when the building was being put up. Today's cook has a much more dependable source of heat than the charcoal which fired these old stoves. Gas is ideal for Chinese cooking, since the flame can be instantly controlled, for fierce temperatures or gentle simmering alike. While an oven is rarely used in a Chinese kitchen, a cooker that incorporates several burners is probably a minimum requirement for the simultaneous production of the various dishes that constitute even a relatively simple Chinese meal.

The Wok

Few people need to be introduced to the wok (鍋), the basic cooking utensil of the Chinese kitchen. Curved, like a shallow bowl, woks come in various sizes. Vast ones, of as much as one metre in diameter, are used for restaurant catering. For the home, however, 35 centimetres or so across is probably enough. Stainless steel and other modern materials are luring people away from the faithful old cast-iron wok. But these old-style pans retain many devotees because, it is claimed, they respond most readily to changes of heat; and, being thinner, they also take less time to heat up in preparation for cooking.

The advantages of the wok over the saucepan or frying pan are numerous. The smooth curve of the pan facilitates the thorough tossing and turning of ingredients — vital during quick-frying and stir-frying. The shape makes deep-frying easier, too, and more economical — just a little oil providing adequate depth to go a long way. Again, the wok is simplicity itself to clean as it has no angle in which food can be trapped. And even if the shape tends to cause the wok to wobble on some cookers, this is no problem either: an inexpensive metal frame (obtainable from most Chinese product stores, or easily run up by a handiman) serves to hold it absolutely steady.

A new wok should be carefully seasoned so that it gives the best service. Wash and dry it thoroughly, and rub the surface with a little cooking oil. Then heat it and allow it to cool, repeating this process several times. As far as maintenance is concerned, a wok rarely needs more than a wipe with a cloth. Use scouring powder to remove any food that has burnt onto the suface; and take a leaf out of the professional cook's book by heating the wok after washing, to ensure that it is completely dry — especially if it is made of cast-iron.

After some time you may notice an accumulated layer of black on the underside of the wok, but there is no need to try to remove this, unless it disturbs you from the aesthetic point of view.

To get best value out of your wok, you will need a long-handled metal spatula (more like a small shovel) with which to turn the contents. Its blade should be curved to follow the curve of the wok exactly for greatest efficiency; and, ideally, it should have a wooden handle to insulate your hand. A strainer (almost any kind of basket or sieve on a handle) is essential in deep-frying, to allow food to be moved up to drain on the side of the pan. A metal lid, to fit snugly inside the rim of the wok, is another useful accessory.

"Good cooks would have more pots and pans and bowls and dishes to allow each kind of food to make one taste."

"Every family cooking-pot has one black spot."

Ancient Chinese Proverbs

The Cleaver

Indispensable is too mild a word to use for the faithful cleaver. The heavy chopper serves dozens of functions in the kitchen and about the house. Usually of carbon steel, the cook's best friend must be kept razor sharp. Old-fashioned kitchens often have a granite sink stone which serves as a knife-stone. You may have to make do with a whetstone to keep your cleaver in the style to which it should be

accustomed. And you will have to be scrupulously careful to wipe it clean and dry after use if disaster, in the form of corrosion, is not to strike overnight.

A good summary of the cleaver's many uses is provided by the book, Food in Chinese Culture, published in 1977 by Yale University Press.

"The large, familiar cleaver — useful for gutting and scaling fish, slicing vegetables, mincing meat, crushing garlic (with the dull side of the blade), cutting one's nails, sharpening pencils, whittling new chopsticks, killing pigs, shaving (it is kept sharp enough, or supposedly is) and setting old and new scores with one's enemies. Not even the machete is more versatile."

Accompanying the cleaver like a faithful shadow is the hardy chopping block, usually a level-sawn cross-section of the soapwood tree (*Sapindus Saponario*). A household-size block will be around 35 centimetres in diameter and so heavy that it will not shift while you are using your cleaver upon it. Cheap, but durable, such a chopping block will last many years with care: it should never be submerged in water, but wiped clean, or scrubbed wih steel wool or a brush, and quickly rinsed. The cross-cut fibres of the wood absorb the impact of the cleaver, blunting it far less quickly than the more familiar Western chopping board.

Additional Utensils and Implements

In addition to the *wok*, the cleaver and the wooden cooking chopsticks in your kitchen, other utensils and implements can be included in your collection, to supplement the basics.

Steamers stand in the *wok*, over boiling water. They come in stackable piles and can be used to cook several dishes at the same time. The largest steamer should be at least two inches smaller in diameter than your *wok*. For the smallest size, you may need to improvise some kind of stand — or simply use an empty steamer on the bottom level — to hold the food above the boiling water. Bamboo steamers are ideal since they are porous, and water does not accumulate in the finished dish. They are decorative as well as practical, and food is often actually served in them — particularly at *dim sum* time, of course. Almost as versatile as the *woks* which they complement, steamers can be used for dumplings, rice dishes, and all kinds of fish, meat and vegetables.

Experts insist on a second cleaver for mincing meat. (They flail the two cleavers alternately — one in each hand — but it requires considerable practice. Take out special insurance before you try it for yourself.)

Two candles,
  a bundle of incense sticks.
The 23rd day is the day to sacrifice to the
  God of the hearth.
There is a dish full of grass
  and a bowl full of water.
When the water is spilt on the ground the
  God ascends to Heaven.
The head of the family comes over and
  knocks his head on the ground.
Then three volleys of fire-crackers go
  'crack'.
God of the hearth
  come back, come back!
We have kept for you Manchurian candy.
Anon

An earthenware cooking pot (沙保 — literally 'sand pot') is hardly a luxury. It is the only way to produce the rich and concentrated stews, favourite food for winter-time in the north of China, especially. The same applies to a Mongolian fire pot. There is no substitute for the authentic vessel, and many fire pots are also pleasingly decorative in themselves, whether they are made of aluminium, brass or (occasionally) copper. The basic principal is for the liquid to boil in the 'moat' around the central chimney, which supplies the source of heat.

The Hunan chicken pot, too, has no real substitute, although a Western casserole with a tight-fitting lid is a fairly good substitute.

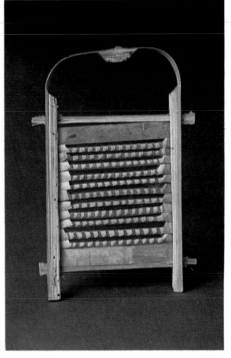

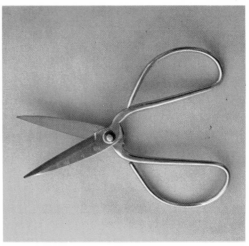

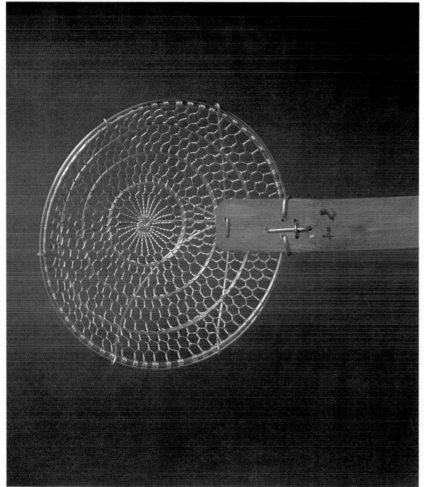

The heavy, flat cast-iron griddle for Mongolian barbecues is efficient, but not really essential: it has no aesthetic attraction of its own, and a regular frying pan serves just as well. A rolling pin and a pastry board, a stone pestle and mortar (some Chinese cooks simply use the cleaver handle and a bowl), cake and biscuit moulds, a grater, a peeler and barbecue hooks can all come in handy. If you already have them, well and good. But if you do not, experiment for a time before you decide to invest.

First came fingers ... then came chopsticks.

As long ago as the days of the Shang people (1766 BC - 1123 BC), chopsticks were to some extent already in use in China. But it is not clear just when they supplanted the fingers completely in the gentle art of eating Chinese food.

Many materials have been tried out by the wealthy as the most suitable to convey food elegantly from dish to mouth. Agate and jade were used, and silver came into great favour at unsettled times as it was popularly believed that the metal turned black if the food was poisoned.

Ivory has long been the firm favourite for refined eating. Even today a set of ten or more pairs of ivory chopsticks makes a common

wedding gift. The Chinese characters for chopsticks (筷子) have the same sound as two other characters (快子), the literal meaning of which is 'quick boys' — adding a symbolic meaning to an acceptable present.

With care ivory chopsticks last a lifetime, but they can become yellow if they are in contact with hot food or liquid at the eating or washing up stage.

These days, chopsticks come in workaday plastic in an imitation ivory colour and texture. However, nothing has yet replaced the versatile long bamboo chopsticks in the kitchen — acting as whisk, tongs and as near to an extra pair of hands as any cook could ever dream of having.

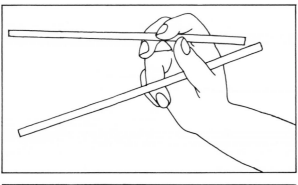

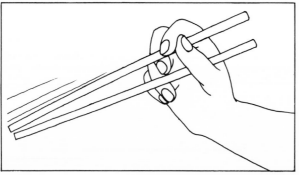

If you find your place set with an uneven pair of chopsticks, you can be sure that you are due to miss a boat, a train or an aircraft. Eat your meal in leisurely style: there is no reason good enough for rushing Chinese food.

Dropped chopsticks herald bad luck, and so do crossed chopsticks — unless they are used by the waiter to indicate that you have already settled the bill for your lunch-time *dim sum*.

Chopsticks have dictated much of the nature of Chinese food, in its bite-sized portions and generally graspable nature. Rice is usually shovelled inelegantly, but efficiently, into the mouth, rather than picked up a few grains at a time. Noodle eating requires no finesse.

Like the correct method of boiling rice, the correct method of manipulating chopsticks is more easily learned through observation and practice than by reading about it. Probably the best advice, then, is to suggest that you arrange your fingers around them as closely as you can get to the way shown in the accompanying illustrations. Think of the chopsticks as nothing more or less than extensions of your hand; and as long as the method that you arrive at works well for you, do not worry if it is a little 'different'. If you are left-handed, chopsticks present fewer problems than a knife and fork. But it could be in your best interests to persevere with your right hand; because it can be conspicuous, not to say uncomfortable for you and the person on your left, if you are the 'odd man out' at a crowded dinner table!

For those who feel qualms about communal eating, with everyone helping himself or herself from the same dishes, serving spoons (as distinct from individual soup spoons) are usually provided. Thus, you can convey the food from the serving plate to your bowl, and then bring your chopsticks to work. At the same time, you might care to reflect that few eating utensils could be more hygienic than chopsticks ... or less hygienic than the fork, with its shoulders and tines resisting all known detergents.

Chapter 4

Preparation & Cooking Methods

An explanation of the preparation of ingredients and of the many and varied ways of making the dishes ready for the table.

Preparation Methods

Most traditional preparation methods utilize the indispensable cleaver.

Slicing

Meats to be sliced should first be cut along the grain into blocks about 5cm (2″) square. Trim off any fat, then cut the meat into very thin slices straight across the grain. This will sever any tough fibres, rendering the meat tender when fast-cooked.

Straight Slicing

Hold the item firmly on the chopping board with the fingers of the left hand. Using the first joints of this hand as a guide, cut straight down with the cleaver. Move the hand back slightly to expose more of the ingredient — adjusting the depth of this move to the required thickness of the slices.

Diagonal Slicing

Hold the item in the same way as above, but angle the cleaver so that it cuts through at an angle of about 45 degrees. Slice right through the item at this same angle to produce uniform slices.

Flat Slicing

Place the item firmly on the chopping board and press down gently on it with the flattened fingers of the left hand. Carefully slice through the item beneath the hand, using a very sharp cleaver, and working slowly so the movement can be felt through the fingers. This is particularly suitable for abalone, kidney and canned bamboo shoots.

Strips

Vegetables and meat to be cut into strips should be of uniform length and width if using in the same recipe — ideally no longer than 5cm (2″) and no wider than 1.5cm (½″). Cut the item thinly, then stack and cut into strips. Meat should first be sliced across the grain.

Shredding

The use of the ingredient will dictate the size of the shreds, which can vary from matchstick size to fine threadlike shreds. Ideally they will never exceed 5cm (2″) in length. Slice the ingredient thinly then stack, slightly overlapping. Cut through the stack to produce the shreds, varying the thickness as needed.

Sticks

To cut vegetables into sticks, peel and cut into slices about 1cm (¼″) thick, then stack the slices and cut through again into uniform sticks.

Dicing/Cubing

Dicing and cubing are done in the same way, the results of the latter being larger in size. Begin by cutting the item into sticks as explained already — the size of the sticks dictated by the required fineness of the dice — then cut through the stacked sticks into cubes. Cubed meat is usually cut to 2cm (¾″) pieces (occasionally larger, though they may then be referred to as chunks). Cubed vegetables of this size would be too large to cook through in quick-frying, unless previously parcooked.

Dice can vary from medium dice — cubes of maximum 1.5cm (½″) — through small dice, which should not exceed 1cm (¼″), to the minute cubes described as fine or very fine, the latter just a little larger than ingredients which have been minced with a cleaver.

Mincing (fine chopping)

Cut the items into dice, or crush, as explained next, holding the tip of the cleaver firmly on the board by pressing with the left hand on top. Work the cleaver in a short up and down motion over the board — moving it from side to side to cover all of the ingredient. From time to time scoop everything together into the centre and continue mincing.

Another method, frequently used, is to quickly and repeatedly chop down on the

board with the whole blade. However this can cause harder items to fly around the kitchen, and the noise does not make one too popular with the neighbours.

As mentioned in the section on the cleaver, two blades can be used in unison for mincing meat, but this does require skill and precision, and is more commonly used in large-scale restaurant cooking.

Crushing

Seasoning ingredients such as ginger, garlic and even scallions are crushed to release their full flavour and to ensure they cook through when stir-fried. Place the peeled item on the board and hit smartly with the flat surface of the cleaver. This step is also preliminary to mincing the same items with the cleaver.

Roll-cut

This method is used to cut long

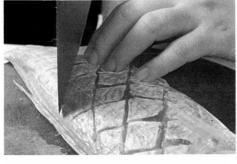

vegetables and other round foods into even sized pieces with a large surface area, desirable for quick frying. Hold the item with the left hand and cut with the cleaver at a diagonal, then turn through one-quarter and cut at the same angle, and so on.

Flower-cut

This does not refer to a traditional preparation method, but has been used here as a convenient term to describe slices of vegetable, and more commonly ginger and carrot, which are cut into decorative shapes purely to enhance the appearance of a dish. This is done simply by cutting the vegetable with ornate metal cutters, which are available in numerous designs. Skilled cooks, however, use age-old techniques to produce these carved vegetable decorations without 'mechanical aids'.

Scoring

Again this technique is important for the appearance of a dish, but it additionally facilitates fast cooking and tenderising. Criss-cross scoring, resulting in a diamond shape pattern on the meat, is the usual rule; liver, kidneys, chewy seafood such as cuttlefish (squid) and whole fish are generally treated to this preparation. The size of the diamonds and the depth of the cuts varies from item to item. Generally the cuts are straight down on fish or kidney and at a distinct angle for firmer meats like squid.

Tenderising

Another method used for tenderising meats is pounding with the blunt top of the cleaver. This is again done in a criss-cross fashion, first working one way, then turning the meat through 180 degrees to work across the first impressions. Pound both sides of the meat. The flat side of the cleaver can also be used to slap down sharply on the meat, softening and breaking fibres.

Grinding

Dry spices, nuts, rice and beans can be ground to a powder in an electric spice grinder, or with a mortar and pestle. However, practical Chinese cook use the heavy handle of a carbon steel cleaver as a pestle, crushing the items in a small rice bowl.

Chopping

The sharp bladed cleaver, with its characteristic heavy weight, is the ideal implement for cutting right through poultry bones and smaller bones of other meats, either cooked or uncooked. Use a straight sharp downwards motion, cutting clear through the meat and bone. Larger bones may also be severed with the cleaver. Hit down as hard as possible, then use the base of the hand to hammer on the blunt top of the blade until forced through.

Preparing Prawns and Shrimps

The Chinese are fond of the taste of prawn heads in certain dishes, and where applicable, it has been recommended that these be left intact. Additionally, mainly for aesthetic reasons, the tail fins may be left on after peeling (these are trimmed to a point by fastidious cooks and the central 'horn' snipped off). Peel prawns and shrimps while fresh, as the shells will slide off easily. Remove all the legs and the head, if preferred. Wash under cold running water, rubbing with a little salt and cornstarch to help eliminate the fishy smell and to whiten the meat. To de-vein prawns, slit along the centre backs and lift out the dark veins. De-veining shrimps is done simply, by inserting a toothpick below the vein in the centre back and gently lifting the whole vein out.

Like every other aspect of the serious business of eating, Chinese cooking covers a multitude of processes and approaches to food. In his erudite and fascinating book, The Chinese Cookery Encyclopedia, Kenneth Lo gives details of almost 40 different terms used for different ways of applying heat to food. He kindly cautions the would-be expert that at least twice as many such terms can be listed. Regional variations and special local expressions would make at least as many again.

For the cook, understanding of these terms is a fundamental requirement: for people who would like to give more precise instructions when ordering food in a restaurant, they are equally valuable. We have summarised some of the more important aspects of each group of terms with a view to assisting both the dedicated cook and the dedicated gourmet — very often one and the same person.

You will soon realise that many of the special methods of cooking must have developed originally with the need to economise on fuel — part of the general principle of making the most of the most that dominates much of the philosophy underlying Chinese food ... and Chinese living. Multiple phases are common in Chinese cooking, even for apparently simple dishes. We have mentioned some of these more significant combinations of technique.

Boiling, Simmering and Stewing

Water (or stock) is the simplest cooking medium, but several different expressions are used by the Chinese to define the intensity of the boil and other details. *Chu* (煮) describes the simmering of whole poultry or other meat in boiling water. Shredded or finely sliced food may be boiled more quickly — *T'ang* (燙) or *T'ang P'ao* (湯爆). Both produce the simplest texture, making the quality of the original food very important. Dips and sauces accompany such food to highlight it. Most people will be familiar with *Shuan* (涮) an extension of the same principle to the hot pot in which food is briefly simmered at the table by the diners, each provided with an individual range of sauces.

Ch'in (浸) carries the technique one stage further. After a brief period of boiling, the food is cooled in its cooking liquid, as a prelude to marinating it later, or perhaps eating it cold with an accompanying sauce or dip. This method is especially suited to young and tender poultry. *Ch'uan* (川) is a similar approach to cooking, but the process of boiling and cooling is repeated several times until the food is thoroughly cooked. Obviously, the tougher the meat, the more times the process must be repeated. Both *Ch'in* and *Ch'uan* can be the sole cooking involved in preparation of a dish, or they may be followed by frying or steaming.

Pao (煲) can best be described as slow simmering, for as long as four hours, in a considerable quantity of water. It forms a direct contrast with several forms of boiling which are intended to evaporate most of the cooking liquid.

Men (燜) is often translated as stewing, and, indeed, it comes very close. Meat is first browned, and then simmered for several hours in water or stock. *Men* is particularly suitable for cooking meats like pig's trotter or beef shin. For a brown stew, brown sugar will be combined with soy sauce, whereas a red stew uses red bean cheese and red wine lees paste to colour the food. *Shao* (燒) is similar to *Men*, except that the stock is reduced at the end of the cooking to produce a small amount of gravy. *Cha Shao* (叉燒) involves spit roasting as the final stage of the cooking, most often encountered with such set pieces as roast suckling pig. *P'eng* (烹) is almost identical, with the final barbecuing a deliberate completion of the drying process. *Lu* (滷) deserves special mention, as it has made more than one restaurant's reputation for half a century. Food — liver, eggs, chicken, fish — is cooked in a strongly aromatic soy stock. The 'master stock' is renewed and enriched with each new food cooked in it and improves with each passing day. The food of course acquires both a

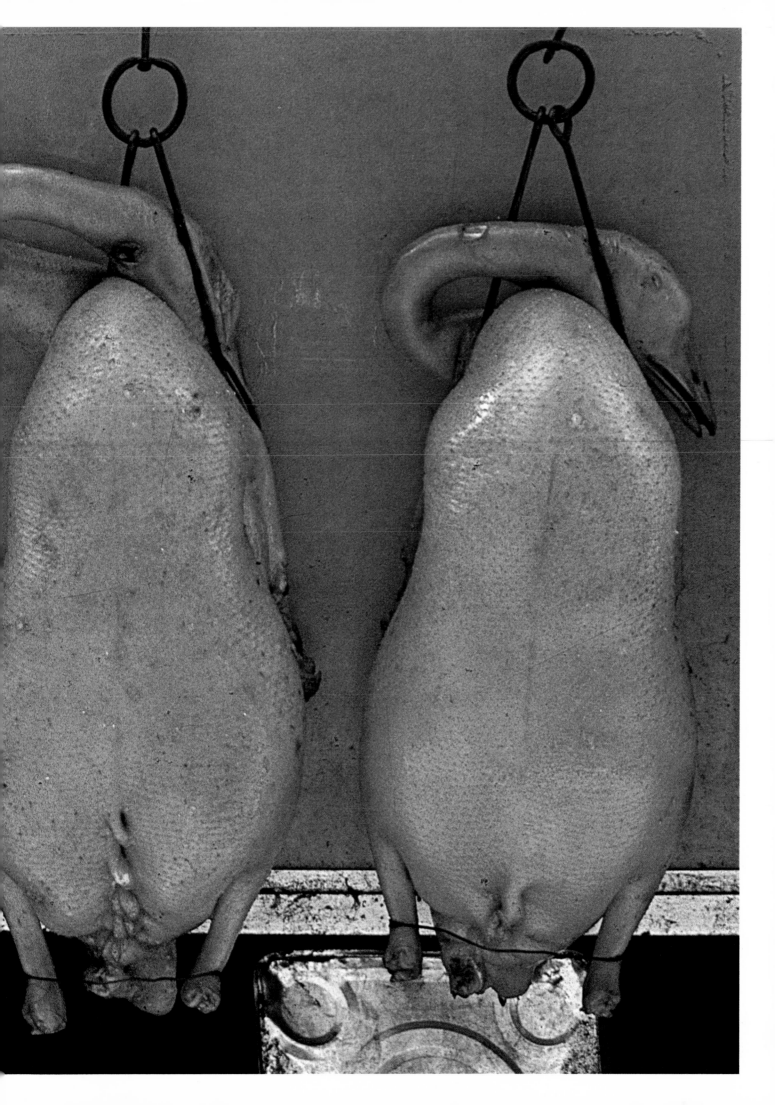

rich brown colour and a wonderful flavour.

Steaming

Quick steaming, *Ch'eng* (蒸), is ideal for quick cooking of pre-marinated food — on an open dish or plate inside a bamboo steamer. Flavour and garnishing are completed .in advance, and the food is served in its cooking dish. Fish responds well to this treatment and so do minced beef dishes. *Tun* (燉), or 'closed something' is usually a long process, in a sealed receptacle, inside the steamer. A flour and water paste, or even paper, may be used to ensure that the seal is tight.

Hui (燴) literally means hot assembly in thickened sauce. Mixed vegetables, with or without meat, and pea-starch noodles are fully cooked, with cornstarch or water chestnut powder added as a thickener at the final stage.

Pan (拌) is sometimes regarded as the equivalent of a hot or cold salad. The foods may be cooked (noodles, meat) or uncooked (cucumber) but everything is finely shredded before being mixed with flavoured oils by way of dressing.

Frying in oil

Deep-frying is the usual translation for *Cha* (炸). Food — plain, coated with batter or rolled in flour — is deep-fried in very hot oil. This may be the final stage of cooking to give a crisp texture to the food, or it may be the prelude to a long or short marinade, perhaps

followed in turn by quick-frying. Sometimes a sauce is added to the drained, deep-fried food. A contrasting method is implied in *Yung* (余), deep-frying for 10-15 minutes.

Chow or *Ch'ao* (炒) can be one of the quickest ways of stir-frying food, often taking less than a minute and seldom taking more than three minutes to complete. Food is cut into small, evenly-sized pieces and the small amount of oil in the wok is there primarily to prevent sticking and burning as the food is vigorously tossed and scraped around the pan.

Pao (爆) is a distinct style of explosive 'plunging' cooking over a high flame, using either oil or stock to heat the food almost instantaneously. It is often the last in a series of cooking stages.

In *Ling* (淋), or splash-frying, the food is suspended over a pan of boiling oil. The cook uses a ladle to pour the oil over the food until it is evenly browned and cooked. This requires considerable dexterity, it will be appreciated, and the 'hand-finished' results make this a special method of cooking, such as might be used to prepare a chicken for a banquet.

A flat pan is used for *Chien* (煎) and *Liu* (溜). A small amount of oil is used and the food is cooked with a minimum of movement, as in frying bread, for instance. *Liu* involves adding a cornstarch-thickened sauce to the dish before the cooking is completed — a favourite way with fish. *T'ieh* (貼) is similar to *Chien*, but the food is cooked on only one side, while the other is deliberately kept soft, by a judicious sprinkling of moisture. The famous Peking dumplings — *kuo t'ieh* — are perhaps the most famous example of this style, with their crisp-fried base and soft interior and top. Occasionally this description is also used for the frying of something like an escalope which is subsequently cut into pieces before serving.

Mixed methods

Pien (爁) sums up the most famous and typical way of cooking vegetables. Onion, garlic and ginger are used to flavour the oil on its own before the vegetables are added. The usual proportion is to use from 10 per cent to 15 per cent of oil in relation to the weight of the vegetables. Stock and water are added to steam the fried vegetables until they are tender. The oil gives them their characteristically shiny appearance and rich flavour. *Ao* (熬) also involves quick frying and quick steaming, although it usually takes less time than *Pien*. It is particularly successful with crab and similar foods.

Nearest approach to the Western concept of braising is to be found in the Chinese *Wen* (炆). After a brief stir-fry over a high heat, the food is covered with water or stock and simmered for about 15 minutes. Before serving, the gravy is thickened with cornflour. Garlic, ginger and onion or chilli are fried in the cooking oil before the main stir-frying starts in *Chueh* (焗). Otherwise the method is similar to *Wen*, but the sauce is produced separately in the pan and poured over the meat or vegetables, which have already been removed and placed on the serving dish.

Chu (焗) means that the food must first be fried over a high heat, before the addition of water, stock or wine. The next stage can be a long, slow simmer or a quick braise; but both must reduce the gravy to the right quantity and consistency. Sometimes *Chu* describes casserole-style cooking, using very little liquid.

Ingredients are stir-fried and cooked first in *Ts'ang* (熗). They are arranged on the serving dish to await the completion of the sauce, prepared in the pan and poured over everything. Sauce and ingredients must be allowed to cool before serving as this is essentially a cold dish: it is a popular treatment of noodles.

T'a (塌) means deep-frying in batter, perhaps preceded by steaming. Braising is the final stage during which flavouring ingredients are thoroughly mixed in.

Other methods

Cooking by convection, as in an oven, is

the usual meaning of *K'ao* (烤), which can occasionally describe pot-roasting. The best-known dish cooked in this way is, of course, Peking duck. *K'ao* is never applied to food heated simply from below: this is described as *Shao*. When food is turned on a spit before a radiant heat source the correct term is *Hung* (烘).

Cooking by burial in a heated substance is *Wei* (煨), which covers the use of heated charcoal, sand, salt, stones and so on as well as lime, which becomes hot when mixed with water. Most foods cooked in this way have a thick crust or skin, which can be easily wrapped in lotus leaves or clay, for example. Sweet potatoes, chicken, chestnuts and eggs all respond well to such treatment.

Smoking — *Hsun* (燻) — is designed to give extra flavour to pre-cooked or at least pre-marinated food. Tea leaves, camphor or pine needles may be used to give a special tang.

K'ou (扣) involves three stages — frying, chopping and steaming in a mould — to produce a meat pudding. The reverse process is *Pa* (扒), in which steaming is followed by frying with extra flavouring agents.

Tsui (醉) is the production of 'drunken' food, with a rice-wine or other alcohol used as a marinade after light cooking. The food — particularly fish or chicken — may soak for several hours or several days. Among the more famous styles of pickling are two rather similar methods, which both involve marinating the food after light cooking, and packing it into an earthen jar for several days or even weeks. *Chiang* (醬) adds soy sauce and soya 'jam', whereas *Chiao* (糟) relies on wine lees paste for extra flavour.

Yien (醃) preserves meat with unrefined salt and a little salt-petre, rubbed in thoroughly before the meat is placed in an earthenware jar. It is turned every third day, and on the ninth day it is pressed under a heavy weight. Heating may precede or follow the salting and pressing. Salt is also the preservative in *Feng* (風), but the food is dried in the wind, rather than compressed. Salt fish is an example of this method and is famous for its smell and flavour when cooked with other foods, or on its own.

Preparing and serving chicken

Arranging 'Spread Eagle' style

Place the head of the chicken at one end of an oval serving plate. (This will be so positioned at the table as to face the guest of honour).

Place the neck sections down the centre of the plate.

Arrange the upper wing pieces below the head of the bird, and place the lower portions of the wings, and the wing tips in position at either side of the head.

Arrange the back sections along the sides of the neck pieces, then pile the breast pieces, skin sides topmost, along the centre.

Arrange the thick pieces over the back

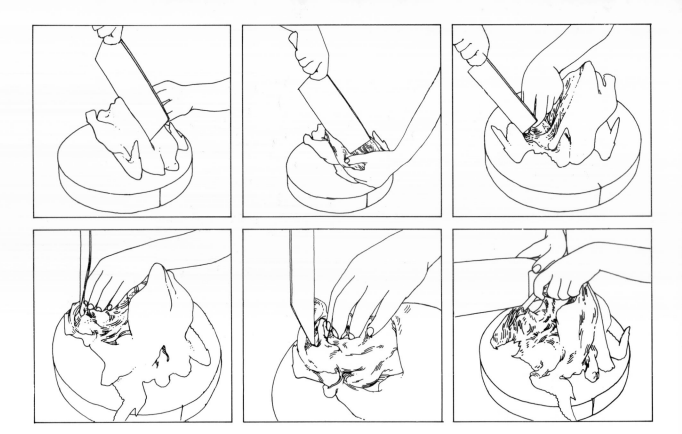

sections, with the lower part of the legs in position on both sides of the parson's nose which has been placed at the centre back.

Boning

Place the bird on its back on the chopping board and cut down the breast bone from neck to tail. Using a sharp cleaver or filleting knife, work the flesh away from the bones until you reach the thigh and wing joints.

Work along the thigh and upper wing bones, removing all the meat. When you reach the first joints, cut through these so that the lower wing sections and the drumsticks remain with the skin and meat.

Continue to carefully cut away the meat from the carcass until they are only connected along the backbone, then very carefully separate, using small strokes of the knife to ensure the skin is not severed. Lift off the carcass and use for stock.

The drumstick bones may be removed, but these are traditionally left intact to reshape the bird when stuffed.

Skinning

This is done in much the same way as boning, except that the meat remains attached to the bones, making the task decidedly more formidable. The bird is not cut open at the breast; work from the neck cavity, using a small sharp knife and a pair of sharp kitchen shears. Leave the wing bones and drumsticks intact, to be cut out after the skin has been completely removed. If any small nicks are made in the skin, these can be repaired with a needle and thread.

Chopping a fowl, traditional method

Use a very sharp cleaver, chopping sharply downwards through the bones. Keep fingers well out of range!

Cut off the head, then chop off the neck and roll-cut into 2cm (¾″) pieces. Cut off wings at the body joints, then cut through central wing joints and cut off wing tips. Chop the upper wing sections into bite-sized pieces. Remove the whole thighs at the body joints. Chop off and discard the lower knuckles. Chop the lower drumstick sections into bite-size pieces, cutting straight through the bones. Chop the upper meaty sections at a diagonal angle, into 2cm (¾″) slices, cutting through the bones. Remove the breast section, then divide the back into two halves. Cut along the backbone. Trim off any bony parts with little meat and discard. Cut the back sections at a diagonal angle into 2cm (¾″) pieces.

Divide the breast in halves down the centre and, cutting right through the thin breast bone, divide at a diagonal angle, into 2cm (¾″) slices.

Chapter 5

The Recipes

A selection of over 200 recipes representing the whole scope of Chinese cuisine — from the most basic home-cooked dishes to the most elaborate banquet offerings.

With the exception of certain dishes using a whole fowl or large cut of meat, most of the recipes yield 6-8 servings. They are intended, in the Chinese tradition, to be served with additional main course dishes, appetizers and soups to make a balanced meal. The number of dishes usually equals the number of diners.

Monosodium glutamate is a traditional flavouring powder called for in many of these recipes. As we have noted elsewhere in this book, it must however be used sparingly, and many cooks will prefer to omit it altogether; or it may be replaced by concentrated chicken essence if an extra flavouring touch is needed.

Shredded Pork with Preserved Vegetables
Hsueh Ts'ai Jou Ssu 雪菜肉絲
Serves 6-8

155 g (5 oz)	lean pork, shredded
125 g (4 oz)	canned bamboo shoots, shredded
125 g (4 oz)	canned preserved Shanghai vegetables, shredded
125 g (4 oz)	Mao Tou green peas, shelled
	few drops sesame oil
	oil for deep-frying

Seasoning A

½ tsp	salt
½ tsp	monosodium glutamate
1½ tsp	cornstarch

Seasoning B

½ tsp	sugar
½ tsp	monosodium glutamate
1 tsp	Shao Hsing wine

Preparation
Mix the pork with the seasoning A ingredients and leave for 15 minutes. Blanch peas in boiling water for 1 minute. Drain well.

Cooking:
Heat the wok, add oil and when very hot, deep-fry the pork shreds for 1 minute. Add the peas and deep-fry briefly. Remove and discard most of the oil.

Stir-fry the bamboo shoots for 1 minute, then add the pork and peas and the seasonings. Stir-fry for 1 minute longer, then add the preserved vegetables and stir-fry until heated through. Sprinkle on sesame oil and serve.

"A proud young husband boasted to a friend of his new bride's expertise in cooking, and assured the friend that his wife could cook "anything". Invited to dinner, the friend decided to test the truth of the husband's allegations and brought along a quantity of pork and a stick of sugar cane, confident that this unlikely combination of ingredients would prove impossible to cook. But by mincing together the sugar cane and pork and combining with flour and the beaten white of an egg, the inventive bride made balls which she then fried, producing a delicious dish. The moral of this story is the very backbone of Chinese cookery — the combination of the most unexpected foods can produce the tastiest of dishes."

Anon

Stir-Fried Pork Kidneys
Chiang Ch'ao Yao Hua 醬炒腰花
Serves 6-8

315 g (10 oz)	pork kidneys
60 g (2 oz)	dried mushrooms, soaked and sliced
60 g (2 oz)	broccoli heads, quartered
30 g (1 oz)	canned bamboo shoots, shredded
½ tsp	ginger, minced
2 tsp	scallion, minced
	few drops sesame oil
	oil for deep-frying

Seasoning

½ tsp	sugar
½ tsp	monosodium glutamate
1 tbsp	dark soy sauce
1 tsp	Shao Hsing wine
1 tbsp	chicken stock
	dash pepper

Thickening — mix together

¼ tsp	cornstarch
2 tsp	water

Preparation
Wash kidneys, remove skin, membranes and fatty cores and blanch in boiling water for 1 minute. Drain, cover with cold water and leave for 1-2 minutes. Drain and slice thinly, then cut criss-cross on one side. Blanch broccoli in boiling water for ½ minute, drain and splash with cold water to brighten the colour. Drain again. Mix the seasoning ingredients and set aside.

Cooking
Heat the wok, add the oil and when hot, deep-fry the mushrooms, broccoli and bamboo shoots for ½ minute. Drain and set aside. Reheat the oil and deep-fry the kidney slices for ½ minute. Remove, drain and discard most of the oil.

Reheat the wok, add ginger and scallion and stir-fry briefly, then add the kidney and vegetables and stir-fry for ½ minute longer. Pour in the seasoning and thickening and stir-fry until sauce thickens. Sprinkle on sesame oil, stir and serve.

In the Eastern Kitchen the meat is sliced
and ready —
Roast beef and boiled pork and mutton,
The Master of the Feast hands round the
wine.
The harp-players sound their clear chords.

Anon

Stir-Fried Pork with Vegetables
Ts'ai Yuan Ch'ao Jou P'ien 菜遠炒肉片
Serves 6-8

185 g (6 oz)	lean pork, thinly sliced
500 g (1 lb)	flowering white cabbage
4-5 slices	carrot, flower-cut
4-5 slices	ginger, flower-cut
1	scallion, coarsely chopped
1 clove	garlic, crushed
2 tbsp	cooked oil
4 tbsp	oil
Seasoning A	
½ tsp	bicarbonate of soda
1 tbsp	water
2 tsp	cornstarch
Seasoning B	
1 tsp	salt
1 tsp	monosodium glutamate
1½ tbsp	chicken stock
½ tsp	cornstarch

Preparation
Mix the pork with the seasoning A ingredients and
leave for 25 minutes. Trim the flowers, and thick
end stems and top of leaves of the cabbage,
retaining only the shoots. Blanch in rapidly boiling
water with 2 tbsp cooked oil added, for 1 minute,
remove and drain. Add the carrot pieces and boil
for a few seconds. Drain. Mix the seasoning B
ingredients and set aside.

Cooking
Heat the wok, add the oil and when very hot
reduce heat slightly and add the garlic and pork.
Stir-fry for 2½ minutes, then remove and drain.
Discard most of the oil and reheat the wok. Stir-fry
the carrot, ginger and scallion for 1 minute. Add the
cabbage and pork, then seasoning B and stir-fry for
1 minute longer. Serve.

Steamed Pork with Salted Cabbage
Mei Ts'ai K'ou Jou 梅菜扣肉
Serves 6-8

625 g (1¼ lb)	fat belly pork
125 g (4 oz)	salted cabbage
1 tbsp	dark soy sauce
	oil for deep-frying
Seasoning A	
1½ tsp	sugar
1 tbsp	cooked oil
Seasoning B	
2 tsp	sugar
¾ tsp	salt
¾ tsp	monosodium glutamate
1 tbsp	light soy sauce
2 tbsp	water
1 tbsp	cooked oil
Thickening — mix together	
1 tsp	cornstarch
1 tbsp	water

Preparation
Wash the pork in cold water, place in a saucepan,
cover with cold water and bring to the boil. Boil for
about 45 minutes on moderate heat, until softened.
Drain and set aside. Soak the salted cabbage in cold
water for 1 hour, trim off stem ends and cut the
vegetables into 2 cm (¾") pieces. Sprinkle on
seasoning A ingredients. Rub the pork with dark
soy sauce when cool. Mix the seasoning B
ingredients and set aside.

Cooking
Heat the wok, add the oil and when very hot deep-
fry the pork until the skin bubbles. (Have the wok
lid ready to cover the pan if it begins to splash oil).
Remove, drain and rinse off the excess oil with
cold water. Cut meat into 1 cm (¼") thick slices and
rub on seasoning B. Arrange in a lightly oiled
shallow bowl and cover with the prepared cabbage.
Place the bowl in a steamer, cover and steam over
moderately high heat for 1 hour. Remove the bowl
and carefully pour off and retain the liquid. Pour
into the wok and bring to the boil. Add the
thickening and stir on high heat until the sauce
thickens. Turn the pork and vegetables out onto a
serving plate with pork on top of the vegetables.
Drain off any excess liquid. Pour on the sauce.

"Good fortune of the mouth is not shallow
— to have good food to eat is important."

Pork Meatballs in Casserole.

Pork Meatballs in Casserole
Sha Kwo Shih Tzu T'ou 砂鍋獅子頭
Serves 8

185 g (6 oz)	lean pork, minced
185 g (6 oz)	lean pork very finely diced
45 g (1½ oz)	canned bamboo shoots, drained
45 g (1½ oz)	dried mushrooms, soaked
45 g (1½ oz)	dried beche-de-mer, soaked*
185 g (6 oz)	Chinese white cabbage
½	egg
375 ml (12 fl oz)	chicken stock
1 tbsp	cooked oil
	cornstarch
	few drops sesame oil
	oil for deep-frying

Seasoning A

½ tsp	salt
¼ tsp	monosodium glutamate
1 tbsp	Shao Hsing wine
1 tsp	ginger, minced
2 tsp	scallion, minced
2 tsp	cornstarch

Seasoning B

¼ tsp	salt
½ tsp	monosodium glutamate
½ tsp	dark soy sauce
1 tbsp	light soy sauce
½ tsp	ginger, minced
1 tsp	scallion, minced
1 tbsp	cooked oil

Thickening — mix together

1½ tbsp	cornstarch
3 tbsp	water

Preparation
Drain and very finely dice bamboo shoots, mushrooms and beche-de-mer. Mix well with the egg and seasoning A ingredients. Add the minced and diced pork and mix well, then divide the mixture and mould into ball shapes, about 5cm (2″) in diameter. Coat the meatballs with cornstarch, wash the cabbage and blanch in boiling water, with 1 tbsp cooked oil added, for 1 minute. Drain and set aside.

Cooking
Heat the wok, add the oil and when very hot, deep-fry the meatballs for 4-5 minutes until light brown. Drain and place in an earthenware pot or casserole. Discard most of the oil.

Reheat the wok, add the chicken stock and seasoning B ingredients and bring to the boil. Pour over the meatballs, place the pot in a steamer and steam for 30 minutes over moderately high heat.

Remove the pot and pour the stock into the wok, leaving the meatballs in the pot. Bring stock to the boil. Add cabbage, sesame oil and the thickening. Stir and boil until the sauce thickens. Pour sauce and vegetables over the meatballs and serve.

*For the method of preparing beche-de-mer, see page 185.

Deep-Fried Pork Intestines
Cha Tai Ch'ang 炸大腸
Serves 8

750 g (1½ lb)	pork intestines
185 g (6 oz)	rock salt
4	anise stars
	salt
	white vinegar
	oil for deep-frying

Seasoning

45 g (1½ oz)	maltose
150 ml (5 fl oz)	white vinegar
100 ml (3 fl oz)	water
	dash orange food colouring powder

Preparation
Wash intestines well. Push inside-out using a chopstick and rub with a paste of equal amounts of salt and white vinegar. Rinse with plenty of cold water to remove the sticky coating. Trim off thin ends and discard. Cut the intestines into 15cm (6″) pieces. Bring a large saucepan of water to the boil, add rock salt, anise stars and the intestines and boil for 45 minutes to 1 hour, until soft. Remove and drain. Place the seasoning ingredients in a double saucepan and heat, stirring occasionally, until the maltose is dissolved. Arrange the intestines in a dish and pour on the seasoning. Soak until well coloured, about 1 hour. Drain and allow the intestines to dry totally.

Cooking
Heat the wok, add oil and when very hot add the intestines. Reduce heat and deep-fry for 2-3 minutes until crispy and bright orange-red. Remove, drain well and cut into 2.5cm (1″) pieces. Slice each piece lengthways and arrange on a serving plate. Serve with spicy salt dip, see recipe page 277.

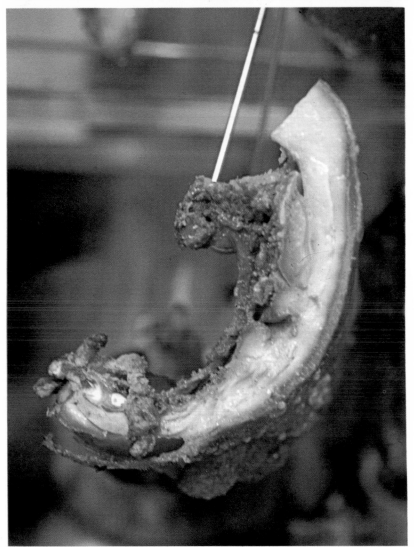

Barbecued Pork
Kan Hsiang Ch'a Shao　甘香叉燒
Serves 12

1½ kg (3 lb)	pork loin
6 tbsp	clear honey

Seasoning

5 tbsp	sugar
1 tbsp	salt
200 ml (6 fl oz)	light soy sauce
1 tbsp	Mue Kwe Lo wine
1 tbsp	ginger juice
	dash red food colouring powder

Preparation
Cut pork meat into 4cm (1½″) wide strips, discarding bone. Score the surface lightly. Mix the seasoning ingredients, adding enough colouring powder to colour the meat a light red. Rub well into the strips of meat and leave for 1-1½ hours. Thread the meat strips on a metal skewer, passing the skewer through one end of each piece of meat. Hang to dry for about ¾ hour.

Cooking
Spit roast the pork in a large oven or over open high heat, for 20-25 minutes. Brush with a little of the honey during cooking to keep the meat moist and to make a clear glaze. When cooked, remove from the heat and brush with the remaining honey and leave until it dries slightly. Slice thinly and arrange on a serving plate. Serve hot or cold.

Fish Flavoured Shredded Pork
Yu Hsiang Jou Ssu 餘香肉絲
Serves 6-8

250 g (8 oz)	lean pork, shredded
60 g (2 oz)	dried cloud ear fungus, soaked, then shredded
125 g (4 oz)	celery, 5cm (2″) thin strips
1 tsp	ginger, minced
1 tbsp	scallion, minced
1 clove	garlic, minced
1-2	chillies, soaked in a solution of brine and wine lees, and cut into thin strips
1 tsp	black vinegar
3 tbsp	cooked oil
	oil for deep-frying

Seasoning A

¼ tsp	salt
½	egg white, beaten
1 tsp	cornstarch

Seasoning B

2 tsp	hot bean paste
1 tsp	wine lees

Sauce

½ tsp	sugar
½ tsp	monosodium glutamate
½ tsp	dark soy sauce
1 tsp	light soy sauce
1 tsp	Shao Hsing wine
2 tbsp	chicken stock

Thickening — mix together

½ tsp	cornstarch
1 tbsp	water

Preparation
Mix the shredded pork with the seasoning A ingredients and leave to marinate for 15 minutes. Mix the sauce ingredients and set aside.

Cooking
Heat the wok, add deep-frying oil and when very hot, deep-fry the pork shreds until cooked through, about 1½ minutes. Stir frequently to prevent sticking together. Drain and discard the oil.

Reheat the wok and add the cooked oil, and when hot, stir-fry the celery and cloud ears for 1 minute. Add the ginger, scallion, garlic and chilli and stir in the seasoning B ingredients. Stir-fry for 1½ minutes longer. Add the pork and the sauce ingredients and stir-fry briefly over high heat. Stir in the thickening and cook for 1 minute. Add the vinegar, stir briefly, then serve.

The Chinese language is monosyllabic, on a character-by-character basis. Consequently, when the language is spoken, word meanings can often be distinguished only by subtle tonal variations.

'Fish-flavoured Pork', for example, is a misnomer, because *yu* — the Chinese word for fish in the Cantonese dialect — is homophonous with another word that means 'surplus'. So the dish should correctly be called 'Many-flavoured Pork'.

Another confusion of a different kind surrounds the well-known dish, 'Gold Coin Pork'.

The Chinese characters used for the name, 'Gold Coin Pork', actually translate as 'Gold Coin Chicken'. One can only assume that the confusion arose because both pork and chicken can be cut into the shape of the ancient Chinese gold coin that is called for in the recipe.

Roast 'Gold Coin' Pork
Shao Chin Ch'ien Chi 燒金錢鷄
Serves 8-10

315 g (10 oz)	pork loin
315 g (10 oz)	pork fat
185 g (6 oz)	pork liver

Seasoning

1 tbsp	sugar
1½ tsp	salt
1 tsp	monosodium glutamate
2 tsp	Rose Dew wine
3 tbsp	yellow bean paste
	dash orange-red food colouring

Preparation
Steam the pork fat over rapidly boiling water for 10 minutes. Remove and cool. Slice pork into 24 circular pieces, each about 1cm (¼″) thick and 5cm (2″) in diameter. Mix the seasoning ingredients, adding food colouring to make a deep orange-red, and marinate the pork for 25 minutes. Cut the pork fat and liver into 24 pieces each to match the pork.

Arrange the pork, pork fat and liver alternately on thin metal rods or skewers.

Cooking
Roast the pork kebabs for about 15 minutes in a hot oven or under a moderate grill, turning the rods frequently to cook evenly. When done, brush with honey or maltose and arrange on a serving plate. Serve.

Diced Pork with Walnuts

Ho T'ao Ch'ao Jou Ting 合桃炒肉丁
Serves 6

220 g (7 oz)	lean pork, 1.5cm (½″) dice
155 g (5 oz)	walnut kernels
4-5 slices	carrot, flower-cut
4-5 slices	ginger, flower-cut
2	scallions, 4cm (1½″) lengths
	oil for deep-frying

Seasoning A

½ tsp	bicarbonate of soda
2 tsp	cornstarch
1 tbsp	water

Seasoning B

½ tsp	salt
½ tsp	monosodiuum glutamate
2 tbsp	chicken stock
½ tsp	cornstarch
	dash white pepper

Preparation

Mix the diced pork with seasoning A ingredients and leave for 10 minutes. Boil the walnut kernels until they soften, about 5-6 minutes. Remove, drain very well and leave until partially dry. Mix the seasoning B ingredients and set aside.

Cooking

Heat the wok, add the oil and when very hot reduce heat slightly and deep-fry the walnuts until they turn a deeper brown, about 2 minutes. Remove, drain and set aside.

Reheat the oil, add the pork and cook on moderate heat for 1½ minutes, until cooked through. Remove and drain. Discard most of the oil. Reheat the wok, and stir-fry the carrot, ginger and scallion for 1 minute, then add the pork. Pour in seasoning B and return walnuts. Stir-fry 1 minute longer. Serve.

Diced Pork with Walnuts.

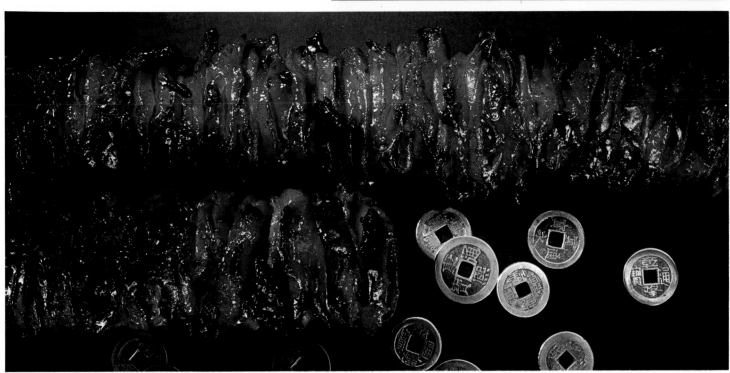

Roast 'Gold Coin' Pork.

Shredded Pork and Dry Beancurd Saute — *recipe on page 112.*

Shredded Pork and Dry Beancurd Saute
Kan Ssu Jou Ssu　乾絲肉絲
Serves 6

155 g (5 oz)	lean pork, shredded
155 g (5 oz)	dry beancurd, shredded
	few drops sesame oil
	oil for deep-frying

Seasoning A

½ tsp	salt
½	egg, beaten
½ tsp	cornstarch

Seasoning B

½ tsp	sugar
¼ tsp	monosodium glutamate
2 tsp	dark soy sauce
½ tsp	Shao Hsing wine

Thickening — mix together

¼ tsp	cornstarch
2 tsp	water

Preparation

Mix shredded pork with seasoning A ingredients and leave to stand for 10 minutes. Mix the seasoning B ingredients and set aside.

Cooking

Heat the wok, add the oil and when very hot deep-fry pork with beancurd for 1½ minutes, until cooked. Remove, drain and discard most of the oil.

Reheat the wok, return pork and beancurd, add seasoning B and the thickening and stir-fry for ½ minute longer. Sprinkle on sesame oil, stir and serve.

Peiping Shredded Pork

Ching Chiang Jou Ssu 京醬肉絲
Serves 6

250 g (8 oz)	lean pork, shredded
5	scallions
	few drops sesame oil
	oil for deep-frying

Seasoning A

½ tsp	salt
2 tsp	water
1 tsp	cornstarch
½	egg white, beaten

Seasoning B

½ tsp	sugar
½ tsp	monosodium glutamate
1 tsp	dark soy sauce
1 tsp	light soy sauce
1 tsp	Shao Hsing wine
1 tsp	sweet bean paste
1 tbsp	chicken stock

Thickening — mix together

½ tsp	cornstarch
1 tbsp	water

Preparation

Mix the seasoning A ingredients with pork and marinate for 10 minutes. Finely shred white parts of scallion, lengthways, discarding green tops. Spread half the shredded scallion on a serving plate and set aside the other half. Mix seasoning B ingredients and set aside.

Cooking

Heat the wok, add the oil and when very hot,

reduce heat slightly. Deep-fry the pork for 1 minute, stirring until the pieces separate. Remove and drain. Discard most of the oil, return the pork to the wok and heat. Add seasoning B and the thickening and stir-fry for ½ minute longer.

Sprinkle on sesame oil, stir and remove. Transfer to a serving plate, scatter remaining shredded scallion on top and serve.

Chopped Soya Bean Sprouts with Pork

Tai Tou Ya Shou Jou Sung 大豆芽瘦肉崧
Serves 6-8

250 g (8 oz)	lean pork, coarsely minced
500 g (1 lb)	soya bean sprouts
1 slice	ginger, finely chopped
2	scallions, finely chopped
75 ml (2½ fl oz)	chicken stock
3 tbsp	oil

Seasoning A

2 tsp	light soy sauce
1	egg white
2 tsp	cornstarch

Seasoning B

1½ tsp	sugar
1 tsp	salt
1 tbsp	dark soy sauce
1 tbsp	oyster sauce
	few drops sesame oil
	dash white pepper

Thickening — mix together

1 tsp	cornstarch
1 tbsp	water

Preparation

Mix the minced pork with seasoning A ingredients and marinate for 7-10 minutes. Wash the bean sprouts and trim the roots. Pluck off any green hoods on the pods and discard any greyish sprouts. Remove pods, if preferred. Chop bean sprouts coarsely. Lightly stir-fry in a dry pan for 1 minute to evaporate excess moisture. Remove and set aside. Mix the seasoning B ingredients and set aside.

Cooking

Heat the wok until it smokes, add the oil and stir-fry the pork for 1 minute. Add the ginger, scallion and chopped bean sprouts and stir-fry for 2 minutes. Add seasoning B and stir-fry for ½ minute longer, then add the chicken stock and the thickening and stir until the sauce thickens. Serve.

Spiced Pork Spare Ribs.

Spiced Pork Spare Ribs
Chiao Yen P'ai Ku 椒鹽排骨
Serves 6-8

500 g (1 lb)	lean pork spare ribs
	oil for deep-frying

Seasoning

¼ tsp	monosodium glutamate
1 tsp	light soy sauce
½ tsp	Shao Hsing wine
½ tsp	curry oil (or chilli oil)
1 tsp	cornstarch
1	egg

Dip

2 tbsp	water
2 tbsp	sugar
¼ tsp	salt
2 tbsp	black vinegar

Thickening — mix together

½ tsp	cornstarch
1½ tbsp	water

Preparation
Wash the spare ribs, divide, trim and chop into 5cm (2″) lengths. Mix the seasoning ingredients and marinate pork ribs for 30 minutes. Prepare the dip in the wok. Over a very low heat, add the water, then the remaining ingredients and stir until sugar is dissolved. Add thickening and stir until smooth. Set aside to cool.

Cooking
Heat the wok, add the oil and when very hot, deep-fry the ribs to a deep brown colour. Drain and arrange on a serving plate. Serve with the dip and a dish of spicy salt, see recipe page 277.

115

Steamed Meat Cake with Salted Fish — *recipe on page 116.*

Steamed Meat Cake with Salted Fish

Hsien Yu Cheng Jou Ping 鹹魚蒸肉餅

Serves 6-8

375 g (12 oz)	semi-fat pork, coarsely minced
60 g (2 oz)	Chao Pai salted fish
20 g (¾ oz)	ginger, long shreds
¼	salted duck egg (optional)
1 tbsp	cooked oil

Seasoning

½ tsp	salt
1	egg white
1 tbsp	cornstarch

Preparation

Mix pork with seasoning ingredients and work with the fingers to make a slightly sticky paste. Spread evenly over a lightly oiled plate to 1cm (¼") thick. Wash the salt fish and dry well. Place in the centre of the meat cake and arrange slivers of ginger on top. Add the diced duck egg, if used.

Cooking

Set the plate in a steamer, cover and steam for 7-8 minutes. The pork will turn a pale colour when cooked. Remove from the steamer, pour on the cooked oil and garnish with sprigs of Chinese parsley. Serve hot.

Deep-Fried Meatballs

Cha Wan Tzu 炸丸子

Serves 6-8

625 g (1¼ lb)	pork, semi-fat
	cornstarch
	oil for deep-frying

Seasoning

½ tsp	salt
1 tsp	monosodium glutamate
1½ tsp	Shao Hsing wine
1 tbsp	sesame oil
½ tsp	ginger, minced
2 tsp	scallion, minced
1	egg, beaten
2 tsp	cornstarch
1 tbsp	water

Preparation

Wash the pork and mince very finely. Add the seasoning ingredients and work until the mixture is very smooth. Divide and mould into ball shapes about 2.5cm (1") in diameter. Coat with cornstarch.

Cooking

Heat the wok, add the oil and when very hot, add the meatballs one at a time to keep the oil bubbling. Deep-fry over moderate heat for about 5 minutes, or until the meatballs turn a light brown colour. Drain and serve with a pepper-salt dip, see page 277.

'Twice Cooked' Pork with Green Peppers

Hui Kwo Jou 回鍋肉

Serves 6-8

500 g (1 lb)	loin pork
1	leek, 5cm (2") thin strips
1	green capsicum, thin strips
1-2	red chillies, thin strips
1 clove	garlic, minced
	oil for deep-frying

Seasoning

¼ tsp	sugar
¼ tsp	monosodium glutamate
½ tsp	dark soy sauce
½ tsp	light soy sauce
1½ tsp	Shao Hsing wine
1½ tsp	hot bean paste
1½ tsp	sweet bean paste
3 tbsp	chicken stock

Thickening — mix together

½ tsp	cornstarch
2 tsp	water

Preparation

Wash the pork and place it in boiling water to cover. Simmer for 1½ hours, until it is thoroughly softened. Drain and allow to cool, then carefully cut into thin slices. Mix seasoning ingredients and set aside.

Cooking

Heat the wok, add the oil and when very hot deep-fry the pork just long enough to lightly color the meat and crisp the fatty parts. Remove and drain. Discard most of the oil.

Reheat the wok and stir-fry the leek, capsicum, chillies and garlic for 1½ minutes. Add the seasoning and return the pork. Stir on moderate heat for 2 minutes longer. Add thickening and stir for a further ½ minute. Serve.

Note: This is a colourful traditional dish of the Szechwan province, "twice cooked" for added flavour and ultimate tenderness.

Sauteed Sliced Beef with Oyster Sauce — *recipe on page 118.*

Stir-Fried Beef with Scallions

Ts'ung Pao Niu Jou 葱爆牛肉
Serves 6-8

375 g (12 oz)	beef fillet
125 g (4 oz)	scallions, 4cm (1½″) lengths
1 tsp	sesame oil
	oil for deep-frying

Seasoning A

½ tsp	bicarbonate of soda
1 tbsp	cornstarch
1	egg white

2 tbsp	cooked oil

Seasoning B

¼ tsp	salt
1 tsp	monosodium glutamate
1 tsp	dark soy sauce
1 tbsp	light soy sauce
1 tsp	Shao Hsing wine

Preparation

Thinly slice the beef across the grain, then cut into thin strips. Mix with the seasoning A ingredients and marinate for 20 minutes. Flatten the scallion pieces with the side of a cleaver so they will cook through. Mix the seasoning B ingredients and set aside.

Cooking

Heat the wok until smoking, add the oil and when very hot, place beef in a wire mesh strainer and plunge into the hot oil for a few seconds. Remove, reheat the oil, then plunge beef in again for several seconds. Remove, drain and set aside. Discard most of the oil.

Reheat the wok, add the scallions and stir-fry for 1½ minutes. Add seasoning B and the beef and stir-fry for ½ minute. Sprinkle on sesame oil, stir and serve.

Stir-Fried Beef with Scallions

Spiced Sliced Beef
Lu Niu Jou 鹵牛肉
Serves 12

625 g (1¼ lb)	shin of beef
1 tbsp	salt
¼ tsp	saltpetre

Seasoning

1 tsp	sugar
¼ tsp	monosodium glutamate
3	anise stars, broken
¾ tsp	fennel, crushed
1 tbsp	dark soy sauce
½ tsp	ginger, minced
2 tsp	scallion, minced

Preparation
Wash the beef, trim and prick all over with a fork. Rub in the salt and saltpetre and leave to stand in a cool place for 2 days, weighted lightly.

Cooking
Blanch the beef in rapidly boiling water to cover, then add the seasoning ingredients. Reduce heat and simmer for 2 hours. Remove the beef and drain well. When cool, slice very thinly and arrange in overlapping rows on a serving plate.

The beef may be kept, refrigerated, for several days.

Sauteed Sliced Beef with Oyster Sauce
Hao Yu Niu Jou 蠔油牛肉
Serves 6

375 g (12 oz)	frying steak
4	dried mushrooms, soaked and sliced
6 slices	carrot, flower-cut
6 slices	ginger, flower-cut
2	scallions, 4cm (1½″) lengths
4 tbsp	cooked oil
	dash Shao Hsing wine

Seasoning A

½ tsp	bicarbonate of soda
1 tsp	light soy sauce
4 tsp	cornstarch
4 tbsp	water
2 tbsp	cooked oil

Seasoning B

1½ tsp	sugar
½ tsp	salt
½ tsp	monosodium glutamate
½ tsp	dark soy sauce
2 tbsp	oyster sauce

Thickening — mix together

½ tsp	cornstarch
1 tbsp	water

Preparation
Steam mushrooms for 10 minutes over moderately high heat. Thinly slice the meat across the grain, then cut into rectangular pieces about 5cm x 1.5cm (2″ x ½″). Mix the seasoning A ingredients and marinate beef for 30 minutes. Blanch carrot in boiling water for ½ minute, drain. Mix seasoning B ingredients and set aside.

Coooking
Heat the wok, add the oil and when very hot add the drained beef. Reduce the heat slightly and stir-fry the beef for 1 minute. Remove and drain. Reheat the wok, add the mushrooms, ginger, carrot and scallions and stir-fry for ½ minute. Return the beef to the wok, add in seasoning B and the thickening and stir-fry for 1 minute longer. Sprinkle on the wine and serve.

"The Chinese also assured us that this City hath an hundred and three score Butchers shambles, and in each of them an hundred stalls, full of all kinds of flesh that the earth produceth, as veal, mutton, pork, goat, the flesh of horses, buffalo, rhinoceros, tygers, lions, dogs, mules, asses, otters, shamois, badgers, and finally of all other beasts whatever ... There are withal many Taverns, where excellent fare is always to be had, and cellars full of gammons of bacon, dried tongues, poudered geese and other savoury viands, for to relish ones drink, all in so great abundance that it would be very superfluous to say more of it; but what I speak is to shew how liberally God hath imparted to these miserable blinded wretches the good things which he hath created on the earth to the end that his holy name may therefore be blessed for ever."

Peking by Pinto

Fillet of Beef with Preserved Mustard Greens
Tai Liang Niu Liu Ssu 大艮牛柳絲
Serves 6

185 g (6 oz)	beef fillet
125 g (4 oz)	preserved mustard greens, soaked
45 g (1½ oz)	canned bamboo shoots, shredded
45 g (1½ oz)	rice stick noodles
1	green capsicum, shredded
1	red chilli, shredded
1 clove	garlic, minced
2 tbsp	cooked oil
	oil for deep-frying

Seasoning A

¼ tsp	bicarbonate of soda
1 tbsp	light soy sauce
2 tsp	cornstarch
2 tbsp	water
2 tbsp	cooked oil

Seasoning B

½ tsp	sugar
½ tsp	salt
1 tsp	monosodium glutamate
1 tbsp	chicken stock
	dash white pepper
	few drops sesame oil

Preparation
Thinly slice the beef across the grain, then cut into long shreds. Mix the seasoning A ingredients and marinate beef for 30 minutes. Drain soaked preserved vegetable and rinse in cold water. Drain again, pressing out excess liquid. Shred finely. Heat the wok without oil and stir-fry shredded mustard greens and bamboo shoots for 1-2 minutes to evaporate excess moisture. Remove and set aside. Mix the seasoning B ingredients and set aside.

Cooking
Heat the wok and add the deep-frying oil and when very hot, drop in small handfuls of broken rice stick noodles to cook until they expand and float to the surface. Remove, drain and arrange on a serving plate. Set aside.

Reheat the oil and when very hot, deep-fry the shredded beef for 1 minute. Remove, drain and set aside. Discard the oil.

Reheat the wok and add 2 tbsp cooked oil. Stir-fry the capsicum, chilli and garlic for 1 minute. Add the shredded vegetables, bamboo shoots and beef and stir-fry on moderately high heat for a few seconds. Add seasoning B and stir-fry for 2-3 minutes longer. Pour onto the fried noodles and serve.

Stir-Fried Beef with Onion and Angled Luffa
Sheng Kua Yang Ts'ung Ch'ao Niu Jou
勝瓜洋葱炒牛肉
Serves 6-8

185 g (6 oz)	frying steak
375 g (12 oz)	angled luffa
1	large onion, 1cm (¼") squares
5-6 slices	carrot, flower-cut
5-6 slices	ginger, flower-cut
1 clove	garlic, crushed
4 tbsp	cooked oil

Seasoning A

¼ tsp	bicarbonate of soda
1 tsp	light soy sauce
2 tsp	cornstarch
1½ tbsp	water
2 tbsp	cooked oil

Seasoning B

½ tsp	salt
½ tsp	sugar
1 tsp	monosodium glutamate
¾ tsp	cornstarch
3 tbsp	chicken stock
	dash white pepper
	few drops sesame oil

Preparation
Thinly slice beef across the grain. Then cut into rectangular pieces about 8cm x 2.5cm (3" x 1"). Mix the seasoning A ingredients and marinate beef for 30 minutes. Remove the ridges from the angled luffa and cut lengthways into 3 pieces. Angle-cut these pieces into 2.5cm (1") lengths. Blanch carrot in boiling water for ½ minute, drain. Mix the seasoning B ingredients and set aside.

Cooking
Heat the wok, add 2 tbsp cooked oil, the onion and luffa pieces and stir-fry on high heat for 1 minute. Reduce heat slightly and stir-fry for 1 minute longer. Remove and drain.

Reheat the wok, add remaining cooked oil and stir-fry the beef for 2-3 minutes, until cooked. Remove and drain. Return the onion and luffa to the wok and add the ginger, carrot and garlic. Stir-fry briefly, adding the beef and seasoning B. Cook until the sauce thickens, serve.

Sesame Beef.

Sesame Beef
Chih Ma Niu Jou 芝麻牛肉
Serves 6

250 g (8 oz)	cold seasoned beef, thin slices (4cm x 2.5cm/1½" x 1")
1 tbsp	white sesame seeds
1½ tsp	oil
½ tsp	sesame oil
	oil for deep-frying

Seasoning

2 tbsp	sugar
½ tsp	monosodium glutamate
½ tsp	dark soy sauce
½ tsp	light soy sauce
½ tsp	Shao Hsing wine
2 tbsp	beef or chicken stock

Cooking

Heat the wok, add 1½ tsp oil and lightly stir-fry the sesame seeds for 1 minute. Remove and set aside. Reheat the wok, add the deep-frying oil and when very hot, place the beef in a wire mesh strainer and plunge into the hot oil for ½ minute. Remove, reheat the oil and repeat this process until meat is very crisp, about 5 times. Drain and set aside. Discard most of the oil. Reheat the wok and stir-fry the beef, adding the seasoning ingredients. Continue to stir-fry over moderate heat until all the liquid evaporates and meat is quite dry and crisp and glazed with the seasonings. Add the sesame seed, sprinkle on sesame oil and stir. Transfer to a serving plate and serve.

Note: For the method of preparing seasoned beef, see page 129.

Tangerine Peel Beef
Chen Pi Niu Jou 陳皮牛肉
Serves 6

250 g (8 oz)	cold seasoned beef, thin slices (4cm x 2.5cm/1½" x 1")
1 tbsp	dried tangerine peel, crumbled
1	dried chilli, seeded and sliced
½ tsp	sesame oil
	oil for deep-frying

Seasoning

2 tbsp	sugar
½ tsp	monosodium glutamate
½ tsp	dark soy sauce
½ tsp	light soy sauce
½ tsp	Shao Hsing wine
2 tbsp	beef or chicken stock

Cooking

Heat the wok, add the oil and when very hot place the beef in a wire mesh strainer and plunge into the hot oil for ½ minute. Remove, reheat the oil and repeat the process until the meat is very crisp, about 5 times. Drain and set aside. Discard most of the oil.

Reheat the wok and stir-fry the tangerine peel and chilli until they darken. Add the beef and seasoning ingredients and continue to stir-fry over a moderate heat until all the liquid evaporates and meat is quite dry and crisp and glazed with the seasoning. Transfer to a serving plate, sprinkle with the sesame oil and serve.

Note: For the method of preparing seasoned beef, see page 129.

Dry Shredded Beef with Vegetables
Kan Pien Niu Jou Ssu 乾煸牛肉絲
Serves 6

220 g (7 oz)	lean beef, cut into thin shreds of equal length
155 g (5 oz)	celery, 5cm (2") thin strips
90 g (3 oz)	carrot, 5cm (2") thin strips
1	leek, 5cm (2") thin strips
1 clove	garlic, finely chopped
2	dried chillies, chopped
½ tsp	salt
1 tsp	black vinegar
4 tbsp	cooked oil

Seasoning

1 tsp	sugar
¼ tsp	monosodium glutamate
1 tsp	dark soy sauce
2 tsp	light soy sauce
2 tsp	Shao Hsing wine
1 tsp	wine lees

Preparation and cooking

Season the beef with salt. Heat the wok until it smokes and add 3 tbsp cooked oil. Stir-fry the beef with chopped chilli for 4 minutes, separating the shreds of beef during cooking. Add remaining oil and stir-fry for 1 minute longer. Remove from the heat and cool slightly, then return to the heat and continue to stir-fry until the beef turns crispy. Add the vinegar and when it evaporates, add the celery, carrot, leek and garlic with the seasoning ingredients. Stir-fry for 3 minutes longer. Serve.

Braised Shin of Beef with 'Cloud Ears' and 'Golden Needles' — *recipe on page 124.*

Braised Shin of Beef with 'Cloud Ears' and 'Golden Needles'
Chin Ts'ai Hsueh Erh Ch'u Niu Chan
金菜雲耳焗牛展
Serves 6

375 g (12 oz)	shin of beef, thickly sliced
60 g (2 oz)	golden needles, soaked
45 g (1½ oz)	cloud ear fungus, soaked
6 slices	ginger, flower-cut
3	scallions, 4cm (1½″) lengths
10	dried red dates, soaked
3 tbsp	cooked oil

Seasoning A

½ tsp	bicarbonate of soda
1 tbsp	light soy sauce
2 tsp	cornstarch
2 tbsp	oil

Seasoning B

2 tsp	sugar
¾ tsp	salt
1 tsp	monosodium glutamate
2 tsp	yellow bean paste
250 ml (8 fl oz)	beef stock

Thickening — mix together

1 tbsp	cornstarch
1½ tbsp	water

Preparation
Mix seasoning A ingredients and pour over the beef, marinate for 45 minutes. Remove heads of golden needles and tie each piece into a knot. Drain and shred cloud ears. Drain dates and remove pips. Mix seasoning B ingredients and set aside.

Cooking
Heat the wok, add oil and when very hot, stir-fry the beef for 4 minutes, until just cooked through. Add the ginger, scallion, golden needles, cloud ears, dates and seasoning B and bring to the boil.

Transfer to an earthenware pot or casserole, cover, return to the heat and cook for 15-20 minutes longer. Add thickening, stir and allow to thicken. Transfer to a serving dish or serve in the same pot.

Note: The golden needles and cloud ears give a slightly musky flavour, the dates a delicate sweetness.

"Don't eat livers of horse or ox"

Chinese Proverb

The grandfather is holding his grandson on his knees.
The grandfather says here are meat buns to dip in vinegar sauce.
When you have finished eating you will be saucy
And will come over to hit your grandfather three blows in the face.

Anon

Beef Balls, Kweilin Style
Kuei Lin Niu Jou Wan 桂林牛肉丸
Serves 6

375 g (12 oz)	lean beef, coarsely minced
75 g (2½ oz)	canned water chestnuts, finely diced
1 sprig	Chinese parsley, finely chopped
	cornstarch
	oil for deep-frying

Seasoning

1½ tsp	salt
1 tsp	monosodium glutamate
4 tbsp	water
2 tbsp	cornstarch

Preparation
Mix the seasoning ingredients with beef to form a thick paste. Add the chopped water chestnuts and parsley and mix well. Divide the mixture into 24 parts, and mould each into a ball. Coat with cornstarch.

Cooking
Heat the wok, add the oil and when very hot reduce heat slightly. Deep-fry the beef balls 6-8 at a time for 4-5 minutes. Remove, drain and serve with a spicy salt dip, see page 277.

"To win the heart of your husband — satisfy his stomach

To uphold the love of your dearest ones — save them a good variety of food.

To expect your children to grow strong — give them appetite."

Confucius

Stewed Lamb with Dry Beancurd

Lamb & Mutton

Jellied Lamb Loaf — recipe on page 129.

Stewed Lamb with Dry Beancurd

Chu Chi Yan Nan Po 竹枝羊腩保
Serves 8

1 kg (2 lb)	breast of mutton
90 g (3 oz)	dried beancurd sticks, 5cm (2″) strips
75 g (2½ oz)	water chestnuts, peeled
90 g (3 oz)	ginger, peeled and lightly crushed
3 cloves	garlic, lightly crushed
1½ lit (40 fl oz)	chicken stock
3 tbsp	cooked oil
	oil for deep-frying

Seasoning

4 tsp	sugar
1½ tsp	salt
1 tsp	monosodium glutamate
½ pc	dried tangerine peel
2 tbsp	Shao Hsing wine
4 tbsp	Chu Hau sauce

Preparation

Trim the mutton and cut into 2.5cm (1″) cubes. Blanch in boiling water for 2 minutes, drain and set aside. Chop ginger and water chestnuts into medium dice. Chop tangerine peel coarsely.

Mix the seasoning ingredients and set aside.

Cooking

Heat the wok, add deep oil and when very hot, reduce heat slightly. Deep-fry the bean curd sticks until expanded and bubbly and a whitish colour. Remove and drain well. Discard the oil.

Reheat the wok, add cooked oil and when hot stir-fry the mutton cubes until lightly browned, about 3 minutes. Add ginger, water chestnuts and garlic and stir-fry briefly.

Pour in the chicken stock and bring to the boil. Add the seasoning. Transfer to a earthenware pot, cover tightly and simmer on moderate heat for 1-1¼ hours. Add the fried beancurd sticks and simmer for 15 minutes longer.

Serve in the pot with a dip of preserved beancurd and small dishes of thinly sliced red chilli and shredded lemon leaves.

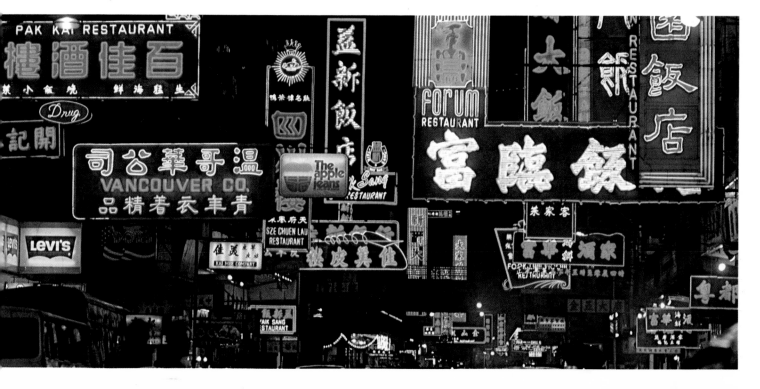

Mongolian Sliced Lamb Hot Pot
Meng Ku Shua Yang Jou Kuo 蒙古涮羊肉鍋
Serves 12

1 kg (2 lb)	lean shoulder or leg of lamb
750 g (1½ lb)	Tientsin cabbage, coarsely chopped
6 squares	soft beancurd, 2.5cm (1") cubes
125 g (4 oz)	bean thread vermicelli, soaked
2 lit (64 fl oz)	chicken stock

Seasoning

1 tsp	salt
½ tsp	monosodium glutamate

Dip

4 tbsp	sugar
8 tbsp	Shao Hsing wine
4 tbsp	red vinegar
4 tbsp	hot chilli sauce
4 tbsp	fish sauce
6 tbsp	sesame paste
60 g (2 oz)	chive shoots, shredded
60 g (2 oz)	Chinese parsley, chopped
60 g (2 oz)	scallion, finely chopped
4 tbsp	sesame oil
8 tbsp	cooked oil

Preparation

Slice the lamb paper thin and arrange on 12 plates. Place cabbage, beancurd and vermicelli on plates. Bring the stock to boil in a large pot over a portable cooker on the table. Add seasonings.

Serve the dip ingredients in small bowls to be mixed to individual taste.

Cooking

Hold slivers of the lamb in the boiling stock until just cooked through. Dip into the sauce before eating. Cook cabbage and beancurd in the same way. Cook the vermicelli last and serve with the stock.

"In winter we should eat beef and mutton. Summer is not the time to eat them. In summer we should eat dried and preserved meats. Winter is not the time to eat them. As for condiments, mustard belongs to summer and pepper belongs to winter."

Yuen Mai.

"Though lamb may be good, it is difficult to cook it to suit everyone's taste."

Ancient Chinese Proverb.

Braised Lamb
Hung Men Yang Jou 紅炆羊肉
Serves 8

1 kg (2 lb)	leg of lamb
30 g (1 oz)	dried mushrooms, soaked and sliced
30 g (1 oz)	canned bamboo shoots, drained and sliced
5 slice	ginger
1	scallion, 4cm (1½") lengths
150 ml (5 fl oz)	chicken stock
1 tbsp	cooked oil
	few drops sesame oil

Seasoning A

2 tbsp	sweet bean paste
1 tbsp	cooked oil

Seasoning B

½ tsp	sugar
¼ tsp	salt
1 tsp	dark soy sauce
1 tbsp	light soy sauce

Thickening — mix together

1½ tsp	cornstarch
1 tbsp	water

Preparation

Wash the lamb and place in a pot. Cover with boiling water, cover the pot and simmer for 1 hour. Drain and cut the meat into 2.5cm (1") cubes. Place in a double boiler and add the seasoning A ingredients, ginger and scallion. Pour in the chicken stock. Mix the seasoning B ingredients and set aside.

Cooking

Simmer the lamb in the double boiler until the meat is very tender, about 1 hour. Remove and drain the lamb, discard scallion and ginger, but retain liquid.

Heat the wok and add 1 tbsp cooked oil. Stir-fry the lamb with mushrooms and bamboo shoots for 1 minute. Add the retained liquid and seasoning B and stir. Add the thickening, stir, cover and braise for 15-20 minutes on moderate heat. Sprinkle on sesame oil, stir and serve.

Jellied Lamb Loaf
Yang Kao 羊羔
Serves 12

875 g (1¾ lb)	lean lamb
310 g (10 oz)	skin of lamb breast and flap
1¼ lit (40 fl oz)	chicken stock
3 slices	ginger
2	scallions, coarsely chopped
1	red chilli, sliced
1	turnip, cubed
1	five-spices bouquet
2 sprigs	Chinese parsley, finely chopped

Seasoning

1 tsp	salt
½ tsp	monosodium glutamate
2 tsp	dark soy sauce
1 tbsp	Shao Hsing wine

Preparation
Wash the lamb skin, blanch in boiling water for 30 seconds, remove and drain. Place the lamb in a pot with water to cover, bring to the boil and simmer briefly, then remove, drain and discard the water.

Cooking
Pour the chicken stock into a large pot, add the lamb and bring to the boil. Add the lamb skin, ginger, scallion, chilli, turnip and seasoning ingredients and bring again to the boil. Lower the heat, add the five-spices bouquet, cover and leave to simmer for 2-3 hours until lamb is completely tender.

Drain the meat, strain stock and discard everything else. Tear the mutton into thin shreds, mix with the chopped parsley and place in a greased shallow dish. Skim the strained stock and boil until reduced to about 250 ml (8 fl oz). Pour enough over the meat to cover, cool and refrigerate until set.

Slice and serve.

"Men eat the flesh of grass-fed and grain-fed animals, deer eat grass, centipedes find snakes tasty, and hawks and falcons relish mice. Of these four, which knows how food ought to taste?"

Wang Ni

"When the host leads on the guests to present the offering to the father of cookery, they will begin with the dishes which were first brought in. Going on from the meat cooked on the bones they will offer some of all the other dishes."

Cold Seasoned Beef
Wu Hsiang Niu Jou 五香牛肉

| 1¼ kg (2½ lb) | shin of beef |
| | sesame oil |

Seasoning

1½ tsp	brown peppercorns
2 tbsp	salt
1½ tsp	saltpetre
2 tsp	Shao Hsing wine
2 slices	ginger, minced

Lu Shui Sauce

2 tbsp	slab sugar, crumbled
1½ tbsp	salt
1	five-spices bouquet
3 tbsp	dark soy sauce
45 g (1½ oz)	old ginger, chopped

Preparation
Wash the beef and prick all over with a fork. Roast the peppercorns in a dry wok over moderately low heat for 1-2 minutes, then grind to a fine powder. Mix with the other seasoning ingredients. Rub well into the meat and leave for 2 days in a cool dry place, turning occasionally. It may be weighted slightly.

Mix the Lu Shui sauce ingredients in a saucepan large enough to hold the meat and add enough water to cover the meat. Stir on high heat until the sugar has completely dissolved. Cover and boil for 15-20 minutes, then discard the bouquet.

Cooking
Blanch the beef in a large pot of boiling water for 5 minutes. Drain and rinse in cold water. Put into the Lu Shui sauce and bring to a gentle boil. Cover and simmer on low heat for 1½-2 hours, for young beef and up to 5 hours for older beef, until the meat is very tender and well flavoured. Remove and drain well, then leave to cool completely. Rub with sesame oil and cut into paper thin slices. Serve cold.

Note: This beef is used to make Sesame Beef and its companion Tangerine Peel Beef.

Sliced Pork with Garlic Sauce— *recipe on page 132;* Cold Seasoned Beef — *recipe on page 129;* Shredded Jelly-Fish Salad — *recipe on page 132.*

Shredded Jelly-Fish Salad
Pan Che P'i 拌蜇皮
Serves 12

250 g (8 oz)	dried jelly-fish, soaked
Seasoning	
2 tsp	sugar
½ tsp	salt
½ tsp	monosodium glutamate
2 tsp	black vinegar
2 tbsp	sesame oil

Preparation
Drain the jelly-fish and clean thoroughly. Roll up and cut into thin strips. Mix the seasoning ingredients and set aside.

Cooking
Place jelly-fish in a large pot, cover with boiling water and leave to soak for at least 10 minutes. Drain well. Place in a colander under running cold water until it loses its fishy smell (about 2 hours). Or soak in cold water, changing the water at least 5 times. Drain until dry, then mix with the seasoning ingredients and leave to stand a short time before serving. Arrange on a plate and garnish with sprigs of parsley.

Sliced Pork with Garlic Sauce
Yun P'ien Pai Jou 雲片白肉
Serves 12

875 g (1¾ lb)	pork shanks
Sweet Soy Sauce	
2 tbsp	dark soy sauce
2 tbsp	slab sugar
¼ tsp	brown peppercorns, powdered
60 g (2 oz)	old ginger, peeled
Sauce:	
¼ tsp	salt
¼ tsp	monosodium glutamate
1 tbsp	black vinegar
1 tbsp	chilli oil
1 tsp	sesame oil
1 tbsp	garlic, minced
2 tbsp	pork stock
	sweet soy sauce

Preparation and Cooking
Shave the pork shanks and wash well. Cut each into two pieces. Place in a large pot of boiling water and return to the boil. Reduce heat and simmer until the pork is completely tender, about 1¾ hours, skimming occasionally. Remove and drain. Leave soaking in the stock until needed.

Stir the soy sauce, crumbled sugar, ginger and pepper in the wok over low heat until the sugar is dissolved. Remove from the heat and leave to cool, then remove the ginger.

Add this sweet soy sauce to the other sauce ingredients, stir well and pour into several small bowls.

Drain the pork and slice paper thin using a very sharp knife. Arrange, overlapping the slices, on a serving plate and serve with the dips of garlic sauce.

"There is nobody who does not eat and drink. But there are few who can distinguish flavours."

Mencius

Cold Meat Combination
Shih Chin Leng Pang 什錦冷盆
Serves 12

90 g (3 oz)	seasoned beef, thinly sliced (*1)
90 g (3 oz)	canned abalone, drained and thinly sliced
90g (3 oz)	chicken fillet
90 g (3 oz)	dried jelly-fish, shredded (*2)
6 stalks	canned asparagus, or 1 green capsicum, 4cm (1½") diagonal slices
90 g (3 oz)	celery, 4cm (1½") diagonal slices
45 g (1½ oz)	dried black mushrooms, soaked and shredded
90 g (3 oz)	Yunnan ham, thinly sliced
90 g (3 oz)	pork sausage, thinly sliced (*3)
90 g (3 oz)	vegetarian goose, thinly sliced (*4)
1	red chilli, thin strips
Seasoning A	
¼ tsp	monosodium glutamate
1 tsp	ginger, minced
1 tsp	scallion, minced
1 tbsp	cooked oil
	pinch of salt
Seasoning B	
½ tsp	salt
¼ tsp	monosodium glutamate
1 tsp	white vinegar
2 tsp	light soy sauce
1 tbsp	sesame oil

Seasoning C

¼ tsp	sugar
¼ tsp	salt
¼ tsp	monosodium glutamate
½ tsp	Shao Hsing wine
¼ tsp	sesame oil

Seasoning D

¼ tsp	sugar
¼ tsp	monosodium glutamate
2 tsp	light soy sauce
1 tbsp	chicken stock

Dip

¼ tsp	monosodium glutamate
4 tbsp	light soy sauce
2 tsp	white vinegar
2 tbsp	sesame oil
4 tbsp	chicken stock

Preparation

Arrange the sliced beef, overlapped, to one side of a serving plate. Arrange thin slices of abalone in a flower shape and place near the beef, with a sliver of red chilli in the centre. Marinate chicken with seasoning A ingredients for 5 minutes, then place in a steamer and cook over rapidly boiling water for 8 minutes. Remove, cool and cut into thin slices. Arrange, overlapped, on the serving plate. Mix prepared jelly-fish with the seasoning B ingredients and pile next to the chicken, or place in the centre of the plate to be covered with the other ingredients. Arrange asparagus or capsicum attractively on the dish. Blanch celery in boiling water for 1 minute. Drain well and mix with the seasoning C ingredients. Arrange in a flower formation on the plate and add a sliver of red chilli to the centre of the flower.

Marinate mushrooms with seasoning D ingredients for 5 minutes steam for 10 minutes, then pile on the serving plate. Arrange ham, pork sausage and vegetarian goose in the remaining spaces on the plate. Mix the dip ingredients and serve in small dishes with the cold meat combination.

Note: *1: For method of making seasoned beef, see page 129.

*2: For preparation of jelly-fish, see previous page.

*3: For method of making pork sausage, see page 223.

*4: For method of making vegetarian goose, see page 227.

Salad with Agar Agar

Leng Pan Liang Ts'ai 冷拌涼菜
Serves 12

15 g (½ oz)	dried agar agar
90 g (3 oz)	cucumber
4	eggs
90 g (3 oz)	boiled or barbecued pork
60 g (2 oz)	dried black mushrooms, soaked
90 g (3 oz)	chicken fillet
90 g (3 oz)	braised or stewed beef
60 g (2 oz)	dry beancurd
2 tsp	cooked oil

Seasoning A

½ tsp	salt
½ tsp	sugar
½ tsp	Shao Hsing wine

Seasoning B

½ tsp	salt
½ tsp	monosodium glutamate
½ tsp	Shao Hsing wine

Salad Dressing

1 tsp	sugar
¼ tsp	salt
½ tsp	monosodium glutamate
2 tbsp	light soy sauce
2 tsp	Shao Hsing wine
2 tsp	white vinegar
2 tbsp	cooked oil
2 tsp	sesame oil

Preparation and Cooking

Soak agar agar for about 30 minutes in warm water, until soft. Drain well and shred the cucumber (peel first if preferred). Heat the wok, add cooked oil and pour in lightly beaten eggs mixed with seasoning A ingredients. Turn pan to make a thin omelette, cover and cook until firm underneath, then turn and cook other side until firm. Remove, leave to cool then shred. Shred boiled or barbecued pork. Steam black mushrooms over high heat for 8-10 minutes. Remove and when cool, shred. Shred chicken, marinate with seasoning B ingredients and steam over moderately high heat for 7 minutes. Cool. Shred braised or stewed beef and dry beancurd. Arrange the agar agar in a salad bowl or on a serving plate and arranged the other ingredients on top. Mix the salad dressing and pour over the salad. Decorate with carved carrots and cucumber.

Cold Meat Combination — *recipe on page 132*

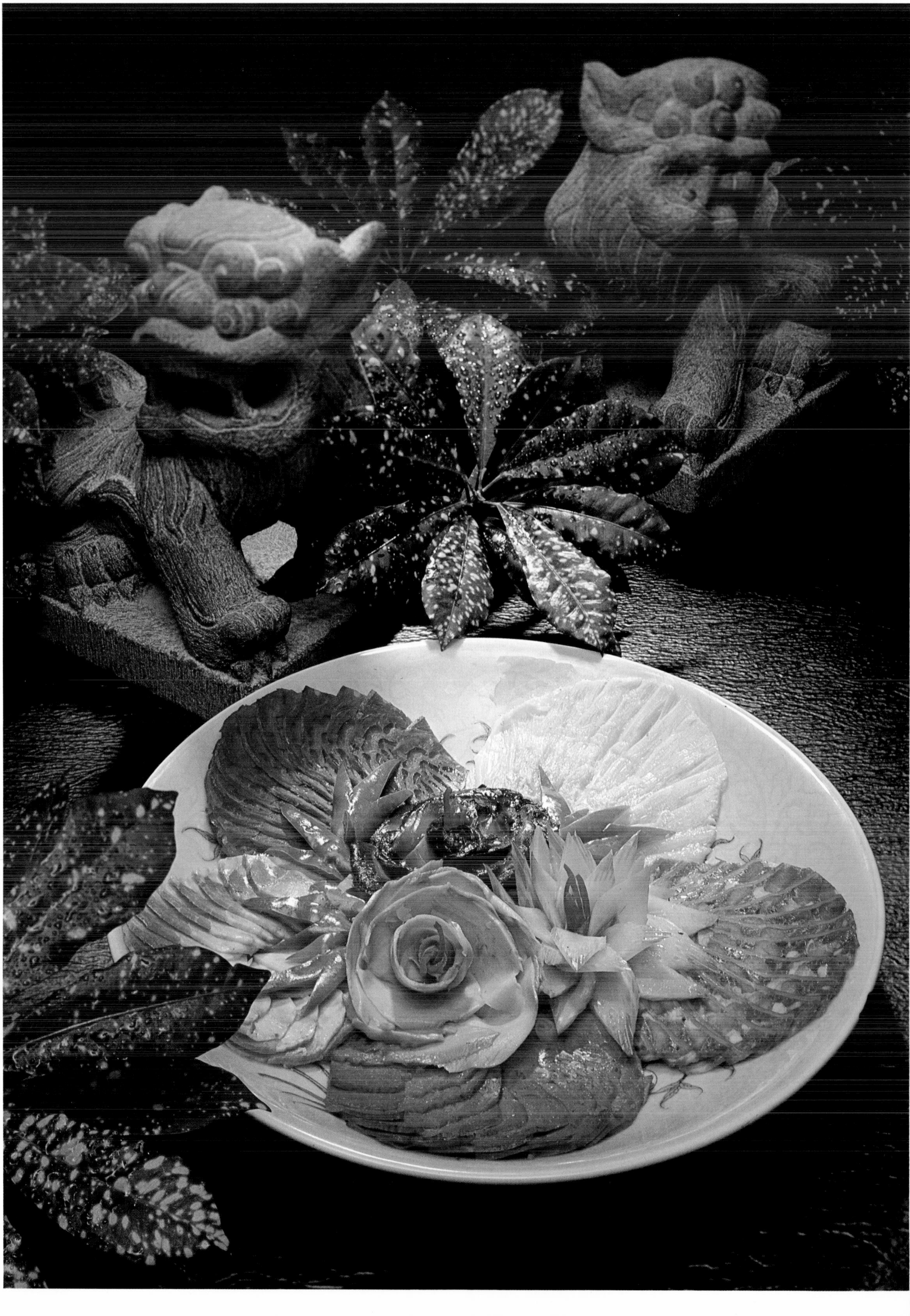

Stir-Fried Diced Chicken with Bean Paste
Chiang Pao Chi Ting 醬爆雞丁
Serves 6

375 g (12 oz)	chicken fillet
2 tbsp	soya bean paste
	few drops sesame oil
	oil for deep-frying

Seasoning A

¼ tsp	salt
½	egg white
1 tbsp	cornstarch

Seasoning B

2 tsp	sugar
½ tsp	monosodium glutamate
½ tsp	dark soy sauce
1 tbsp	Shao Hsing wine

Preparation

Cut chicken fillets into 1.5cm (½″) cubes. Mix with seasoning A ingredients and leave for 10 minutes. Mix the seasoning B ingredients and set aside.

Cooking

Heat the wok, add the oil and when moderately hot, add the chicken and fry gently for 1 minute. Remove, drain and set aside. Discard most of the oil.

Reheat the wok and stir-fry bean paste briefly, then add chicken and seasoning B. Sprinkle on sesame oil and stir-fry for ½ minute longer. Serve.

"From the moment I get up in the morning, I am busy about seven things: fuel, rice, oil, salt, soy sauce, vinegar and tea."

A Housewife in a Yuan Dynasty Drama

Stir-Fried Diced Chicken with Bean Paste.

'Bon Bon' Chicken
Pang Pang Chi 棒棒鷄
Serves 12

1	whole chicken (about 1½ kg/3 lb)
1 tbsp	white sesame seeds
1½ tsp	oil
2 tsp	sesame oil

Dip

2½ tbsp	sesame or peanut paste
1-2 tbsp	chilli sauce (to taste)
2½ tbsp	cooked oil
2 tsp	sesame oil
1½ tbsp	sugar
¼ tsp	monosodium glutamate
1½ tbsp	light soy sauce
1½ tsp	black vinegar
2 tbsp	chicken stock

Preparation

Wash and clean the chicken. Lightly stir-fry the sesame seeds in 1½ tsp oil, remove and set aside. Prepare the dip, first mixing the peanut paste, chilli sauce, cooked oil and sesame oil to a smooth paste. Stir in remaining ingredients a little at a time to make a smooth sauce. Set aside.

Cooking

Place the chicken in a pot and cover with water. Bring to the boil, cover and simmer for 10 minutes over moderate heat. Add 100 ml (3 fl oz) cold water, turn chicken over, bring to the boil again and simmer for 10 minutes longer. Add another 100 ml (3 fl oz) cold water and repeat this process.

Remove pot from the heat and leave to stand for 1 hour. Drain the chicken and brush the skin with sesame oil. Debone and tear into thin shreds. Arrange the chicken on a plate with skin pieces topmost. Sprinkle on fried sesame seeds and serve cold with the dip.

136

Chicken with Ham and Green Vegetables
Chin Hua Yu Shu Chi 金華玉樹雞
Serves 6-8

½	chicken (about 750 g/1½ lb)
90 g (3 oz)	Yunnan ham, thinly sliced
125 g (4 oz)	kale or leaf mustard
	chicken stock
2 tbsp	cooked oil

Seasoning

1 tsp	salt
½ tsp	monosodium glutamate

Sauce

½ tsp	sugar
½ tsp	salt
½ tsp	monosodium glutamate
1 tsp	oyster sauce
150 ml (5 fl oz)	chicken stock

Thickening — mix together

2 tsp	cornstarch
1 tbsp	water

Preparation and Cooking

Clean and wash the chicken. Bring enough chicken stock to cover the chicken to a rapid boil. Add the chicken, cover and bring back to the boil. Uncover, reduce the heat and simmer for 20 minutes. During this time, lift the chicken out of the stock two or three times to drain. Remove from the pan, drain and allow to cool. Reserve some of the stock for the sauce. Debone and cut into 24 pieces, each about 5 x 1.5cm (2″ x ½″). Cut the ham into 24 pieces to match the chicken. Arrange the chicken and ham pieces alternatively in rows on an oval serving dish. Mix the sauce ingredients and set aside.

Trim and wash kale or mustard and blanch in boiling water for 1 minute, add the seasoning ingredients and boil for 2 minutes longer. Arrange around the rim of the dish.

Heat the wok and add oil. When very hot pour in the sauce and bring to the boil. Add thickening and stir until the sauce clears, then pour over the dish. Serve hot.

"The chicken, the pig, the fish, the duck — these are the four heroes of the table."

Yuen Mai

"Everyone's tastes in food are different."

Ancient Chinese Proverb

Diced Chicken with Mixed Meat and Vegetables
Pa Pao Chi Ting 八寶雞丁
Serves 6-8

155 g (5 oz)	chicken fillet
30 g (1 oz)	pork kidney
30 g (1 oz)	raw shrimps, peeled
30 g (1 oz)	ham, strips 4cm x 1.5cm (1½″ x ½″)
60 g (2 oz)	broccoli heads, chopped
30 g (1 oz)	button mushrooms, diced
30 g (1 oz)	raw cashew nuts
	oil for deep-frying

Seasoning A

½ tsp	salt
½	egg, beaten
½ tsp	cornstarch

Seasoning B

½ tsp	sugar
¼ tsp	monosodium glutamate
1 tsp	dark soy sauce
½ tsp	Shao Hsing wine
1 tbsp	chicken stock

Thickening — mix together

½ tsp	cornstarch
1 tbsp	water

Preparation

Wash the chicken, wipe dry and cut into medium dice. Mix with seasoning A ingredients and let stand for 10 minutes. Wash kidneys, remove skin, membranes and fatty cores and cut into small dice. Drop into a pot of boiling water to blanch for 1 minute. Drain and cover with cold water. Drain again. Blanch broccoli in boiling water for ½ minute, drain and splash with cold water to brighten colour. Drain again. Mix the seasoning B ingredients and set aside.

Cooking

Heat the wok, add the oil and when fairly hot, deep-fry the chicken over moderate heat for ½ minute. Add the diced kidney, shrimps, ham, broccoli and mushrooms and deep-fry for 1 minute. Put in cashew nuts and deep-fry for 2 minutes. Remove, drain and discard most of the oil.

Reheat the wok, return the meat and vegetables, add seasoning B and the thickening and stir-fry for ½ minute longer, then serve.

137

Salt-Baked Chicken — *recipe on page 140*

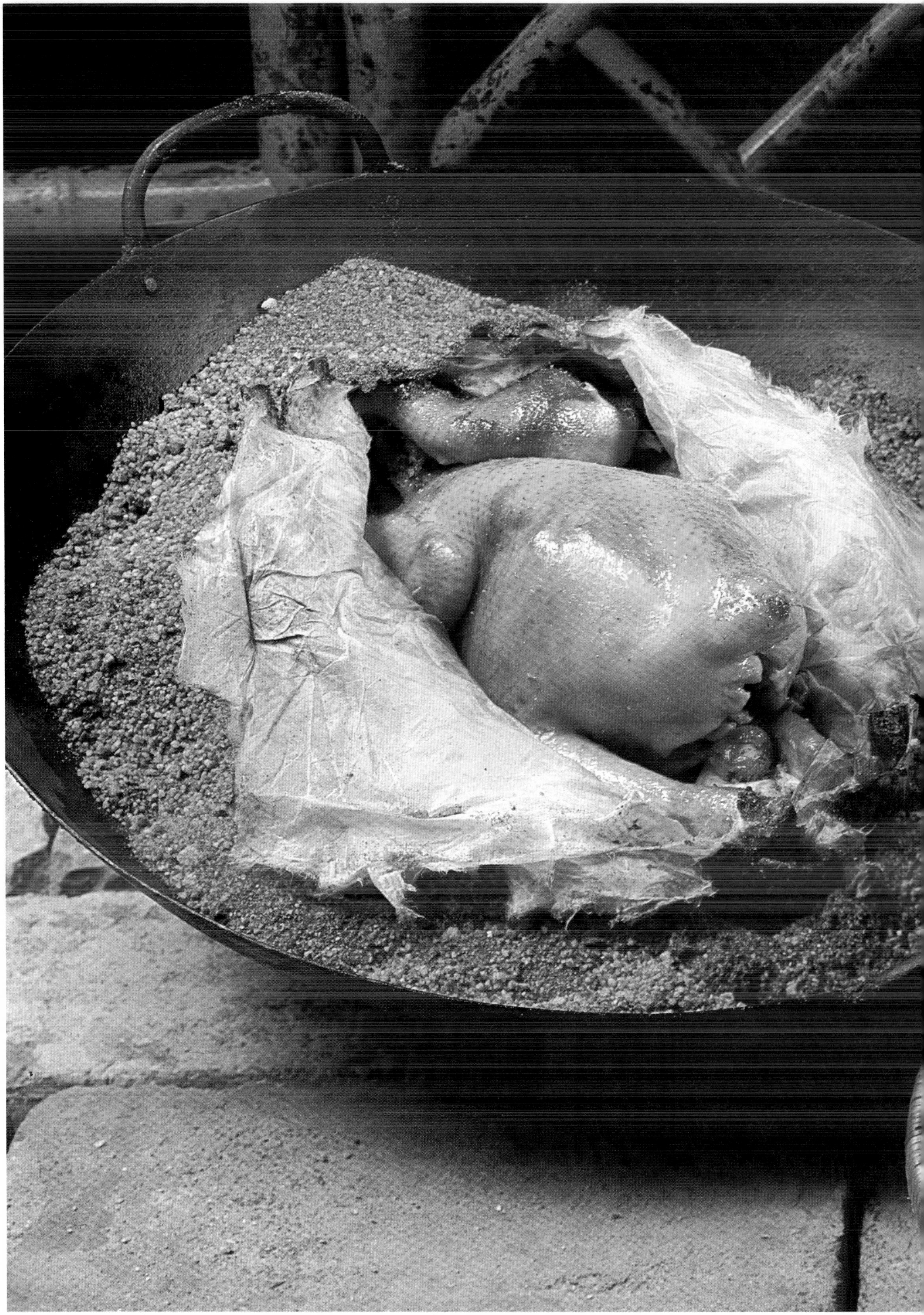

Salt-Baked Chicken
Ku Fa Yen Chu Chi 古法鹽焗鷄
Serves 12

1	chicken (about 1½ kg/3 lb)
3 kg (6 lb)	rock salt
3 sheets	mulberry paper (72cm x 65cm/28″ x 25″)
	dark soy sauce

Stuffing

1 tsp	salt
3	anise stars, broken
1 tsp	monosodium glutamate
2 tbsp	Rose Dew wine
2 knobs	ginger, coarsely chopped
2	scallions, coarsely chopped
4	shallots, coarsely chopped

Preparation and Cooking

Heat the rock salt in a large wok or pan for 20 minutes over a very hot flame — or longer if flame is not very hot — stirring constantly. Wash and clean the chicken, rub the skin with soy sauce. Mix the stuffing and place in the cavity. Secure with a metal pin.

Meanwhile continue to stir the rock salt until it becomes quite black. Lay the three sheets of mulberry paper together and oil the top sheet generously. Wrap the chicken, one sheet at a time, with the paper and rub the outer paper with a little cold water to seal. Scoop a cavity in the rock salt and insert the wrapped chicken. Cover with the salt. Leave on moderate heat for 10 minutes, then remove the chicken, reheat the salt and replace chicken with the other side downwards. Cover with salt and cook for another 10 minutes.

Remove the chicken, strip away the paper and cut the chicken in halves. Discard stuffing and cut the chicken into bite-size slices. Arrange on a serving plate and serve hot with a ginger and scallion dip, see next recipe.

"A black chicken should never be used for food."

Imperial Cookery Book of the Mongol Dynasty — *Yin Shan Cheng Yao*

"A good cure for pains in the back is chicken with foxglove. Half a pound of foxgloves, five ounces of sugar, and one black chicken are the ingredients required. Pluck the chicken and draw it in the usual way; cut up the foxgloves and stuff the bird with them and the sugar. Stew in a bronze vessel and eat with rice. Neither salt nor vinegar should accompany this dish, and only the flesh should be eaten."

Imperial Cookery Book of the Mongol Dynasty. — *Yin Shan Cheng Yao*

'White-Cut' Chicken with Ginger and Scallion Dip
Pai Ch'ieh Fei Chi 白切肥鷄
Serves 12

1	chicken (about 1½ kg/3 lb)
	chicken stock

Dip

1 tsp	salt
6-8 slices	ginger, minced
1-2	scallions, minced
5 tbsp	cooked oil

Preparation and Cooking

Clean and wash chicken, drain well. Bring enough chicken stock to completely cover the chicken to boil in a large saucepan. When bubbling, put in chicken, cover pan and boil for 2-3 minutes. Skim the surface of the stock, reduce heat and simmer for about 20 minutes, then remove from the heat and leave the chicken in the hot stock until cooked through. To test if done, gently squeeze the thigh. The flesh should feel firm, but springy.

Remove from the stock and leave to cool for 10 minutes, then cut into bite-size pieces and arrange 'spread eagle' on a serving plate. Decorate with scallion curls.

Warm the cooked oil, add salt and remove from the heat. Pour over the minced ginger and scallion and transfer to small dishes. Serve with the chicken.

'White-Cut' Chicken with Ginger and Scallion Dip.

Smoked Chicken, Peiping Style
Hsun Chi 燻雞
Serves 12

1	chicken (about 1½ kg/3 lb)
1 tbsp	sugar
1 tbsp	jasmine tea leaves (optional)
2 tbsp	camphor wood chips

Stock:

4 tbsp	salt
1 tsp	monosodium glutamate
2	five-spices bouquets
150 ml (5 fl oz)	dark soy sauce
1½ lit (48 fl oz)	water

Dip

1 tbsp	sugar
1 tbsp	dark soy sauce
1 tsp	white vinegar
2 tsp	sesame oil
2 tsp	garlic minced

Preparation and Cooking

Mix the dip ingredients and pour into several sauce dishes.

Clean and throughly wash the chicken. Drain well.

Bring stock ingredients to the boil and simmer for 5 minutes. Put in the chicken and poach on moderate heat for 20 minutes. Lift out and drain well.

Place the sugar, tea leaves (if used) and wood chips in a wok and set over high heat. When smoking, place the chicken on the pan on a rack and cover tightly.

Smoke on one side for 7 minutes then turn and smoke the other side for 5 minutes. Remove, cut into bite-size pieces and arrange "spread eagle" style on a serving plate. Serve with the dip.

Deep-Fried Spiced Chicken
Hsiang Su Ch'uan Chi 香酥全鷄
Serves 10-12

1	whole chicken (about 1½ kg/3 lb)
1 tsp	ginger, minced
2 tsp	scallion, minced
1	anise star
½ tsp	brown peppercorns
	oil for deep-frying

Seasoning

2 tsp	salt
1 tsp	brown peppercorns, powdered
3	anise stars, ground

Preparation

Wash and clean the chicken, leaving head on. Mix the seasoning ingredients and rub well into the skin. Place ginger, scallion, anise star and brown peppercorns inside the bird, and leave to stand for 25 minutes. Place on a lightly oiled plate and steam over gently boiling water for 1½ hours. Remove, discard the seasonings inside, and leave to cool, then place on a rack in an airy place to dry for several hours.

Cooking

Heat the wok, add the oil (it should be quite deep) and when very hot, carefully put in the chicken to deep-fry on high heat until it is crispy and golden brown. Ladle the hot oil over the bird and turn several times during cooking. Remove, drain and chop chicken into bite-size pieces. Arrange, skin side upwards in the original shape of the chicken, on a serving plate lined with shredded lettuce. Garnish with shrimp crackers and serve with a spicy salt dip, see page 277.

"It is against the will of God, to eat delicate food hastily."

Chang Ch'ao

Fried Shedded Smoked Chicken
Chiang Pao Hsun Chi Ssu 醬爆燻雞絲
Serves 6-8

½	smoked chicken Peiping style, see above left.
	oil for deep-frying

Seasoning

1 tbsp	soya bean paste
2 tbsp	cornstarch

Preparation

Debone the chicken and tear the meat into slivers about 5cm (2″) long. Thoroughly coat with the soy bean paste, then with cornstarch.

Cooking

Heat the wok, add the oil and when very hot, reduce heat slightly. Place the chicken in a wire mesh strainer and lower into the oil. Deep-fry for 2 minutes, separating the pieces of chicken with chopsticks during cooking.

Lift out, drain well and serve.

Tangerine Peel Chicken
Ch'en P'i Chi 陳皮鷄
Serves 6-8

500 g (1 lb)	chicken fillet
1 slice	ginger, minced
1	scallion, minced
2	dried chillies, chopped
1 pc	dried tangerine peel (5cm x 1.5cm/2" x ½"), crumbled
	oil for deep-frying

Seasoning A

½ tsp	salt
½ tsp	monosodium glutamate
½ tsp	dark soy sauce
½ tsp	Samshu wine
2 tsp	cornstarch

Seasoning B

1½ tsp	sugar
½ tsp	monosodium glutamate
½ tsp	dark soy sauce
2 tsp	light soy sauce
1 tsp	Shao Hsing wine
2 tsp	black vinegar
	few drops sesame oil

Thickening — mix together

½ tsp	cornstarch
1 tbsp	water

Preparation
Wash the chicken and cut into 2cm (¾") cubes. Mix thoroughly with the minced ginger and scallion, then add the seasoning A ingredients and marinate for 15 minutes. Mix the seasoning B ingredients and set aside.

Cooking
Heat the wok until smoking, add the oil and when very hot deep-fry the chicken pieces for 1½ minutes, until golden. Drain. Discard most of the oil.

Reheat the wok and stir-fry the chillies and tangerine peel until they darken. Add the chicken pieces and stir. Add seasoning B and the thickening and stir-fry until the seasoning coats the chicken. Serve.

"The dinner then began. We had, in succession, sharks fins: a stew of goose: tendons of deer: birds nest soup: turtle: ham (very good): fowl and quails: pigeons made up like faggots: fish sounds: small puddings of pork fat, as at the eating house: a soup of rose leaves, with a strong twang of garlic: and many unknown things. There were sixteen courses!"

To China and Back — *Albert Smith*

Deep-Fried Crispy Chicken
Tang Hung Cha Tzu Chi 當紅炸子鷄
Serves 12

1	chicken (about 1½ kg/3 lb)
	oil for deep-frying

Seasoning A

1 tsp	salt
½ tsp	five spices powder

Seasoning B

45 g (1½ oz)	maltose
150 ml (5 fl oz)	white vinegar
30 ml (1 fl oz)	red vinegar
100 ml (3 fl oz)	water

Preparation
Clean and wash the chicken. Tie a string around the neck and hang to drain and dry the skin. Pour boiling water over the chicken several times to partially cook the skin, making it crisper when cooked. Rub the seasoning A ingredients into the cavity.

Heat seasoning B ingredients together in a double saucepan until the maltose dissolves. Pour over the chicken several times, catching it in a drip tray placed beneath the chicken. Leave to hang for another 1½-2 hours until dry, with a smooth shiny glaze.

Cooking
Heat the wok and add oil. When very hot reduce heat slightly and deep-fry the chicken for 6-7 minutes. Ladle the hot oil over the chicken continually while cooking. Raise heat and continue to cook until the chicken is a deep golden brown and the skin has puffed slightly and come away from the meat.

Remove and drain. When slightly cool, chop into bite-size pieces and arrange "spread-eagle" on a serving plate. Serve with a spicy salt dip, see recipe page 277.

Drunken Chicken
Tsui Chi 醉鷄
Serves 8-10

½	chicken (about 750 g/1½ lb)
Sauce	
¼ tsp	sugar
1 tsp	salt
¼ tsp	monosodium glutamate
5 tbsp	Shao Hsing wine

Preparation
Wash and clean the chicken. Mix the sauce ingredients.

Cooking
Place the chicken in a pot and cover with cold water. Bring to the boil, cover and simmer for 20 minutes. Drain and allow to cool.

Chop into bite-size pieces and arrange in a bowl. Pour the sauce over the chicken and leave to marinate for several hours. Serve cold.

Shantung Chicken
Shan Tung Shao Chi 山東燒鷄
Serves 8-10

1	whole chicken (about 2½ lb/1¼ kg)
1 slice	ginger, minced
3-4	scallions, minced
1 tsp	salt
2 tsp	five-spices powder
	oil for deep-frying
Seasoning	
1 tbsp	dark soy sauce
1 tbsp	Shao Hsing wine
½ tsp	salt
1 tbsp	oil

Preparation
Wash, clean and dry the chicken. Rub the salt and five-spices powder well into the skin and leave for 20 minutes.

Cooking
Heat the wok, add the oil and when very hot, deep-fry the chicken over high heat for 5-8 minutes or until the skin turns golden. Transfer the chicken to a shallow dish and rub with minced ginger and scallion. Mix the seasoning ingredients and pour over the chicken, rubbing lightly into the skin. Place the dish in a steamer and steam over moderate heat for 30 minutes.

Remove and tear the meat from the bones in slivers. Arrange on a serving plate with the skin pieces topmost and garnish with sprigs of Chinese parsley. Serve with a garlic dip, see page 277.

The literal translation of the Chinese name of the next dish is "Ridiculous in Taste Chicken".

Exotic-Tasting Chicken
Kuai Wei Chi 怪味鷄
Serves 6-8

625 g (1¼ lb)	chicken thighs
1 tbsp	white sesame seeds
2 tsp	cooked oil
1 tsp	sesame oil
Sauce	
1½ tsp	sugar
¼ tsp	salt
½ tsp	monosodium glutamate
3 tbsp	dark soy sauce
½ tsp	light soy sauce
1 tsp	black vinegar
1 tsp	sesame oil
¾ tsp	chilli oil
1 tbsp	ginger, minced
1 tsp	scallion, minced
1 clove	garlic, minced

Preparation
Wash and dry the chicken thighs. Wash and thoroughly dry the sesame seeds. Heat the wok, until very hot and stir-fry the sesame seeds over a low heat until crackling and golden brown. Drain and grind half to a paste. Set other half aside. Mix the sauce ingredients, adding the ground sesame seeds and set aside.

Cooking
Place the chicken thighs in a pot with enough water to cover. Cover the pot and bring to the boil. Reduce heat and simmer for 20 minutes, or until chicken thighs are cooked right through. Test by pinching the thickest part of the thighs. The meat should be firm and springy. Remove. Drain, de-bone and cut meat into bite-size pieces.

Arrange chicken on a serving plate, skin side topmost and sprinkle with sesame oil and remaining sesame seeds. Serve the sauce separately, or pour over the chicken before adding the sesame seeds. Serve.

Steamed Chicken on Lotus Leaf
Ho Yeh Cheng Hua Chi 荷葉蒸滑鷄
Serves 6-8

625 g (1¼ lb)	chicken pieces
90 g (3 oz)	fresh straw mushrooms, sliced
6-8 slices	ginger, flower-cut
2	scallions, sliced
1	fresh lotus leaf

Seasoning

½ tsp	sugar
1½ tsp	salt
½ tsp	monosodium glutamate
2 tsp	light soy sauce
1 tbsp	cornstarch
2 tbsp	cooked oil

Preparation

Wash the chicken, dry, debone, and cut into 2cm (¾") cubes. Rinse straw mushrooms and drain well. Blanch in boiling water for 1 minute. Drain.

Wash the lotus leaf and dry. Trim to fit a shallow dish, brush with oil and place on the dish.

Mix the seasoning ingredients and pour over the chicken. Leave for 5 minutes, then add the mushrooms, ginger and half the scallion. Spread over the lotus leaf.

Cooking

Place the plate in a steamer, cover and steam over high heat for 15 minutes. Remove, sprinkle with the remaining scallion and serve.

Paper-Wrapped Chicken, Wu Chou Style
Wu-Chou Chih Pao Chi 梧州紙包鷄
Serves 12

1	chicken (about 1½ kg/3 lb)
2 sheets	edible rice paper or cellophane (120cm x 90cm/48" x 36")
	oil for deep-frying

Seasoning

1½ tsp	sugar
1 tsp	salt
1 tsp	five-spices powder
1 tsp	monosodium glutamate
2 tbsp	oyster sauce
1 tbsp	cornstarch
3 tbsp	cooked oil

Preparation

Wash and clean the chicken. De-bone and cut into 24 equal pieces. Mix the seasoning ingredients, pour over chicken and marinate for 1 hour, turning occasionally.

Oil the paper and cut into 24 equal rectangular pieces. Fold into envelopes and place a piece of chicken in each. Tuck the flap securely inside the envelope.

Cooking

Heat the wok, add oil and when very hot, reduce heat to moderate and deep-fry the wrapped chicken several pieces at a time to keep the oil bubbling, for 2½ minutes. Remove and drain. Serve hot.

Steamed Chicken on Lotus Leaf

Chicken Meatballs Garnished with Glutinous Rice
Chen Chu Chi Chiu 珍珠鷄球
Serves 6-8

375 g (12 oz)	chicken fillet
60 g (2 oz)	glutinous rice, soaked
2	scallions, minced
4 sprigs	Chinese parsley, minced
1 tbsp	Yunnan ham, minced
Seasoning	
1½ tsp	salt
½ tsp	monosodium glutamate
1 tbsp	cornstarch

Preparation
Drain rice, place on a cloth and set in a steamer to cook for 20 minutes. Sprinkle on several tablespoons of cold water every 3-4 minutes while cooking.

Coarsely mince chicken or cut into very small dice. Mix with scallion, seasoning ingredients and half the parsley. Work with the fingers until it becomes a sticky paste. Mould into ball shapes, about 3cm (1¼″) in diameter. Arrange on an oiled plate. Cover each meatball with a spoonful of steamed rice and garnish with minced ham and remaining parsley.

Cooking
Place the plate in a steamer and cook over high heat for 15 minutes. Remove and serve hot.

Poached Chicken with Hot Sesame Sauce
Chiao Ma Chi 椒麻鷄
Serves 6-8

1	chicken (about 1½ kg/3 lb)
90 g (3 oz)	celery, 4cm x 1cm (1½″ x ½″) sticks
90 g (3 oz)	cucumber, 4cm x 1cm (1½″ x ½″) sticks
	white sesame seeds, dry-fried (optional)
Sauce	
1 tbsp	brown peppercorns
1 tsp	sugar
½ tsp	salt
2 tsp	dark soy sauce
1 tbsp	ginger, minced
2 tbsp	scallion, minced
2 tbsp	sesame oil
2 tbsp	chicken stock
1 tbsp	cooked oil

Preparation
Wash and clean the chicken.

Roast the peppercorns in a dry wok for 1-2 minutes over low heat, then grind to a fine powder. Mix with the sugar and salt, then add the remaining ingredients and stir well. Pour into a sauce bowl or jug and set aside.

Cooking
Bring enough water to cover the chicken to a rapid boil, reduce heat and put in the chicken. Cover and bring back to a gentle boil. Cook on moderate heat, turning once, until the chicken is almost cooked through, about 20 minutes. Remove from the heat and leave in the hot stock until just cooked through. Pinch the thigh to test if done. The flesh should be firm and springy.

Remove, drain and leave to cool slightly, then de-bone and cut the meat into bite-size pieces.

Place the celery and cucumber sticks on a serving plate and arrange the chicken, skin pieces topmost, over the vegetables. Garnish with carrot flowers and parsley sprigs.

Serve the sauce separately to be poured over the chicken at the table or used as a dip.

Beggar's Chicken
Chiao Hua Chi 教化鷄
Serves 6-8

1	chicken (about 1½ kg/3 lb)
125 g (4 oz)	fat pork, shredded
90 g (3 oz)	canned preserved Shanghai vegetable, shredded
30 g (1 oz)	ginger, shredded
3	lotus leaves, soaked in boiling water
2 kg (4 lb)	pond mud*
Seasoning A	
¼ tsp	salt
2 tsp	Shao Hsing wine
2 tsp	sesame oil
Seasoning B	
1 tbsp	sugar
¼ tsp	salt
¾ tsp	monosodium glutamate
1 tbsp	dark soy sauce
1 tbsp	light soy sauce
1 tbsp	Shao Hsing wine
2 tsp	sesame oil
2 tsp	cooked oil

*Modelling clay or flour and water dough can be used.

148

Preparation

Clean and thoroughly wash the chicken and drain well. Rub with the seasoning A ingredients and leave for 1 hour. Mix the seasoning B ingredients.

Cooking

Heat the wok and stir-fry the fat pork for ½ minute, then add the ginger and seasoning B ingredients and stir-fry for a further ½ minute.

Add the preserved vegetables and stir-fry for 1 minute longer. Stuff into the chicken, then wrap in the drained lotus leaves. Tie firmly with string.

Chicken Meatballs Garnished with Glutinous Rice

Spread the mud thickly over a piece of newspaper and wrap around the chicken, to encase it entirely.

Roast in a very hot oven, at 550 deg F for 1¼ hours, then reduce heat to moderately hot, 400 deg F and bake until the mud is dark and dry, about 1 hour longer.

Crack open the hardened mud case and remove. Place chicken on a serving plate and unwrap the lotus leaves. Serve.

Unlike many of the famous Chinese dishes which were created in the Imperial Kitchens and later adapted for home cooking, Beggar's Chicken, as the name implies, had quite humble beginnings.

One story has it that an old beggar, on successfully poaching a plump chicken, hit upon an ingenous method for cooking it without detection.

On his way home to his hut in a grove by the side of a pond, he plucked a few scallions to use as seasonings, and some Lotus leaves to wrap the chicken and prevent it burning.

In a hole scooped out of the soft mud at the edge of the pond he kindled a small fire. His prize was disguised in a thick coating of the mud and placed over the blaze, then a modest fire — just big enough to warm a chilled and tired old man — was lit on top. Thus it was left to cook.

But little did the beggar appreciate that the tell-tale delicious smells would herald the opening of his makeshift oven!

149

Roast Peking Duck
Peh Ching K'ao Ya 北京烤鴨
Serves 12

1	whole Peking duck, (about 3 kg/6 lb)
2 tbsp	maltose
250 ml (8 fl oz)	boiling water
12	scallions, 5cm (2″) lengths
24	Mandarin Pancakes*

Dip

4 tbsp	sugar
4 tbsp	sweet bean paste
2 tbsp	sesame oil
125 ml (4 fl oz)	water

Preparation

Wash duck, cut off feet and discard. Make a slit in the neck, insert a small rubber pipe and blow air in to separate the skin from the meat of the bird. Slit duck open near the neck and remove intestines. Wash thoroughly inside and out with cold water. Drain off water. Force a small bamboo stick into the cavity and wedge it horizontally inside the breast. Cut off wingtips. Tie a strong string around the neck and hold duck over a basin. Pour about 1 litre (32 fl oz) boiling water over the bird and hang to dry slightly. Melt maltose in 250 ml (8 fl oz) boiling water and pour slowly over the duck. Leave the duck hanging in a dry, sunny place for about 4 hours until the skin dries.

Cooking

Place duck breast down on a rack in a large baking tray. Place in a preheated moderately hot oven at 375°-400°F and bake for 20 minutes. Turn and roast breast meat for 20 minutes. Remove from the oven and place the baking rack holding the duck in a large bain marie. Return to the oven and continue baking, turning once only, until duck is done, about 20 minutes longer. Remove from the oven and place on a cutting board. Slice skin from the breast area and thighs, then cut thin slices of meat. Arrange skin and meat on a serving plate and serve with scallion, Mandarin Pancakes and the dip. To prepare dip mix sugar with beanpaste and water. Heat the wok and add sesame oil and when warm, add the mixed ingredients and stir until the sugar is completely dissolved. Pour into small dishes.

Note: The carcass can be used for soup, see recipe page 199.

*For method of preparing Mandarin Pancakes see recipe page 253.

Sliced Duck with Winter Bamboo Shoots
Hsien Tung Sun Ch'ao Ya P'ien 鮮冬筍炒鴨片
Serves 6-8

½	small duck (about 750 g/1½ lb)
155 g (5 oz)	winter bamboo shoots, cube-cut
185 g (6 oz)	flowering white cabbage
4-5 slices	ginger, flower-cut
4-5 slices	carrot, flower-cut
1 clove	garlic, finely chopped
	oil for deep-frying

Seasoning A

¾ tsp	monosodium glutamate
1½ tsp	cornstarch
1 tbsp	water
2 tbsp	oil

Seasoning B

½ tsp	sugar
½ tsp	salt
½ tsp	monosodium glutamate
2 tbsp	chicken stock
	few drops Shao Hsing wine
	few drops sesame oil
	dash white pepper

Thickening — mix together

½ tsp	cornstarch
1 tbsp	water

Preparation

Clean and wash the duck. De-bone and cut the meat into bite-size strips. Mix the seasoning A ingredients with the meat and leave to marinate for 30-45 minutes.

Boil bamboo shoots until softened, about 25 minutes. Trim cabbage, discarding any damaged leaves. Blanch in boiling water for 1 minute, then rise in cold water and drain well. Mix the seasoning B ingredients.

Cooking

Heat the wok, add oil and when very hot, reduce heat slightly. Deep-fry the duck slices for 1-1½ minutes, then drain. Discard most of the oil. Reheat the wok and stir-fry the bamboo shoots, cabbage, carrot, ginger and garlic for 1½ minutes on high heat. Add the duck and seasoning B and stir-fry briefly, then add the thickening and stir until the sauce thickens and becomes clear. Serve.

"For the people, food is heaven."

Chinese Proverb

Camphor and Tea Smoked Duck
Chang Ch'a K'ao Ya 樟茶烤鴨
Serves 12

1	duck (about 2 kg/4 lb)
90 g (3 oz)	jasmine tea leaves
125 g (4 oz)	camphor wood chips
185 g (6 oz)	rice
1 pc	dried tangerine peel, crumbled
	oil for deep-frying

Seasoning

2 tbsp	salt
2 tsp	saltpetre
1½ tsp	brown peppercorns
1 tsp	pepper
½ tsp	monosodium glutamate
1 tbsp	Dai Chu wine
2 tsp	ginger, minced
1 tbsp	scallion, minced

Preparation
Clean and wash duck, drain well and pat dry. Mix seasoning ingredients and rub onto duck, inside and out. Leave to marinate for 12 hours. Blanch in boiling water for 5 minutes. Drain and hang in an airy place until very dry.

Cooking
Place half the tea leaves, wood chips and rice in a wok and set over high heat. When smoking set duck in the pan on wire rack. Cover and smoke for 5 minutes. Turn the duck over to the other side and add the remaining tea, wood chips and rice and cover.

Smoke for 5 minutes longer. Remove. Place duck on a dish in a steamer and steam over high heat for 2 hours. Remove and leave to cool. Pat the skin dry, and drain away any liquid inside.

Heat the wok, add oil and when very hot, deep-fry duck until skin is deep brown and very crisp, about 15 minutes. Ladle the oil over the duck constantly while cooking.

Chop into bite-size pieces and arrange on a serving plate. Serve with a pepper salt dip and steamed bread, see pages 277 and 248.

This may also be served with scallion curls, sweet bean paste sauce and Mandarin Pancakes, see pages 278 and 253.

Braised Duck with Lo Han Vegetables — *recipe on page 156.*

Fried Spiced Duck

Hsiang Su Fei Ya 香酥肥鴨

Serves 12

1	duck (about 2 kg/4 lb)
2 slices	ginger, minced
1	scallion, minced
1	red chilli, minced (optional)
2 tbsp	dark soy sauce
	oil for deep-frying

Seasoning

1 tbsp	brown peppercorns
1 tbsp	salt
1½ tsp	five-spices powder
½ tsp	monosodium glutamate
1 tsp	Dai Chu Wine

Preparation

Clean duck, wash well, drain and pat dry.

Roast brown peppercorns in a dry pan over low heat for 2 minutes, until fragrant, add salt and remove from the heat. Add remaining seasonings and mix with minced ginger, scallion and red chilli, if used. Rub seasonings over the duck, inside and out and leave for about 6 hours to marinate.

Cooking

Place the duck on a dish in a steamer and steam over moderately high heat for 2½ hours, or until very tender. Remove and wipe. Leave to cool. Drain away any liquid inside. Heat the wok, add oil and when very hot, deep-fry the duck over high heat until deep brown and crispy. Ladle oil over the duck constantly as it cooks.

Remove, drain and cut into bite-size pieces. Arrange on a serving plate and serve with a pepper salt dip, see recipe page 277, and with scallion curls, sweet bean paste sauce and steamed silver thread rolls, see recipes pages 249.

Braised Duck with Lo Han Vegetables

Lo Han P'a Tai Ya 羅漢扒大鴨

Serves 6-8

½	duck (about 825 g/1¾ lb)
2 tbsp	dark soy sauce
2-3 slices	ginger
2	scallions
2	anise stars
3-4 tbsp	dark soy sauce
	oil for deep-frying

Lo Han Vegetables

45 g (1½ oz)	golden fungus, soaked
45 g (1½ oz)	dried black mushrooms, soaked
45 g (1½ oz)	fresh straw mushrooms, halved
45 g (1½ oz)	frozen peas, thawed
45 g (1½ oz)	carrot, sliced
185 g (6 oz)	flowering white cabbage, 8cm (3″) strips
75 g (2½ oz)	fresh bean sprouts, trimmed
75 g (2½ oz)	canned bamboo shoots, thinly sliced
45 g (1½ oz)	canned button mushrooms
60 g (2 oz)	fried beancurd cubes
3-4 tbsp	cooked oil
200 ml (6 fl oz)	chicken stock

Seasoning

1 tsp	sugar
1 tsp	salt
1 tsp	monosodium glutamate
2 tsp	dark soy sauce
2 tbsp	oyster sauce

Thickening — mix together

2 tsp	cornstarch
1½ tbsp	water

Preparation and Cooking

Wash the duck and rub the 2 tbsp dark soy sauce well into the skin. Leave to dry for 2 hours. Heat the wok, add deep-frying oil and when very hot deep-fry the duck until the skin turns a deep red brown and is crisp.

Remove, drain and place in a casserole. Cover with hot water, and add ginger, scallions, anise stars and dark soy sauce. Bring to the boil, cover and stew for 45 minutes. Lift out and drain. Cut into serving portions and arrange in a shallow serving dish. Set aside.

Blanch the golden fungus and the mushrooms in boiling water for 5 minutes. Drain and set aside. Boil carrots until soft, then drain and cover with cold water until needed. Blanch white cabbage for 2 minutes in boiling water with a little salt and oil added. Drain, rinse with cold water and drain again. Stir-fry the bean sprouts in a dry wok for 1 minute, add a pinch of salt and stir-fry for ½ minute longer. Remove. Heat the wok, add cooked oil and stir-fry white cabbage for ½ minute. Arrange around the rim of the serving dish. Add all remaining Lo Han ingredients and stir-fry for 2 minutes. Add the seasoning ingredients and stir-fry for 2 minutes longer. Pour in the stock, add thickening and cook until the sauce thickens and becomes clear. Pour over the duck and serve hot.

'Lu Shui' Goose
Lu Shui Ngo 鹵水鵝
Serves 12

1	goose (about 3 kg/6 lb)

Lu Shui sauce

250 g (8 oz)	sugar
250 g (8 oz)	salt
2	five-spice bouquets
250 ml (8 fl oz)	light soy sauce
10 slices	ginger

Cooking

Mix the sauce ingredients in a large cooking pot and bring to the boil. Put in the goose and return to the boil. Remove the spice bouquets, then reduce heat and simmer until the goose is cooked through, about 50 minutes. Ladle the sauce frequently over the goose while cooking, and carefully turn several times. Test if done by inserting a thin skewer into the thigh, if no pink liquid runs off it is ready.

Remove from the sauce and drain well. Leave to cool, then cut into bite-size pieces. Arrange on a serving plate and garnish with Chinese parsley sprigs.

Serve with a garlic dip, see recipe page 277, or sour plum sauce.

157

'Lu Shui' Goose.   Double-Boiled Pigeons with Mushrooms — *recipe on page 159.*

Roast Crispy Duck
Kua Lu Tai Ya 掛爐大鴨
Serves 12

1	whole duck (about 2 kg/4 lb)
Seasoning	
2 tsp	salt
1 tsp	five-spices powder
Glaze	
3 tbsp	maltose
1 tsp	white vinegar
2 tsp	red vinegar
3 tbsp	water

Preparation

Wash and clean the duck. Mix the seasoning ingredients and rub well into the cavity. Close the cavity by stitching the skin. Hang the duck by its neck over a drip tray and pour boiling water over it several times.

Pour the glaze ingredients to the wok and bring to the boil. Pour this mixture over the duck several times to thickly glaze. Again hang the duck by its neck and leave for 3-4 hours to dry.

Cooking

Spit-roast the duck for 25 minutes over a high flame, or roast for 25 minutes in a hot oven, 500 deg F, turning continuously. Chop the duck into bite size pieces and arrange 'spread-eagle' style on a serving dish. Serve hot.

Main Course Dishes

A dish of fat chicken, pot-boiled duck and bean curd, cooked by Cheng Erh

A dish of swallows' nests and julienned smoked duck, cooked by Cheng Erh

A bowl of clear soup, cooked by Jung Kui

A dish of julienned pot-boiled chicken, cooked by Jung Kui

A dish of smoked fat chicken and Chinese cabbage, cooked by Chang Erh

A dish of salted duck and pork, cooked by Jung Kui

A dish of court-style fried chicken

Pastries

A dish of bamboo-stuffed steam dumplings

A dish of rice cakes

A dish of rice cakes with honey

Pickles (served in a ceramic container patterned with hollyhock flowers)

Chinese cabbage pickled in brine

Cucumbers preserved in soy

Pickled eggplant

Rice

Boiled rice

The Menu of a Meal served to Emperor Ch'ien-lung in 1754

Steamed Duck in Wine Sauce
Chiu Cheng T'ien Ya 酒蒸塡鴨
Serves 12

1	whole Peking duck (about 2½ kg/5 lb)*
Seasoning	
1 tsp	sugar
1 tsp	salt
½ tsp	monosodium glutamate
125 ml (5 fl oz)	Kaoliang wine
3 slices	ginger
3	scallions
375 ml (12 fl oz)	chicken stock

*If Peking Duck is unavailable, use any well fattened duck.

Preparation

Clean and wash the duck. Place in a large pot of rapidly boiling water and cook for 5 minutes, remove and drain. Mix seasoning ingredients.

Cooking

Transfer the duck to a deep bowl and add the seasonings. Place the bowl in a steamer, cover and steam for 3 hours over extremely low heat. (Cooking time can be shortened to about 1½ hours over medium heat, but the texture of the duck will not be as fine and tender). Lift out the duck, drain. Skim fat and froth from the stock and discard ginger and scallion. Place duck, whole, on a serving plate. Reboil stock and strain about one-third over the duck. The duck will be tender enough to serve slivers of meat with chopsticks.

Pigeons Braised in Soy Sauce
Shih Yu Huang Ju Ko 豉油皇乳鴿
Serves 6-8

3	pigeons (about 375 g/12 oz each)

Lu Shui sauce

500 g (1 lb)	sugar
1	five-spices bouquet
200 ml (6 fl oz)	dark soy sauce
500 ml (16 fl oz)	light soy sauce
1¼ lit (40 fl oz)	water

Preparation
Clean pigeons and wash well. Drain.

Cooking
Mix the sauce ingredients in a large cooking pot and bring to the boil. Add pigeons and return to the boil, then reduce heat, cover and simmer until the pigeons are tender and cooked through, about 20 minutes. Test if done by inserting a thin skewer into the thighs, if no pink liquid runs off they are ready.

Drain, cut into bite-size pieces and arrange 'spread eagle' style on a serving plate. Serve.

Note: 'Lu Shui' sauce can be used several times. Store in a screw top jar in the refrigerator.

Double-Boiled Pigeons with Mushrooms
Peh Ku Tun Ju Ko 北菇燉乳鴿
Serves 6

2	pigeons (about 250 g/8 oz each)
60 g (2 oz)	dried black mushrooms, soaked
20 g (¾ oz)	Yunnan ham, very thinly sliced
1½ lit (48 fl oz)	chicken stock

Seasoning

2 tsp	salt
1 tsp	monosodium glutamate
1 tbsp	Shao Hsing wine

Preparation
Clean and wash pigeons. Blanch in boiling water for 5 minutes. Remove and drain. Remove mushroom stems.

Cooking
Place pigeons in a casserole set in a double-boiler or steamer. Add ham slices and pour in hot chicken stock. Cover and steam over moderate heat for 1 hour. Add mushrooms and seasoning ingredients and steam for 20-30 minutes longer. Serve in the casserole.

Deep-Fried Rice Birds
Shao Chu Ho Hua Ch'iao 燒焗禾花雀
Serves 12

24	rice birds
	oil for deep-frying

Seasoning A

2 tsp	sugar
½ tsp	salt
1 tsp	monosodium glutamate
4 tbsp	light soy sauce
1 tbsp	Rose Dew wine
1 tsp	ginger, minced
1 tbsp	scallion, minced
4 tbsp	water
	dash red food colouring powder

Seasoning B

2 tsp	sugar
1 tbsp	tomato ketchup
2 tbsp	chicken stock

Preparation
Clean, pluck and wash rice birds. Place in a dish with the seasoning A ingredients and leave to marinate for 1 hour.

Cooking
Heat the wok, add oil and when very hot reduce heat slightly. Put in rice birds and deep-fry for 3-4 minutes. Remove and drain well. Discard most of the oil. Return rice birds with seasoning B and stir-fry until the birds are well glazed with the seasonings. Serve on a bed of washed watercress and garnish with lemon wedges.

"A good cook cannot with the utmost application produce more than four successful dishes in one day, and even then it is hard for him to give proper attention to every detail; and he certainly won't get through unless everything is in its right place and he is on his feet the whole time. It is no use to give him a lot of assistants; each of them will have his own ideas, and there will be no proper discipline."

Yuan Mei

Deep-Fried Rice Birds — *recipe on page 159.*

Fried Stuffed Dace
Niang Ling Yu 釀鯪魚
Serves 6-8

2	dace (about 375 g/12 oz each)
30 g (1 oz)	dried shrimps, soaked
30 g (1 oz)	Yunnan ham, finely diced
1	scallion, finely chopped
2 sprigs	Chinese parsley, chopped
6 tbsp	cooked oil

Seasoning

½ tsp	salt
1 tsp	monosodium glutamate
2 tsp	cornstarch
	few drops sesame oil
	dash white pepper

Sauce

¾ tsp	sugar
¼ tsp	salt
1 tsp	dark soy sauce
1 tbsp	light soy sauce
2 tsp	Shao Hsing wine
200 ml (6 fl oz)	chicken stock
1½ tsp	cornstarch

Preparation

Scale, gut and wash fish. Cut along the stomach and carefully slice out the meat, leaving bones and skin intact. Finely chop the fish fillets and mix with drained and finely chopped dried shrimps, Yunnan ham, scallion and parsley. Add seasoning ingredients and work with the fingers into a sticky paste. Stuff into the fish, and smooth the filling at the openings. Mix the sauce ingredients and set aside.

Cooking

Heat the wok until smoking, add 2 tbsp oil and when very hot reduce heat slightly and fry fish for 2-3 minutes on one side. Turn, add another 2 tbsp oil and fry for 3-4 minutes or until cooked through.

Remove, drain and discard the oil. Place fish on a serving plate. Add remaining oil to the wok, reheat and pour in the sauce. Bring to the boil and simmer for 1 minute. Pour over the fish and serve.

"It's the skill of the cook, not the quality of the food that counts."

Chinese Proverb

Braised Fish with Beancurd and Vegetables
Ts'ao Yu Tou Fu 草魚豆腐
Serves 8

220 g (7 oz)	fillets of grass carp (or other white fish)
4 squares	soft beancurd
125 g (4 oz)	Chinese white cabbage, trimmed and coarsely chopped
1 tsp	ginger, minced
1 tsp	scallion, minced
2 tbsp	cooked oil

Seasoning A

½ tsp	salt
¼ tsp	Shao Hsing wine
1½ tbsp	cornstarch

Seasoning B

½ tsp	sugar
¼ tsp	salt
2 tsp	Shao Hsing wine

Sauce

2 tsp	sugar
¼ tsp	salt
¼ tsp	monosodium glutamate
3 tbsp	dark soy sauce
1 tbsp	Shao Hsing wine
900 ml (30 fl. oz)	chicken stock

Thickening — mix together

1½ tbsp	cornstarch
1 tbsp	water

Preparation

Cut fish fillets into pieces about 5cm x 2.5cm (2" x 1") and mix well with the seasoning A ingredients. Leave for 10 minutes.

Cut beancurd into pieces 5cm x 1.5cm (2" x ½") and soak in cold water for 1 minute. Drain well. Mix the sauce ingredients and set aside.

Cooking

Heat the wok, add oil and when very hot stir-fry the cabbage with seasoning ingredients for 1½ minutes. Remove and drain well. Add ginger and scallion and stir-fry for ½ minute. Add sauce to the wok and bring to the boil. Drop in the fish pieces and return to the boil, then add beancurd, cover and simmer on moderate heat for 5 minutes, or until the beancurd becomes spongy. Add thickening and stir until the sauce thickens slightly and becomes clear. Add the cabbage, re-cover and simmer for 2 minutes longer. Serve.

Braised Carp Tails
Hung Shao Yu Wei 紅燒魚尾
Serves 6-8

500 g (1 lb)	grass carp tails (cut from below stomach cavity)
1 tbsp	ginger, shredded
1 tbsp	scallion, minced
½ tsp	sesame oil
1	scallion, shredded (optional)
4 tbsp	cooked oil
Sauce	
½ tsp	sugar
¼ tsp	salt
½ tsp	monosodium glutamate
1 tbsp	dark soy sauce
2 tsp	Shao Hsing wine
275 ml (9 fl. oz)	chicken stock or water
	few drops sesame oil
	dash white pepper

Thickening — mix together

1½ tsp	cornstarch
1 tbsp	water

Preparation

Scale and thoroughly wash the carp tails and trim tails to points. Mix the sauce ingredients and set aside.

Cooking

Heat the wok and add 3 tbsp oil. When hot add the fish tails with ginger and minced scallion. Colour lightly on one side, then turn and colour other side.

Pour in the sauce, bring to the boil, then cover and simmer on reduced heat for 5 minutes, until fish tails are cooked through.

Lift out tails and arrange on a serving plate. Cover with shredded scallion, if used. Add thickening to the sauce and bring to the boil. Simmer for 2 minutes. Add remaining oil and sesame oil, pour over the fish tails and serve hot.

"Don't eat carp with dog meat"

Chinese Proverb

Hilsa Herring on Hot Plate
T'ieh Pan Shih Yu 鐵板鰣魚
Serves 6-8

½	hilsa herring (about 1 kg/2 lb), sliced in half along the backbone, retaining half the head and tail
75 g (2½ oz)	fat pork, finely shredded
1	leek, shredded
1	red capsicum, thinly sliced
4 slices	ginger, shredded
4 sprigs	Chinese parsley
1½ tsp	five-spices powder
250 ml (8 fl oz)	chicken stock
Seasoning A	
½ tsp	salt
½ tsp	monosodium glutamate
1 tbsp	Shao Hsing wine
2 tbsp	cooked oil
Seasoning B	
1 tbsp	sugar
½ tsp	salt
½ tsp	monosodium glutamate
1 tbsp	dark soy sauce
1 tbsp	light soy sauce
2 tbsp	Shao Hsing wine

Preparation

Wash the fish, leave scales on and blanch in boiling water for a few seconds. Remove and drain. Place the fish on an oven-proof tray and scatter shredded pork on top. Sprinkle with the seasoning A ingredients and leave for 10 minutes. Arrange shredded leek, capsicum, ginger and parsley sprigs on the fish and sprinkle on five-spices powder. Mix the seasoning B ingredients, and pour into the tray with fish.

Cooking

Place tray in a preheated moderately hot oven and bake for 30 minutes, basting occasionally. Transfer fish to a well heated metal serving plate, lift off scales and arrange the vegetable garnish over the fish. Pour on the sauce from the cooking tray and serve.

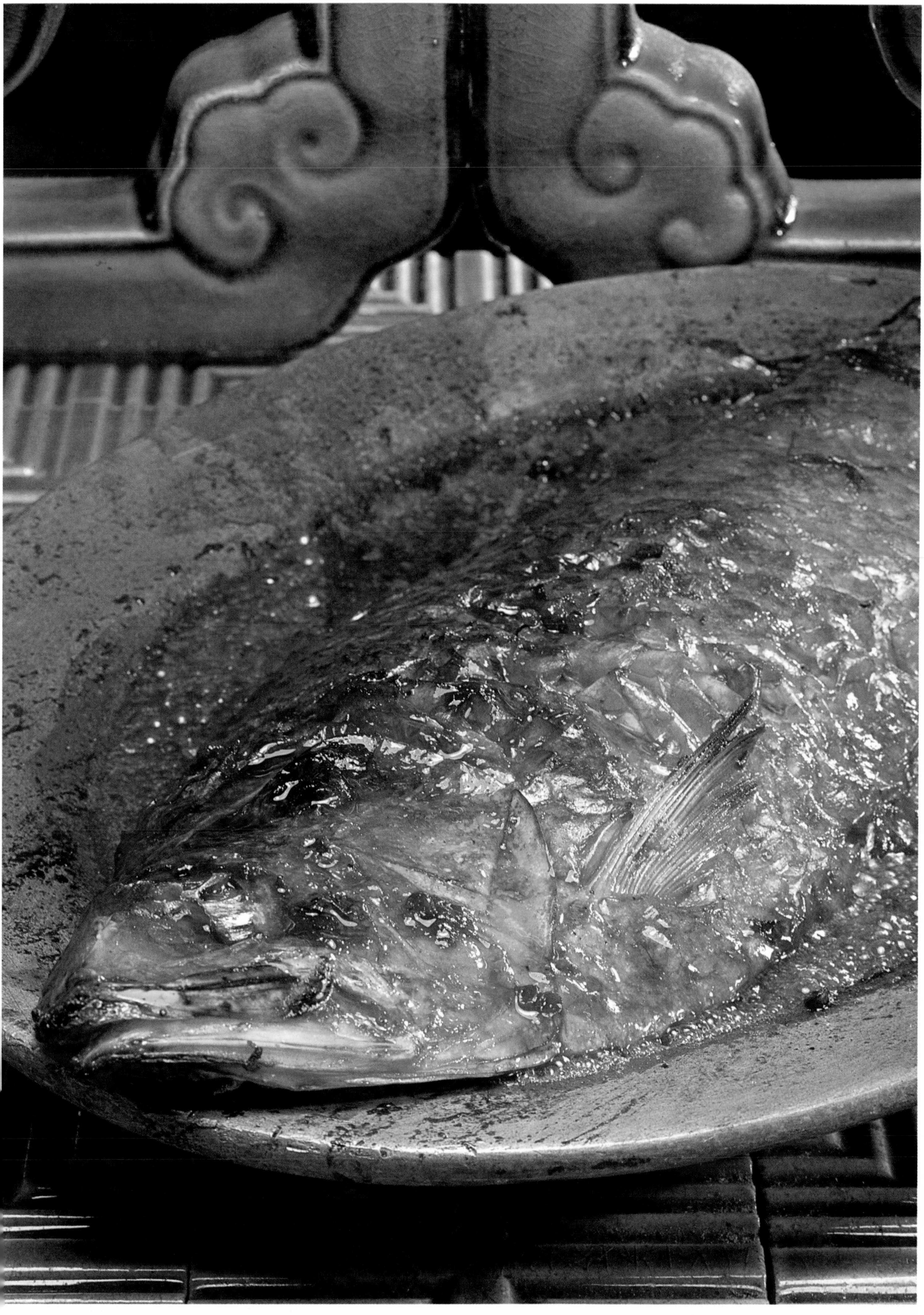

Crispy Yellow River Carp
Ts'ui P'i Huang Yu　脆皮黃魚
Serves 6-8

1	grass carp (about 750g/1½ lb)
20 g (¾ oz)	carrot, small dice
20 g (¾ oz)	dried black mushroom, soaked and diced
20 g (¾ oz)	water chestnut, small dice
20 g (¾ oz)	green capsicum, small dice
20 g (¾ oz)	onion, small dice
20 g (¾ oz)	frozen peas, thawed
20 g (¾ oz)	pineapple, small dice
1 large	tomato, chopped
1 tsp	ginger, finely chopped
1	scallion, minced
1 clove	garlic, minced
	cornstarch
	oil for deep-frying

Seasoning

1 tsp	salt
½ tsp	monosodium glutamate
1 tbsp	Shao Hsing wine
2	eggs
	dash white pepper

Sauce

6 tbsp	sugar
1 tsp	salt
½ tsp	monosodium glutamate
3 tbsp	tomato ketchup
5 tbsp	white rice vinegar
6 tbsp	chicken stock
1 tbsp	cornstarch
1 tsp	sesame oil
2 tbsp	cooked oil

Preparation
Scale, gut and thoroughly wash the fish. Slice off the fillets, leaving the head and tail attached to the backbone. Trim tail to a point. Wash the carcass and dry thoroughly. Coat with cornstarch and set aside. Cut the fillets into fingers, cutting through the meat, but leaving the slices held together by the skin. Sprinkle with the seasonings, well mixed together, and rub in lightly. Leave for 5 minutes, then coat with cornstarch.

Blanch the carrot, mushroom, water chestnut, capsicum, onion and peas in boiling water for 1 minute. Remove and drain well.

Cooking
Bring the sauce ingredients to boil in a small saucepan. Simmer for 2 minutes then add the blanched ingredients and boil for 2 minutes longer. Add pineapple, tomato, ginger, scallion and garlic and boil for a further 2 minutes. Set aside, keeping warm.

Heat the wok, add oil and when very hot, deep-fry the carcass until lightly coloured. Lift out, drain well and arrange on a serving plate. Surround with finely shredded cabbage or lettuce.

Reheat the oil, add the two fish fillets and deep-fry until cooked through and crisp on the surface, about 2-2½ minutes. If preferred, cook until the meat is very crispy, about 5 minutes. Drain well and arrange on the carcass in the original shape of the fish, but with the skin next to the bone.

Reheat the sauce to boiling, pour into a jug and serve separately, or pour over the fish just before serving.

Fish Heads in Casserole
Sha Kwo Yu T'ou　砂鍋魚頭
Serves 6-8

4	large fish heads (about 500 g/ 1 lb)
125 g (4 oz)	canned bamboo shoots, thinly sliced
3	dried black mushrooms, soaked and sliced
30 g (1 oz)	fat pork, thinly sliced
1 tsp	ginger, minced
1 tsp	scallion, minced
45 g (1½ oz)	bean thread vermicelli, soaked
3 tbsp	cooked oil
	few drops sesame oil

Sauce

1 tsp	sugar
¼ tsp	monosodium glutamate
3 tbsp	dark soy sauce
1½ tbsp	Shao Hsing wine
1¼ lit (40 fl oz)	chicken stock

Thickening — mix together

2 tbsp	cornstarch
3 tbsp	water

Preparation
Wash the fish heads well. Drain and wipe dry.

Mix the sauce ingredients and set aside.

Cooking
Heat the wok, add the oil and when very hot fry the fish heads on all sides until golden. Remove and drain. Place in a casserole. Reheat the wok, add

Fried Salted Fish

the bamboo shoots, mushroom, fat pork and stir-fry for several seconds, then add the ginger and scallion and stir-fry together for 1½ minutes longer. Add the sauce and boil for 5 minutes on moderate heat.

Pour the sauce into the casserole and bring to the boil. Simmer for 10 minutes, then add the drained bean thread vermicelli and simmer for a further 10 minutes.

Add thickening and cook until the sauce thickens, then sprinkle on sesame oil and serve.

Fried Salted Fish
Chien Hsien Yu 煎鹹魚
Serves 6-8

1 piece	Chao Pai salted fish (125-185 g/4-6 oz)
4 tbsp	cooked oil
	vegetable oil

Preparation
Wash the salted fish, wipe dry and place in a dish. Cover with vegetable oil and leave to soak for 2-3 hours. Drain well.

Cooking
Heat the wok until it smokes, add half the cooked oil and reduce heat slightly. Fry the fish for 1-2 minutes until it turns a light golden brown. Turn, add remaining oil and cook other side for 1 minute. Remove, drain and serve with a dip of red vinegar.

Note: This makes an excellent appetiser.

"Food has no taste if you eat too much."

Ancient Chinese Proverb

Crispy Yellow River Carp

Sliced Fish in Wine Sauce.

Sliced Fish in Wine Sauce
Tsao Liu Yu P'ien 糟溜魚片
Serves 6-8

315 g (10 oz)	yellow river carp fillets, thinly sliced
15 g (½ oz)	cloud ear fungus, soaked and roughly chopped
150 ml (5 fl oz)	chicken stock
2 tsp	rendered chicken fat (optional)
	oil for deep-frying

Seasoning A

¼ tsp	salt
½	egg white
1½ tsp	cornstarch

Seasoning B

2 tsp	sugar
¼ tsp	salt
¼ tsp	monosodium glutamate
3 tbsp	wine lees

Thickening — mix together

2 tsp	cornstarch
1 tbsp	water

Preparation

Wash the fish slices and marinate with the seasoning A ingredients for 10 minutes. Simmer cloud ear fungus in boiling water for 3-4 minutes, drain and set aside. Mix the seasoning B ingredients.

Fish Heads in Casserole — *recipe on page 164.*

Steamed Garoupa with Ham and Vegetables — *recipe on page 168.*

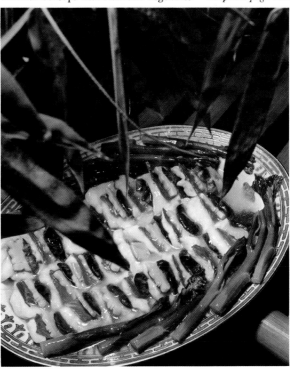

Cooking

Heat the wok and add deep-frying oil. When very hot, reduce heat slightly and add the fish, one slice at a time to keep the oil bubbling. Deep-fry until the fish turns white, about 1 minute. Remove, drain and set aside. Pour off the oil.

Add chicken stock to the wok and bring to the boil, then add the seasoning B and thickening and when boiling again, return the fish and simmer until the sauce thickens. Add the chicken fat, if used, and the cloud ear fungus and heat through. Serve.

"Certainly to have a fresh fish and to cause it to become unfresh is a terrible act."

"To know right from wrong, a man must be sober. And only a sober man can distinguish good flavours from bad. It has been well said that words are inadequate to describe the various shades of taste. How much less then must a stuttering sot be able to appreciate them!"

Yuen Mai.

Steamed Garoupa With Ham and Vegetables
Yu Shu Chi Lin Pan 玉樹麒麟斑
Serves 6-8

375 g (12 oz)	garoupa fillets
125 g (4 oz)	canned bamboo shoots
125 g (4 oz)	cooked ham or Yunnan ham
8	dried black mushrooms, soaked
185 g (6 oz)	leaf mustard or kale
½ tsp	salt
1 tbsp	cooked oil

Seasoning

½ tsp	sugar
1 tsp	salt
½ tsp	monosodium glutamate
2 tsp	cornstarch
1 tbsp	cooked oil
	few drops sesame oil
	dash white pepper

Sauce

¾ tsp	salt
½ tsp	monosodium glutamate
150 ml (5 fl oz)	chicken stock
2 tsp	cornstarch
2 tsp	cooked oil
	few drops sesame oil
	dash white pepper

Preparation

Wash fish and cut into 12-16 slices. Mix with the seasoning ingredients and leave for 10 minutes. Cut bamboo shoots and ham into 12-16 slices to match the fish. Drain mushrooms and cut each in half.

Brush a serving plate with oil and arrange fish, ham, bamboo shoots and mushrooms alternately in two or three rows on the plate. Mix the sauce ingredients and set aside.

Cooking

Set the plate in a steamer over high heat, cover and steam for 6-7 minutes until cooked. Remove from the heat.

Trim mustard or kale and blanch in boiling water with salt for 1 minute. Remove and drain.

Heat the wok, add cooked oil and when very hot stir-fry vegetables for 1½ minutes. Drain and arrange around the rim of the serving plate.

Reheat the wok, pour in the sauce and bring to the boil. Simmer for 1 minute, then pour over the dish and serve.

Fried Crispy Pomfret
Chien Ts'ang Yu 煎鎗魚
Serves 6-8

1	pomfret (about 750 g/1½ lb)
2	scallions, shredded
1 stalk	Chinese parsley, 4cm (1½″) strips
6-7 tbsp	cooked oil

Seasoning

1 tbsp	light soy sauce
2 tsp	ginger juice

Sauce

2 tsp	sugar
¼ tsp	salt
1 tsp	monosodium glutamate
½ tsp	dark soy sauce
1 tbsp	light soy sauce
200 ml (6 fl oz)	chicken stock
1 tsp	cornstarch
	few drops sesame oil
	dash white pepper

Preparation

Clean and gut fish, cutting open only on one side. Cut a criss-cross pattern on the other side and sprinkle with the seasoning ingredients. Rub in lightly. Mix sauce ingredients and set aside.

Cooking

Heat the wok, add 3 tbsp oil and fry fish on one side over high heat for 3-4 minutes. Turn, add 2-3 tbsp oil as needed and fry for 4 minutes longer, or until cooked through. Remove, drain and place on a serving dish. Garnish with scallion and parsley strips. Discard the oil, wipe out wok and reheat. Add remaining oil and pour in the sauce. Bring to the boil and simmer for 1 minute, then pour over the fish. Serve.

We mind the furnaces, treading softly;
Attend to the food-stands so tall....
Our lord's lady hard at work
Sees to the dishes, so many,
Needed for guests, for strangers.

The Book of Songs

Sauteed Prawns with Chinese Broccoli
Chieh Lan Hsia Chiu 芥蘭蝦球
Serves 6-8

750 g (1½ lb)	medium prawns, in shell
250 g (8 oz)	Chinese broccoli
5-6 slices	ginger, flower-cut
5-6 slices	carrot, flower-cut
1 clove	garlic, crushed
2 tbsp	cooked oil
	oil for deep-frying

Seasoning

½ tsp	sugar
½ tsp	salt
½ tsp	monosodium glutamate
2 tsp	cornstarch
2 tbsp	cooked oil

Sauce

1 tsp	sugar
½ tsp	salt
½ tsp	monosodium glutamate
5 tbsp	chicken stock
1½ tsp	cornstarch
	few drops sesame oil
	dash white pepper

Preparation

Rinse and peel the prawns. Slit down centre backs and remove dark veins. Rinse again and dry in a kitchen towel. Mix with the seasoning ingredients and leave for 5 minutes.

Remove any damaged leaves and the flower pods from broccoli, cut into 8cm (3") pieces. Blanch in boiling water for 1 minute, drain and rinse in cold water to brighten the colour. Drain again. Mix the sauce ingredients and set aside.

Cooking

Heat the wok, add oil and when very hot reduce heat slightly. Deep-fry prawns for 1-1½ minutes until cooked through, then remove and drain. Pour off the oil, reheat the wok and add cooked oil. Stir-fry ginger, carrot and garlic for ½ minute, then add broccoli and stir-fry for ½ minute longer. Add prawns and the sauce and bring to the boil. Stir on high heat until the sauce thickens and becomes slightly clear. Transfer to a serving dish. Serve.

"If an article of food is in itself bad, the greatest chef of all ages could not cook a flavour into it."

Yuen Mai.

Fried Shrimp on Croutons with Sesame Seeds
Cha Chih Ma Hsia 炸芝蔴蝦
Serves 12

185 g (6 oz)	shrimp meat
2	egg whites
3 slices	white bread, crusts removed
45 g (1½ oz)	white sesame seeds
	oil for deep-frying

Seasoning

½ tsp	salt
½ tsp	monosodium glutamate
2 tsp	cornstarch
1 tbsp	water

Preparation

Pound the shrimp meat to a smooth paste in a mortar or on a chopping board and mix with the seasoning ingredients. Beat egg whites to soft peaks and fold into the shrimp paste, mixing well. Spread thickly over the bread and coat with sesame seeds.

Cooking

Heat the wok, add oil and when very hot, reduce heat slightly. Deep-fry the bread, shrimp side downwards for 1 minute. Turn and fry for another minute, then drain and cut into pieces about 5cm x 2cm (2" x ¾"). Serve with a pepper salt dip, see recipe page 277.

Steamed Prawns
Pai Cho Hsien Hsia 白灼鮮蝦
Serves 6-8

| 750 g (1½ lb) | medium prawns, in shell |

Sauce

3 tbsp	dark soy sauce
3 tbsp	light soy sauce
4 slices	ginger, shredded
2	scallions, shredded
1	red chilli, shredded (optional)
4 tbsp	cooked oil

Preparation and Cooking

Wash prawns well and leave in iced water for 10 minutes. Place in a wire mesh strainer in a steamer and steam over high heat for 8-10 minutes. Mix sauce ingredients and pour into several small bowls.

Transfer prawns to a serving plate and serve with the sauce dips.

169

Steamed Prawns — *recipe on page 169.*

Fried Shrimps in Scrambled Egg

Hsia Jen Ch'ao Tan　蝦仁炒蛋
Serves 6-8

185 g (6 oz)	fresh shrimps, peeled
6	eggs
4-5 tbsp	cooked oil
	oil for deep-frying

Seasoning A

¼ tsp	salt
¼ tsp	monosodium glutamate
½ tsp	cornstarch

Seasoning B

½ tsp	salt
½ tsp	monosodium glutamate

Preparation

Slit shrimp down centre backs and remove veins. Wash well in cold water and dry. Marinate with seasoning A ingredients, adding 1 tbsp of egg white. Leave for at least 1 hour before cooking. Beat eggs lightly, adding the seasoning B ingredients.

Cooking

Heat the wok, add deep-frying oil and when very hot deep-fry the shrimp for 20 seconds. Remove and drain well. Pour off the oil.

Reheat the wok, add half the cooked oil and pour in the egg mixture.

Cook until beginning to firm underneath. Add shrimps, and pour a little more oil around the edge of the egg. When firm, turn the omelette, add the remaining oil around the edge of the omelette, and cook on reduced heat until just firm. Lift out and place on a serving plate. Garnish with shredded scallion and Chinese parsley. Serve.

"The Cantonese pronounce the Chinese character for prawn (蝦) as 'ha' — the same 'ha' that is an element of the almost universally-accepted 'ha, ha' sound of laughter. This is considered to be a rather auspicious coincidence, and many Chinese hosts insist, therefore, that a prawn dish be featured in every banquet that is arranged on their behalf."

Fried Shrimp Balls

Hsueh Hua Hsia Chiu　雪花蝦球
Serves 6-8

440 g (14 oz)	fresh baby shrimps, peeled
30 g (1 oz)	pork fat, steamed and finely chopped
2 tsp	ginger, minced
2 tsp	scallion, minced
2	egg whites
125 g (4 oz)	fresh white breadcrumbs
	oil for deep-frying

Seasoning

½ tsp	sugar
¼ tsp	salt
¼ tsp	monosodium glutamate
1 tsp	Shao Hsing wine
1 tbsp	cornstarch

Preparation

Wash shrimp, pat dry and pick out dark veins. Pound to a smooth paste in a mortar or on a chopping board. Mix in seasonings, ginger, scallion and pork fat and work with the fingers until completely amalgamated. Beat egg whites to soft peaks and stir into the shrimp mixture. Mould into ball shapes, about 2.5cm (1″) in diameter. Coat with breadcrumbs, shaking off excess.

Cooking

Heat wok, add oil and when very hot reduce heat slightly and put in shrimp balls, several at a time to keep the oil bubbling, and deep-fry for about 4 minutes, or until they turn golden and have expanded slightly. Increase heat and cook for a further ½ minute. Drain and serve with a spicy salt dip, see page 277, or sweet and sour sauce, see page 278.

Fried Prawns in Hot Sauce

Kan Shao Ming Hsia　干燒明蝦
Serves 6-8

6-8	king prawns, in shell
2 tsp	Chinese celery, minced
1 tsp	ginger, minced
2 tsp	scallion, minced
1-2 cloves	garlic, minced
	oil for deep-frying

Seasoning

1 tsp	Shao Hsing wine
1 tsp	wine lees
1 tsp	black vinegar

Sauce

1½ tsp	sugar
1 tsp	salt

¼ tsp	monosodium glutamate
1 tsp	Shao Hsing wine
1 tsp	hot bean paste
1½ tsp	tomato paste
5 tbsp	chicken stock
2 tbsp	cooked oil
Thickening — mix together	
½ tsp	cornstarch
1 tbsp	water

Preparation

Wash the prawns and cut off the whiskers and legs. Snip the shells with scissors along the back, but do not remove. Devein and rinse in cold water. Cut off heads and cut bodies into two pieces. Do not discard heads. Mix the sauce ingredients and set aside.

Cooking

Boil the prawns for 2 minutes, then drain well.

Heat the wok, add deep-frying oil and deep-fry the prawns for about 1 minute, until the shells are crisp and the prawns are cooked through. Remove and drain. Discard most of the oil.

Stir-fry the celery, ginger, scallion and garlic for ½ minute. Add the prawns with the sauce and bring to the boil. Simmer for 2 minutes. Add the thickening and boil until the sauce thickens. Add in the seasonings, stir and serve.

Prawn Cutlets

Kao Li Tai Hsia 高力大蝦
Serves 6

6	large raw prawns
8	egg whites
2 tbsp	all purpose flour
2 tsp	cornstarch
105 g (3½ oz)	breadcrumbs
	oil for deep-frying
Seasoning	
½ tsp	salt
⅓ tsp	monosodium glutamate
1 tsp	Shao Hsing wine
1 tsp	sesame oil

Preparation

Peel prawns, leaving the tails intact. Slit down centre backs to divide into halves. Sprinkle on seasoning ingredients and leave for 5 minutes. Beat egg whites to soft peaks and mix to a smooth batter with flour and cornstarch. Beat again until the egg white mixture stands in stiff peaks. Dip in

each prawn piece to coat thickly, then sprinkle with breadcrumbs.

Cooking

Heat the wok, add oil and when very hot reduce heat slightly. Deep-fry the prawns, two at a time, to a deep golden colour and cooked through, about 3 minutes. Drain and serve.

The sun is sinking in the west,
Bidding the fishermen think of rest.
"Today," they cry, "no need to search,
The people rush to buy our perch;
Of shell-fish, too, we are bereft,
We've scarcely half a basket left!"
And at the piles of silver bright
They laugh, and shout: "Good wine tonight!"

Cheng-cheng

Fried Fresh Prawns

Ch'ing Ch'ao Hsia Jen 清炒蝦仁
Serves 6-8

750 g (1½ lb)	medium prawns, in shell
1 tsp	salt
1 tsp	cornstarch
	oil for deep-frying
Seasoning A	
¼ tsp	salt
¼ tsp	monosodium glutamate
2	egg whites
1 tsp	cornstarch
Seasoning B	
¼ tsp	monosodium glutamate
2 tsp	Shao Hsing wine
1 tsp	ginger juice
1½ tbsp	cooked oil

Preparation

Peel prawns, slit down centre backs and remove dark veins. Rinse well in cold water with salt and cornstarch added. Drain and dry in a kitchen towel. Beat egg whites and mix with remaining seasoning A ingredients. Mix with the prawns and marinate for 1-2 minutes.

Cooking

Heat the wok, add oil and when very hot deep-fry prawns for 45 seconds. Drain well. Pour off the oil, reheat the wok and add the seasoning B ingredients and the prawns. Stir-fry for 30 seconds. Serve.

Fried Prawns in Hot Sauce — *recipe on page 172.*

Prawn Cutlets — *recipe on page 173.*

Fried Shrimp Balls — *recipe on page 172.*   Fried Shrimp on Croutons with Sesame Seeds — *recipe on page 169.*

Sauteed Squid with Celery
Chieh Lan Hsien Yu 芥蘭鮮魷
Serves 6-8

375 g (12 oz)	fresh squid
185 g (6 oz)	celery
5-6 slices	ginger, flower-cut
5-6 slices	carrot, flower-cut
1 clove	garlic, finely chopped
4 tbsp	oil
Sauce	
½ tsp	sugar
1 tsp	salt
1 tsp	monosodium glutamate
½ tsp	cornstarch
3 tbsp	chicken stock

Preparation
Clean the squid, removing heads, intestines and pink skin. Cut open and flatten, then score the meat deeply using an angled cut, criss-cross fashion. Cut into 4cm x 1.5cm (1½″ x ½″) pieces. Blanch in boiling water until they curl and turn opaque, then drain and set aside.

Wash the celery and cut into strips about 5cm x 1.5cm (2″ x ½″). Blanch in clean boiling water for 1 minute, then drain well. Mix the sauce ingredients.

Cooking
Heat the wok, and add 1 tbsp oil. Lightly stir-fry the celery, then remove, drain and set aside. Add remaining oil to the wok and stir-fry ginger, carrot and garlic for ½ minute. Pour in the sauce and stir until it thickens. Add celery and squid and stir for 2 minutes on moderately high heat. Serve.

Pan-Fried Oyster Cake
Chien Hao Ping 煎蠔餅
Serves 6-8

250 g (8 oz)	small oysters, removed from the shell
8 tbsp	all purpose flour
2½ tbsp	cornstarch
150 ml (5 fl oz)	water
1	duck egg
4	scallions, finely chopped
1	stalk Chinese parsley, finely chopped
4 tbsp	cooked oil
Seasoning	
1 tsp	salt
½ tsp	monosodium glutamate
¼ tsp	white pepper

Preparation
Wash the oysters in cold running water, then blanch in boiling water for ½ minute. Drain well.

Sieve the flour and cornstarch into a mixing bowl and make a well in the centre. Add the water and duck egg, with the seasoning ingredients and mix well, then add the scallions and Chinese parsley and beat the batter well.

Cooking
Heat the wok, add 2 tbsp cooked oil and when very hot pour in the batter. Reduce heat to moderate, cover and fry for 1 minute, then remove cover and leave to cook for 1 minute longer. Turn, pour remaining oil around the edge of the pancake and continue to cook until the pancake is cooked through and golden brown, 3-4 minutes. Cut into wedges and serve.

"A little injustice in the breast can be drowned by wine; but a great injustice in the world can be drowned only by the sword."

Chang Ch'ao

Drunken Crabs
Tsui Hsieh 醉蟹
Serves 6-8

6	fresh Shanghai crabs (about 155g/5 oz each)
1 pc	dried tangerine peel, crumbled
1 tsp	ginger, minced
1 tsp	scallion, minced
Sauce	
1 tsp	sugar
2 tbsp	salt
625 ml (20 fl oz)	Shao Hsing wine dash monosodium glutamate

Preparation
Wash the crabs thoroughly, scrubbing with a soft brush to clean the muddy undersides. Place the tied crabs, still alive, in a large jar. Mix the sauce ingredients and pour over the crabs. Sprinkle in tangerine peel, ginger and scallion, cover and leave to stand for 1 week, in a cool place.

Serving
Cut off the tips of the crab legs. Lift off the shells and cut in halves. Cut off the undershells and remove inedible parts. Cut the crabs into four pieces each and arrange on a serving plate with the shells on top, yellow yolks upwards. Serve.

177

Crispy Rice Crackers with Seafood and Vegetables
San Hsien Kwo Pa 三鮮鍋巴
Serves 6-8

125 (4 oz)	crispy rice crackers*
195 g (6 oz)	fresh shrimps, peeled
75 g (2½ oz)	canned abalone, thinly sliced
60 g (2 oz)	cooked ham, shredded
60 g (2 oz)	canned bamboo shoots, thinly sliced
60 g (2 oz)	canned button mushrooms, horizontally sliced
1 tsp	ginger, minced
2 tsp	scallion, minced
1 tsp	rendered chicken fat
	dash white pepper
	oil for deep-frying

Seasoning A

½ tsp	salt
½ tsp	cornstarch
½	egg white, beaten
	dash white pepper

Sauce

¼ tsp	salt
½ tsp	monosodium glutamate
½ tsp	Shao Hsing wine
625 ml (20 fl oz)	chicken stock
1 tsp	cooked oil

Thickening — mix together

| 1 tbsp | cornstarch |
| 2 tbsp | water |

Preparation
Rinse shrimps, slit down centre backs and remove dark veins. Rinse again and cut large pieces in halves. Dry in a kitchen towel and marinate with seasoning A ingredients for 5 minutes. Mix the sauce ingredients and set aside.

Cooking
Heat the wok, add oil and when very hot, reduce heat slightly. Deep-fry the rice crackers until golden and crisp. Remove, drain and place in a serving bowl. Add shrimps and deep-fry for 20 seconds. Remove and drain, discard most of the oil. Reheat the wok, add ginger and scallion and stir-fry for a few seconds, then add abalone, ham, bamboo shoots and mushrooms and return the shrimps. Stir-fry for a few seconds, then pour in the sauce and bring to the boil. Add thickening and stir until sauce thickens and becomes clear. Add chicken fat and pepper and pour over the crispy rice crackers. Serve immediately.

Fish Lips with Crispy Rice Crackers
Yu Chun Kwo Pa 魚唇鍋巴
Serves 6-8

155 g (5 oz)	dried 'fish lips', soaked
125 g (4oz)	crispy rice crackers*
90 g (3 oz)	lean pork, thinly sliced
60 g (2 oz)	canned bamboo shoots, thinly sliced
6	dried black mushrooms, soaked
1 tsp	ginger, minced
2 tsp	scallion, minced
3 tbsp	cooked oil
	dash Shao Hsing wine
	oil for deep-frying

Sauce

1½ tsp	sugar
½ tsp	salt
½ tsp	monosodium glutamate
2 tsp	dark soy sauce
½ tsp	black vinegar
½ tsp	Shao Hsing wine
625 ml (20 fl oz)	chicken stock

Thickening — mix together

| 1 tbsp | cornstarch |
| 2 tbsp | water |

Preparation and Cooking
Drain fish lips and place in a saucepan with boiling water to cover. Add a dash of wine and boil until completely softened. Drain and cut into pieces about 5cm x 2cm (2″ x ¾″).

Heat the wok, add cooked oil and stir-fry ginger and scallion for ½ minute. Remove. Add pork and stir-fry for 1 minute, then lift out. Add bamboo shoots and mushroom and stir-fry for 1 minute. Remove.

Pour in the sauce ingredients, well mixed, and bring to the boil. Return the fried ingredients and add fish lips. Bring to the boil. Cover and cook for 5 minutes. Skim the stock, add thickening and simmer, stirring occasionally, until the sauce has thickened and become clear. Keep hot.

Wipe out the wok, reheat and add deep-frying oil. When very hot, reduce heat slightly and deep-fry rice crackers until golden and crisp.

Remove, drain well and arrange in a serving bowl or tureen. Pour on the hot fish lips and sauce and serve immediately.

Note: *For method of making crispy rice crackers, see page 227.

Fish Lips with Crispy Rice Crackers; Crispy Rice Crackers with Seafood and Vegetables; Beche-de-Mer with Crispy Rice Crackers — *recipe on page 183.*

Braised Crabs in Ginger Sauce
Ch'iang Ts'ung Chu Hsieh　羗葱焗蟹
Serves 6

1-2	fresh crabs (about 1 kg/2 lb)
90 g (3 oz)	ginger, sliced and lightly crushed
90 g (3 oz)	scallions, 8cm (3″) lengths
2 cloves	garlic, crushed
4 tbsp	cooked oil
Seasoning	
1 tsp	salt
1 tsp	monosodium glutamate
100 ml (3 fl oz)	chicken stock
Thickening — mix together	
1½ tsp	cornstarch
1 tbsp	water

Preparation
Thoroughly clean the crab shells and rinse in cold water. Prise off the back shells, remove inedible parts, then chop the undershells each into 6 with the legs and claws attached. Break off top parts of claws and crack the shells. Mix the seasoning ingredients and set aside.

Cooking
Heat the wok, add the oil and when hot stir-fry the ginger, scallion and garlic for a few seconds. Add the crab pieces and stir-fry for 2 minutes. Stir in the seasoning, cover and cook for 2-3 minutes on moderate heat. Add thickening and stir until the sauce thickens. The crab shells should turn a bright orange colour. Arrange on a serving plate with the back shells on top.

Deep-Fried Oysters
Su Cha Sheng Hao　酥炸生蠔
Serves 6

12	large fresh oysters (about 375 g/12 oz)
1 tsp	salt
	oil for deep-frying
Seasoning	
½ tsp	salt
½ tsp	monosodium glutamate
	few drops sesame oil
	dash pepper
Batter	
75 g (2½ oz)	all purpose flour
1 tbsp	cornstarch
1½ tsp	bicarbonate of soda
125 ml (4 fl oz)	water
2 tbsp	oil

Preparation
Wash and clean the shelled oysters, then blanch them in salted boiling water for a few seconds. Remove, drain and mix with the seasoning ingredients. Prepare the batter, mixing the ingredients except oil, to a smooth consistency.

Cooking
Heat the wok, add the oil and when very hot add the 2 tbsp oil to the batter and beat in well. Dip the oysters into the batter, coating well, and drop them one at a time into the oil. Deep-fry 6 at a time, for ½ minute then turn and deep-fry for 1 minute longer, until golden brown. Remove, drain and serve with a pepper salt dip, see page 277.

Braised Turtle
Pai Shao Shui Yu　白燒水魚
Serves 12

1	whole turtle (about 2kg/4 lb)*
125 g (4 oz)	Yunnan ham, thinly sliced
60 g (2 oz)	canned bamboo shoots, thinly sliced
90 g (3 oz)	fresh straw mushrooms, trimmed
3 slices	ginger
2	scallions
3 tbsp	cooked oil
	dash white pepper
Seasoning	
2 tsp	sugar
2 tsp	salt
½ tsp	monosodium glutamate
1 tbsp	Shao Hsing wine
Thickening — mix together	
1½ tbsp	cornstarch
3 tbsp	water

*Prepare the turtle, following the recipe on page 196. Cut into 4cm (1½″) chunks.

Cooking
Heat the wok, add 2 tbsp oil and stir-fry ginger and scallion for ½ minute. Transfer to a casserole. Add the seasoning ingredients, the turtle and enough hot water to completely cover it.

Bring to the boil, cover and simmer for 1½ hours. Skim the stock, add ham, bamboo shoots and mushrooms and simmer for 1½ hours longer, until half the water has evaporated and the turtle is very tender. Discard the ginger and scallion. Add thickening, pepper and remaining oil and stir until the sauce thickens. Serve in the casserole or transfer to a deep serving dish. Serve hot.

Fu Yung Crab in Cabbage Rolls

Fu Yung Hsieh Ju Tsai Ch'uan 芙蓉蟹肉菜卷
Serves 6-8

6 large leaves	Tientsin cabbage
8	egg whites
60 g (2 oz)	fillet of dace or other white fish, shredded
30 g (1 oz)	conpoy, steamed to soften
45 g (1½ oz)	cooked crabmeat
3 tbsp	cooked oil

Seasoning

1 tsp	salt
¼ tsp	monosodium glutamate
¼ tsp	Shao Hsing wine
1 tsp	cornstarch

Sauce:

¼ tsp	salt
1 tsp	Shao Hsing wine
125 ml (4 fl oz)	chicken stock
1 tsp	cornstarch

Preparation

Blanch cabbage leaves in boiling water for 1½ minutes to soften. Drain and leave to partially dry. Beat egg whites to soft peaks. Stir in shredded fish, flaked conpoy, crabmeat and seasoning ingredients.

Cooking

Heat the wok, add oil and when very hot reduce heat slightly and stir-fry the mixture until egg is just firm. Remove from the pan and leave to cool. Divide the mixture between the cabbage leaves and roll up, tying with cotton or securing with toothpicks. Place the cabbage rolls on a lightly oiled plate and set in a steamer to cook over high heat for 5 minutes. Wipe out the wok, add mixed sauce ingredients and bring to the boil.

Cut the cabbage rolls into 2.5cm (1″) thick slices. Pour on the hot sauce and serve.

"... as far as crabs are concerned, my mind is addicted to them, my mouth enjoys the taste of them, and not a single day in my life have I ever forgotten about them."

Li Li-weng

Beche-de-Mer with Crispy Rice Crackers

Hai Shen Kwo Pa 海參鍋巴
Serves 6-8

125 g (4 oz)	beche-de-mer, soaked*1
90 g (3 oz)	crispy rice crackers* 2
30 g (1 oz)	lean pork, thinly sliced
3	dried mushrooms, soaked
60 g (2 oz)	canned bamboo shoots, thinly sliced
1 tsp	ginger, minced
1 tsp	scallion, minced
3 tbsp	cooked oil
	oil for deep-frying
	dash Shao Hsing wine
	dash white pepper

Sauce

¼ tsp	salt
¼ tsp	monosodium glutamate
1½ tsp	dark soy sauce
1 tsp	light soy sauce
1 tbsp	Shao Hsing wine
375 ml (12 fl oz)	chicken stock

Thickening — mix together

1 tbsp	cornstarch
1 tbsp	water

Preparation

Shred the beche-de-mer and blanch in boiling water for 2 minutes with the dash of wine. Mix the sauce ingredients.

Cooking

Heat the wok and add the oil for deep-frying. When very hot, deep-fry the rice crackers over high heat until they are golden brown and float to the surface. Place the crackers in a serving bowl. Pour off the oil.

Reheat the wok and add 3 tbsp cooked oil. When the oil is very hot, stir-fry the ginger and scallion for a minute or two, then discard.

Add the pork, mushrooms and bamboo shoot. Stir-fry for 2 minutes. Add the sauce ingredients and the beche-de-mer. Cover and bring to the boil. Simmer for 10 minutes. Skim the stock then add the thickening and the pepper and return to the boil. Cook until the sauce thickens slightly. Pour over the rice crackers and serve.

Note. *1 For the method of preparing beche-de-mer, see page 185.

—— *2 Use the crusty rice scraped from the bottom of the saucepan after cooking white rice, or see page 277 for method of preparation.

Noodles with Braised Eel — *recipe on page 233*; Deep-Fried Eel, Wu Hsi Style.

Braised Beche-de-Mer with Scallions.

Braised Crabs in Ginger Sauce — *recipe on page 182.*

Deep-Fried Eel, Wu Hsi Style

Wu Hsi Ts'ui Shan　無錫脆鱔

Serves 6-8

750 g (1½ lb)	live eels
2 tsp	sesame oil
	oil for deep-frying
Seasoning A	
1½ tsp	salt
1½ tsp	black vinegar
Seasoning B	
2 tbsp	sugar
¼ tsp	monosodium glutamate
3 tbsp	dark soy sauce
2 tsp	black vinegar
1 tsp	ginger, minced
2 tsp	scallion, minced
2 cloves	garlic, minced

Preparation

Place the live eels in a deep bowl and cover with boiling water. Cover and leave for 1 minute. Transfer the eels to a wok, add seasoning A ingredients and cold water to cover. Bring to the boil, reduce heat and simmer for 5 minutes. Remove the wok from the heat, cover and let stand for 3 minutes. Pour off the water, rinse eels with cold water, then drain. Take each eel and de-bone, gripping the head and using a sharp knife to slice down the length of the body. (Cutting at an angle to the bone the meat can be taken off in 3 strips). Discard all except the meat and rinse thoroughly in cold water. Cut into 13cm (5") strips. Mix the seasoning B ingredients and set aside.

Cooking

Heat the wok, add the oil and when very hot, place the eels in a wire mesh strainer and plunge into the oil for a few seconds. Remove, drain and reheat the oil.

Repeat this process about 5 times over high heat, gradually separating the pieces of eel and deep-frying until they are very crisp. Remove and drain. Discard most of the oil.

Reheat the wok, return the eel with seasoning B and stir-fry over high heat until the eel is well glazed with the seasonings. Sprinkle on sesame oil, Stir and serve.

"Better than sea-slugs if not first rate, is a dish of bamboo shoots." —— *Yuen Mai*

"Some animals are good for food; others are not. But avoid even those which are normally edible if there be anything unnatural in their appearance."

Imperial Cookery Book of the Mongol Dynasty—*Yin Shan Cheng Yao*

Braised Beche-de-Mer with Scallion

Ts'ung Shao Hai Shen　葱燒海參

Serves 6-8

250 g (½ lb)	dried beche-de-mer, soaked
4	scallions, 5cm (2") lengths
3 tbsp	cooked oil
Seasoning	
½ tsp	sugar
½ tsp	salt
½ tsp	monosodium glutamate
¼ tsp	dark soy sauce
1 tbsp	light soy sauce
2 tsp	Shao Hsing wine
3 tbsp	chicken stock
Thickening — mix together	
½ tsp	cornstarch
1 tbsp	water

Preparation

Place drained beche-de-mer in cold water to cover, bring slowly to the boil and boil for 5 minutes. Remove from heat and cool for 20 minutes. Drain, cover with more cold water and bring to the boil again. Remove from the heat, drain and cover with cold water and leave for some hours (or overnight). Drain, slit in halves and scrub clean. Bring to the boil again, cook over moderate heat until softened, then drain and rinse in cold water. (The beche-de-mer should be soft and with a gelatinous texture when ready). Cut into 5cm (2") squares. Mix the seasoning ingredients and set aside.

Cooking

Heat the wok, add the oil and when very hot reduce heat slightly. Stir-fry the beche-de-mer pieces with scallion for 1 minute. Add the seasoning, cover and braise over moderate heat for 4 minutes. Add the thickening and stir until the sauce thickens. Serve.

185

Stuffed Crab Claws.

Stuffed Crab Claws

Pai Hua Niang Hsieh Ch'ien　百花釀蟹鉗

Serves 12

12	fresh crab claws
440 g (14 oz)	prawn or shrimp meat
	cornstarch
	oil for deep-frying

Seasoning

1 tsp	salt
¼ tsp	monosodium glutamate
2 tsp	cornstarch
	few drops sesame oil
	dash white pepper

Preparation

Pound the prawn or shrimp meat to a paste using the flat side of the cleaver on a chopping board. Mix well with the seasoning ingredients, then divide into 12 equal portions, dusting each with a little cornstarch.

Crack the shells of the crab claws and, keeping the tips of the claws attached to the meat, remove the rest of the shells. The meat must remain intact. With well floured hands mould a portion of the prawn or shrimp paste around each claw, leaving the shell tip exposed. Form into ball shapes, dusting with more cornstarch if necessary. Set aside.

Cooking

Heat the wok, add the oil and when very hot reduce heat slightly. Deep-fry the crab claws, several at a time, for about 5 minutes until golden brown. Remove, drain and arrange on a serving plate.

Serve with a red vinegar dip, see page 277.

187

Deep-Fried Oysters — *recipe on page 182.*

Shark's Fin

Shark's Fin in Brown Sauce
Hung P'a Yu Ch'ih 紅扒魚翅
Serves 6-8

250 g (8 oz)	dried shark's fin
250 ml (5 fl oz)	chicken stock
2 tbsp	cooked oil
Sauce	
¾ tsp	sugar
¾ tsp	salt
¾ tsp	monosodium glutamate
2 tsbp	dark soy sauce
1 tbsp	light soy sauce
1 tbsp	Shao Hsing wine
625 ml (20 fl oz)	chicken stock
	dash white pepper
Thickening — mix together	
2 tbsp	cornstarch
2 tbsp	water

Preparation
Soak shark's fin in cold water for 2 hours, then bring to the boil and boil for ½ hour on low heat. Drain and cover with more cold water. Repeat the soaking and boiling process three or four times until the fins are softened. Scrub with a brush to clean thoroughly and rinse well in cold water. Mix sauce ingredients and set aside.

Cooking
Heat the wok, add chicken stock and the drained shark's fin and simmer for 3-4 minutes. Drain.

Reheat the wok, add 1 tbsp oil and the sauce and bring to the boil. Add thickening and stir until the sauce begins to thicken. Add the shark's fins and bring to the boil. Reduce heat and simmer for 5 minutes. Sprinkle on remaining oil. Transfer to a serving dish. Serve hot with a red vinegar dip.

"There is a popular saying that a woman and her husband should be compatible. The 'Book of Etiquette' by Li Chi, also said that one is judged by the company one keeps. Cookery is no different. Food cooked must need something to go along with it. Clear should go with clear, thick with thick, hard with hard, and soft with soft. Only then would there be a perfect blending."

Yuen Mai.

"A well-prepared Chinese dish is expected to appeal to more senses than the one of taste. Its colours should be pleasing to the eye, the ingredients should be of uniform size, and it should be fragrant. There should be contrasting tastes and textures within the meal; if one dish is crisp, it should be offset by another that is smooth; a bland dish is paired with a spiced one. Always the effort is to create a balance."

The Cooking of China
Tai Te Ching

Shark's Fin and Chicken in Soup
Sha Kwo Chi Pao Ch'ih 砂鍋鷄鮑翅
Serves 6-8

250 g (8 oz)	dried shark's fin*
250 g (8 oz)	chicken fillet, shredded
30 g (1 oz)	Yuannan ham, shredded
250 ml (8 fl oz)	chicken stock
Soup	
1 tsp	salt
½ tsp	monosodium glutamate
2 tsp	light soy sauce
1 tbsp	Shao Hsing wine
1½ lit (48 fl oz)	chicken stock

Preparation
*For method of preparing shark's fins, see previous recipe.

Cooking
Heat the wok, add chicken stock and drained shark's fin and simmer for 3-4 minutes. Drain.

Bring the soup ingredients to the boil. Add shredded chicken and ham and cook for 2 minutes, then add the shark's fins and cook for 1-2 minutes. Transfer to a soup tureen and serve hot with a red vinegar dip.

Note: Thinly sliced canned abalone, or dried abalone boiled until softened, can also be added here.

Shark's Fin in Brown Sauce.

Eight-Treasure Beancurd Soup — *recipe on page 193;* Chinese Parsley and Sliced Fish Soup — *recipe on page 193;* Double-Boiled Chicken with White Fungus in Soup —

page 192; Sliced Pork Liver and Matrimony Vine Soup — *recipe on page 193.*

Soups

Double-Boiled Chicken with White Fungus in Soup
Hsueh Erh Tun Chi T'ang 雪耳燉鷄湯
Serves 6-8

½	chicken (about 750 g /1½ lb)
30 g (1 oz)	Yunnan ham, 1.5cm (½″) cubes
30 g (1 oz)	white fungus, soaked
2 slices	ginger
2 tbsp	ginger wine
1¼ lit (40 fl oz)	chicken stock

Seasoning

1½ tsp	salt
1 tsp	monosodium glutamate

Preparation and Cooking
Clean chicken, wash well and drain. Cut into several large pieces and blanch in boiling water for 3 minutes. Drain. Place chicken and ham in a double boiler and add the stock. Cover and double-boil for 1 hour.

Drain fungus and add to the pot. Add ginger and ginger wine and return to the boil. Continue to double-boil for 45 minutes longer. Add seasonings in last 15 minutes of cooking. Serve in the double-boiler, or transfer to a deep serving dish.

Double-Boiled Winter Melon Soup — *recipe on page 268.*

Eight-Treasure Beancurd Soup
Pa Chen Tou Fu Keng　八珍豆腐羹
Serves 6-8

4 squares	soft beancurd
60 g (2 oz)	fresh shrimps, peeled and diced
60 g (2 oz)	chicken fillet, diced
45 g (1½ oz)	chicken liver, diced
45 g (1½ oz)	barbecued pork, diced
45 g (1½ oz)	fresh straw mushrooms, diced
45 g (1½ oz)	frozen green peas
6-8	chive shoots, 1.5cm (½″) pieces
1¼ lit (40 fl oz)	chicken stock
1 tbsp	cooked oil

Seasoning

1 tsp	salt
1 tsp	monosodium glutamate
	dash white pepper

Thickening — mix together

4 tsp	cornstarch
2 tbsp	water

Preparation
Cut beancurd into medium dice. Blanch in hot water for a few seconds and drain well. Blanch shrimps, chicken, chicken livers, pork, mushrooms and peas for 1 minute. Drain.

Cooking
Heat the wok, add cooked oil and the chicken stock and bring to the boil. Add seasonings and the blanched ingredients and bring back to the boil. Reduce heat and simmer for 5 minutes. Add thickening and chive shoots and stir until thickened. Pour into a serving bowl or tureen. Serve.

Sliced Pork Liver with Matrimony Vine Soup
Kou Ch'i Chu Kan T'ang　枸杞豬肝湯
Serves 6-8

250 g (8 oz)	pork liver
500 g (1 lb)	matrimony vine
5 slices	ginger, flower-cut
1¼ lit (40 fl oz)	water
2 tsp	salt
1½ tbsp	cooked oil

Seasoning

½ tsp	salt
2 tsp	cornstarch

Preparation
Wash liver, remove skin and all tendons and cut into thin slices, then into strips about 4cm x 1cm (1½″ x ¼″). Sprinkle with the seasoning and leave for 10 minutes, then blanch in boiling water for 2-3 minutes. Drain well and leave to cool.

Strip leaves from the matrimony vine stems and wash in cold water. Drain well.

Cooking
Bring water to the boil, adding ginger, salt and cooked oil. Add in matrimony vine leaves, cover and simmer on moderate heat for 3-4 minutes. Add in the liver, stir well, and simmer for 2 minutes longer. Serve.

Note:　This soup is taken to improve blood circulation.

"Eat too much at one meal, and you'll have to drink soup for ten meals."

Chinese Proverb

Chinese Parsley and Sliced Fish Soup
Yuan Hsi Ch'a Kua Yu P'ien T'ang　芫茜茶瓜魚片湯
Serves 6-8

250 g (8 oz)	fresh grass carp fillets
3 stems	Chinese parsley
60 g (2 oz)	sweet cucumber pickle, shredded
3 slices	ginger, shredded
1¼ lit (40 fl oz)	water or fish stock
2 tsp	salt
1 tbsp	cooked oil

Seasoning

½ tsp	salt
2 tsp	cooked oil
	dash white pepper

Preparation
Wash fish and cut into 1.5cm (½″) strips, cutting diagonally through the fillets. Place the fish pieces into a serving dish or soup tureen. Sprinkle with seasoning and leave for 10 minutes. Remove roots from Chinese parsley and cut into 2.5cm (1″) pieces. Rinse pickle in cold water and drain well.

Cooking
Bring stock to boil, adding salt, cooked oil, ginger and pickle. Bring back to the boil again and put in Chinese parsley. Cover and simmer on moderately high heat for several seconds. Pour over the fish, cover and serve.

Mushrooms with Crispy Rice Crackers in Soup.

Mushrooms with Crispy Rice Crackers in Soup

K'ou Mo Kwo Pa T'ang 口蘑鍋巴湯
Serves 6-8

60 g (20 oz)	dried brown mushrooms, soaked
125 g (4 oz)	crispy rice crackers*
1 lit (32 fl oz)	chicken stock
	oil for deep-frying

Seasoning

½ tsp	salt
¼ tsp	monosodium glutamate
1 tbsp	light soy sauce
2 tsp	Shao Hsing wine

*For method of making crispy rice crackers, see page 227.

Preparation and cooking:
Drain brown mushrooms and remove stems.

Heat deep-frying oil and deep-fry rice crackers until golden brown. Remove and drain well. Place in a serving dish or soup tureen.

Bring chicken stock to the boil and add the mushrooms and seasoning ingredients. Boil for 2-3 minutes, then pour over the rice crackers. Serve.

"Do not try to gulp down soup with vegetables in it, nor add condiments to it. Do not keep picking the teeth, nor swill down the sauces. If a guest adds condiments, the host will apologize for not having had the soup prepared better. If he swills down the sauces the host will apologize for his poverty."

Li Chi

Pork Tripe and Gingko Nut Soup — *recipe on page 196.*

Pork Tripe and Gingko Nut Soup

Pai Kuo Chu Tu T'ang 白菓豬肚湯

Serves 6-8

625 g (1¼ lb)	pork tripe
105 g (3½ oz)	gingko nuts, in the shell
45 g (1½ oz)	dried beancurd skin
2 tsp	salt
2 tbsp	white vinegar
2 tsp	dark soy sauce
2 lit (64 fl oz)	water

Seasoning

2½ tsp	salt
½ tsp	monosodium glutmate
1 tbsp	Shao Hsing wine
2 tsp	cornstarch
1 tsp	sesame oil

Preparation

Wash tripe well, turn inside out and remove any fat. Rub with salt and vinegar and rinse with cold water. Repeat four or five times until the surface is shiny and clean. Rinse well in cold water and drain. Shell gingko nuts and remove skin.

Cooking

Bring the water to boil in a large pot. Add tripe, gingko nuts and beancurd skin and return to the boil. Reduce heat and simmer for at least 1½ hours. Then add the seasoning and cook for 15 minutes longer. Remove tripe and cut into bite-size pieces. Return to the soup, add soy sauce. Reheat and serve.

"Everything has its own taste and should not be mingled and mixed. It is just like the Great Sage, whose teaching methods varied according to the level of the learner. There was no obligatory uniformity, for "a good man would help others to achieve perfection". The cooks of today think nothing of mixing in one soup the meat of chicken, duck, pig, and goose, rendering all skills unnecessary, all tastes waxen. Had these chickens, ducks, pigs and geese souls, they would most certainly file plaints in the netherworld as to the injustice they had received."

Yuen Mai.

"And pickled suckling pig,
And flesh of whelps, floating in liver sauce,
With salad of minced radishes in brine."

Double-Boiled Clear Turtle Soup

Ch'ing Tun Shui Yu 清燉水魚

Serves 6-8

1½ kg (3 lb)	whole turtle
125 g (4 oz)	Yunnan ham, thinly sliced
1 slice	ginger, shredded
1	scallion, shredded
1 lit (32 fl oz)	water

Seasoning

1½ tsp	salt
1 tsp	monosodium glutamate
1 tsp	Shao Hsing wine

Preparation

Place the turtle on a chopping board, stomach upwards. Remove head and drain off the blood. Discard. Place the turtle in boiling water and boil until skin begins to flake, about 5 minutes. Remove from the water, drain and scrape off skin. Slit open stomach and remove intestines. Chop off claws. Wash the turtle very well and return to clean boiling water for another 5 minutes. Drain and scrub under cold water to clean thoroughly and remove the remaining fishy odour.

Cooking

Place the turtle in a heavy casserole, pour in the water and add seasonings. Scatter on the shredded ginger and scallion and arrange the sliced ham on top. Cover the casserole with rice paper or greaseproof paper (glue in place with a paste of flour and water, or tie with string). Set in a steamer over rapidly boiling water and boil for 1½ hours. Remove ham and set aside. Recover the casserole and boil for another 1½ hours. Transfer turtle to a soup tureen and strain soup over it. Discard ginger and scallion. Arrange the ham on the turtle and serve.

"Next are brought fresh turtle, and sweet chicken cooked in cheese. Pressed by the men of Ch'u."

Ch'u Yuan

Chicken Soup with Bamboo Fungus in Hot Pot — *recipe on page 198.*

Double-Boiled Clear Turtle Soup

Chicken Soup with Bamboo Fungus in Hot Pot
Ch'i Kwo Chu Sheng Chi T'ang 汽鍋竹笙鷄湯
Serves 6-8

½	chicken, (about 750 g/1½ lb)
15 g (½ oz)	bamboo fungus, soaked
1 slice	ginger
1	scallion

Seasoning

½ tsp	salt
¼ tsp	monosodium glutamate
1 tsp	Shao Hsing wine

Preparation

Drain bamboo fungus, then soak in boiling water for 15 minutes. Drain again.

Cut chicken into 4cm (1½″) cubes. Place all the ingredients except seasonings into a hot pot steamer.

Cooking

Place the hot pot in a large pot and pour in boiling water to about 4cm (1½″) below the lid of the hot pot. Cover the pot and double-boil for 6 hours. The water will boil up into the hot pot through the central spout and will almost fill the hot pot.

Add the seasonings just before serving.

Bamboo Fungus Soup
Chu Sheng Szu Pao T'ang 竹笙四寶湯
Serves 6-8

15 g (½ oz)	bamboo fungus, soaked
45 g (1½ oz)	fresh straw mushrooms
60 g (2 oz)	chicken gizzard, diced
60 g (2 oz)	chicken fillet, diced
60 g (2 oz)	pork loin, diced
60 g (2 oz)	ham, diced
45 g (1½ oz)	bamboo shoots, diced
1¼ lit (40 fl oz)	water
	rice paper

Seasoning

1 tsp	salt
¼ tsp	monosodium glutamate
½ tsp	Shao Hsing wine

Preparation

Drain bamboo fungus, then soak in boiling water for 15 minutes. Drain again.

Thoroughly wash the straw mushrooms and trim the bases. Cut into dice.

Place all the diced ingredients in a casserole and add the seasoning, ginger and scallion. Pour in the water and cover the bowl with rice paper. Tie in place with string or use a flour and water paste to glue it to the bowl.

Cooking

Place the bowl in a steamer and steam over moderately high heat for 3 hours. Skim off any excess oil before serving.

"Tung-po's soup is a vegetable soup that he cooked when he was living in retirement. It did not contain fish or meat or the five flavourings, but it had a natural sweetness."

In Praise of Tung-po's Soup — *Su Shih*

Cubed Chicken and Noodles in Soup
Nun Chi Wei Mien 嫩鷄煨麪
Serves 6-8

440 g (1 4 oz)	thin Shanghai noodles
375 g (12 oz)	cooked chicken, 2cm (¾″) cubes
625 g (1¼ lb)	Chinese white cabbage, chopped
2 tbsp	cooked oil

Seasoning

½ tsp	sugar
½ tsp	salt
2 tsp	Shao Hsing wine

Soup

1 tsp	salt
½ tsp	monosodium glutamate
2 tsp	light soy sauce
1½ lit (48 fl oz)	chicken stock

Preparation

Drop noodles into boiling water and bring back to the boil. Stir to loosen the bundles, add in several tablespoons cold water and boil for 3-4 minutes until noodles are just tender. Drain and divide between 6-8 large soup bowls. Set aside.

Cooking

Heat the wok, add the oil and stir-fry chicken for 1½ minutes. Remove, add the cabbage and stir-fry for 1 minute. Add the seasoning ingredients and stir-fry briefly, then return the chicken and stir-fry together until chicken and vegetables are cooked.

Note: If preferred, the noodles may be simmered in the soup stock until tender.

Duck Carcass Soup
Ya Ku T'ang 鴨骨湯
Serves 12

1	whole duck carcass (normally from a carved Peking duck)
155 g (5 oz)	winter melon, thinly sliced
1 slice	ginger
1	scallion, 5cm (2") pieces
1½ lit (48 fl oz)	chicken stock
1 tbsp	evaporated milk
1 tbsp	cooked oil
Seasoning	
½ tsp	salt
½ tsp	monosodium glutamate
1 tbsp	Shao Hsing wine

Preparation
Chop the duck carcass into 4cm (1½") pieces.

Cooking
Bring chicken stock to the boil and add oil, ginger and scallion. Boil for 1-2 minutes, then add seasoning ingredients and the duck and melon pieces. Cover and simmer for 4-5 minutes. Skim fat and froth from the surface of the soup. Stir in evaporated milk and serve.

Chicken Blood in Soup
Chi Hung T'ang 鷄紅湯
Serves 6-8

185 g (6 oz)	coagulated chicken blood, thinly sliced
45 g (1½ oz)	chicken fillet, thinly sliced
30 g (1 oz)	chicken gizzard, boiled and sliced
30 g (1 oz)	fresh shrimps, peeled
30 g (1 oz)	broccoli heads, quartered
30 g (1 oz)	canned bamboo shoots, sliced
2	dried black mushrooms, soaked and sliced
1 tsp	ginger, minced
1 tsp	scallion, minced
1 lit (32 fl oz)	chicken stock
1 tbsp	cooked oil
Seasoning	
1 tsp	salt
¼ tsp	white pepper
¼ tsp	monosodium glutamate
1 tsp	Shao Hsing wine

Preparation
Blanch chicken blood, chicken fillet, chicken gizzard and shrimp in boiling water for 1 minute. Drain well.

Cooking
Bring chicken stock to the boil, add oil and seasonings, then add blanched ingredients with broccoli, bamboo shoots and drained mushrooms. Bring to the boil and simmer until the broccoli is tender, about 2 minutes. Add scallion and ginger and heat through. Transfer to a serving bowl or tureen and serve.

"No food is really enjoyed unless it is keenly anticipated, discussed, eaten and then commented upon."

Lin Yutang

Vermicelli and Fried Beancurd Soup
Yu Tou Fu Fen Ssu T'ang 油豆腐粉絲湯
Makes 6-8 servings

315 g (10 oz)	dried bean thread vermicelli
18	fried beancurd cubes
125 g (4 oz)	lean pork, shredded
125 g (4 oz)	dried shrimps, soaked
6	dried black mushrooms, soaked and sliced
1½ lit (48 fl oz)	chicken stock
Seasoning	
1 tsp	monosodium glutamate
2 tbsp	dark soy sauce
1 tbsp	Shao Hsing wine
1 tsp	sesame oil

Preparation
Soak bean thread vermicelli in warm water to soften, about 5 minutes. Drain well.

Cooking
Bring stock to the boil and add beancurd cubes, pork, shrimps and mushrooms. Boil for 1 minute, then add in seasoning ingredients and boil for another minute.
Add vermicelli and simmer until tender. Serve in separate bowls.

On the third day, I enter the kitchen,
Washing my hands to prepare the soup.
I do not know my mother-in-law's palate yet,
So I ask my husband's sister to have a taste first.

Wang Chien

Beancurd with Shredded Pork in Soup — *recipe on page 201.*

A bowl of fish soup isn't worth more than a
    few cents;
Yet, made as in the days of the former
    capital, it brings smiles to the imperial
    face.
So people come in droves to buy it at twice
    the price;
In part, they are buying the imperial
    gesture, and in part they buy the
    soup.

Ming Dynasty Poem

"For each meal, be it congee or rice, think of
its origin and the hardship."

Chinese Proverb

Beancurd with Shredded Pork in Soup
Jou Ssu Tou Fu Keung 肉絲豆腐羹
Serves 6-8

90 g (3 oz)	lean pork, shredded
250 g (8 oz)	soft beancurd, 1.5cm (½″) dice
30 g (1 oz)	dried black mushrooms, soaked and sliced
2 slices	ginger, shredded
3	chive shoots, 5cm (2″) pieces
1¼ lit (40 fl oz)	water
1 tbsp	cooked oil
	few drops sesame oil

Seasoning

½ tsp	salt
½ tsp	monosodium glutamate
1 tbsp	dark soy sauce
1 tsp	Shao Hsing wine

Thickening — mix together

1 tbsp	cornstarch
2 tbsp	water

Preparation and Cooking
Soak beancurd in cold water for 1 minute, drain
well. Bring stock to boil and add pork. Boil for 2
minutes, then reduce heat slightly and add
seasonings with mushroom, ginger and oil.
Simmer on moderate heat for 2 minutes, then
skim the surface of the soup and add in thickening.
Stir until the soup has become clear, then add
beancurd and chive shoots and simmer until
heated through. Sprinkle on sesame oil and serve.

Hot and Sour Soup
Suan La T'ang 酸辣湯
Serves 6-8

2 squares	soft beancurd, thinly sliced
60 g (2 oz)	coagulated chicken blood, thinly sliced
15 g (½ oz)	lean pork, shredded
15 g (½ oz)	dried beche-de-mer, soaked, cleaned and shredded*
30 g (1 oz)	canned bamboo shoots, sliced
5 g (⅙ oz)	cloud ear fungus, soaked
45 g (1½ oz)	fresh shrimps, peeled
1	scallion, minced
1	egg, beaten

Stock

½ tsp	salt
½ tsp	monosodium glutamate
½ tsp	dark soy sauce
1 tbsp	light soy sauce
½ tsp	Shao Hsing wine
625 ml (20 fl oz)	chicken stock

Seasoning

1½ tsbp	black vinegar
1 tsp	chilli oil
¼ tsp	sesame oil

Thickening — mix together

1 tbsp	cornstarch
2 tbsp	water

Preparation
Blanch beancurd in hot water for a few seconds
and drain well. Blanch chicken blood, pork, beche-
de-mer, bamboo shoot and cloud ear fungus in
boiling water for 1 minute. Drain.

Cooking
Mix stock ingredients in a large saucepan and add
the blanched ingredients. Bring to the boil, then
add thickening, seasoning ingredients and beancurd.
Bring back to the boil, stirring, then add shrimps
and minced scallion and cook for 1 minute.
Remove from the heat and pour in beaten egg,
stirring gently. Leave to set in threads in the soup,
then reheat briefly and serve.

Note: *For method of preparing beche-de-mer,
    see page 185.

"To quench the thirst, drink broth; to dispel
melancholy, drink wine; to obtain voluptous
sleep, drink tea."

Su I

Yellow Fish in Soup
Tai T'ang Huang Yu 大湯黃魚
Serves 6-8

500 g (1 lb)	yellow river carp
60 g (2 oz)	canned bamboo shoots, shredded
60 g (2 oz)	preserved Shanghai vegetable, shredded
3 slices	ginger
2	scallions
1¼ lit (40 fl oz)	water
3 tbsp	cooked oil

Seasoning

½ tsp	salt
¼ tsp	monosodium glutamate
2 tsp	Shao Hsing wine

Preparation
Scale, clean and thoroughly wash the fish. Score diagonally across the body, then cut in halves at the same angle.

Cooking
Heat the wok, add oil and when very hot stir-fry ginger and scallion briefly, then put in the fish pieces and fry on both sides until lightly coloured. Move to one side of the pan, then add the bamboo shoots and preserved vegetable with the seasoning

ingredients. Add water, cover and bring to the boil. Reduce heat and simmer for 10 minutes.

Remove ginger and scallion before serving.

"Don't eat yellow fish with buckwheat".

Chinese Proverb.

Vermicelli and Fried Beancurd Soup — *recipe on page 19*

Vegetables Braised with Chicken Fat
Chi Yu Pai Ts'ai 鷄油白菜
Serves 6-8

750 g (1½ lb)	Chinese white cabbage
45 g (1½ oz)	Yunnan ham, thinly sliced
4 tsp	rendered chicken fat*
2 tbsp	cooked oil

Sauce

½ tsp	salt
¼ tsp	monosodium glutamate
125 ml (4 fl oz)	chicken stock

Thickening — mix together

| 1 tsp | cornstarch |
| 1 tbsp | water |

Preparation
Wash cabbage, discard damaged leaves and cut stems into 8cm (3″) pieces. Cut thick stalks in halves lengthways. Blanch in boiling water for ½ minute and drain well. Mix sauce ingredients.

Cooking
Heat the wok, add cooked oil and half the chicken fat and when very hot stir-fry the cabbage for ½ minute. Arrange sliced ham on top, pour in the sauce, cover and simmer on low heat for 5 minutes. Increase heat, uncover and baste cabbage with the sauce, for ½ minute. Pour in thickening and cook until sauce thickens. Add chicken fat and heat briefly.

Arrange vegetables on a serving plate with ham overlapped on top. Pour on the sauce. Serve.

Note: *For method of preparing rendered chicken fat, see page 278.

Vegetables Braised with Chicken Fat

Braised Marrow with Conpoy Sauce

Yao Chu P'a Chieh Kua 瑤柱扒節瓜
Serves 6-8

750 g (1½ lb)	Chinese marrow (hairy gourd)
45 g (1½ oz)	dried conpoy, soaked
30 g (1 oz)	dried shrimps, soaked
2 tsp	salt
	oil for deep-frying

Sauce

½ tsp	sugar
½ tsp	monosodium glutamate
1 tsp	Shao Hsing wine
1 tbsp	oyster sauce
100 ml (3 fl oz)	chicken stock

Thickening — mix together

1 tsp	cornstarch
1 tbsp	water

Preparation and Cooking

Remove skin and seeds from marrow and cut into 10cm (4″) strips. Heat the wok, add the oil and when very hot deep-fry marrow for 1 minute. Remove and place in a saucepan. Add drained dried shrimps and salt and cover with cold water. Bring to the boil and cook on moderate heat for 20-25 minutes. Steam conpoy until softened, then break into shreds. Remove marrow from the pot, drain and place in a serving dish. Discard ingredients remaining in the pot.

Pour off oil from the wok. Heat the wok, add sauce ingredients and conpoy and bring to the boil. Add thickening and stir until the sauce thickens. Pour over the marrow and serve.

Stir-Fried Seasonal Vegetables

Ch'ao Yu Ts'ai 炒油菜
Serves 6

1 kg (2 lb)	flowering white cabbage
2 tsp	salt
5 tbsp	cooked oil

Preparation

Wash vegetables and cut off flowers and thick ends of stems, leaving about 10cm (4″) of the shoots (they will weigh about 375 g/12 oz).

Cooking

Blanch vegetables in boiling water with 2 tbsp oil added, for 1 minute. Remove, drain until dry.

Heat the wok and add remaining oil. Add vegetables with salt and stir-fry for 2 minutes on high heat, until the vegetables turn a deeper green. Serve.

Fried Beancurd

Kwo T'a Tou Fu 鍋蹋豆腐
Serves 6-8

6 squares	soft beancurd
3 tbsp	all purpose flour
2-3	eggs
1 tsp	ginger, minced
1 tsp	scallion, minced
2 tsp	dried shrimp caviar (roe)
½ tsp	sesame oil
	oil for deep-frying

Seasoning A

½ tsp	monosodium glutamate
1 tsp	Shao Hsing wine
1 tsp	sesame oil
	pinch of salt

Seasoning B

¼ tsp	sugar
¼ tsp	salt
¼ tsp	monosodium glutamate
¼ tsp	dark soy sauce
1 tbsp	light soy sauce
100 ml (3 fl oz)	chicken stock

Preparation

Cut beancurd into 2.5cm x 1.5cm (1″ x ½″) pieces. Mix the seasoning A ingredients, pour over the beancurd and leave for 5 minutes. Coat each cube of beancurd with flour, then dip into beaten egg.

Mix the seasoning B ingredients and set aside.

Cooking

Heat the wok, add oil and when very hot reduce heat slightly and deep-fry beancurd, several pieces at a time to keep oil bubbling, until golden. Drain and set aside.

Discard most of the oil, reheat the wok and stir-fry ginger and scallion for ½ minute. Add shrimp caviar and seasoning B and bring to the boil. Return the beancurd. Add sesame oil, cover and simmer for 2 minutes. Remove the lid and continue to cook until the liquid is absorbed. Transfer to a serving plate. Serve.

Bitter Melon Rings Stuffed with Shrimp Paste

Pai Hua Chien Niang Liang Kua Fu

百花煎釀涼瓜甫

Serves 6-8

4	fresh bitter melons (about 440 g/14 oz)
185 g (6 oz)	shrimp meat
1 clove	garlic, sliced
2 tbsp	cooked oil
	large pinch bicarbonate of soda
	cornstarch

Seasoning A

1 tsp	salt
2 tsp	cornstarch
⅓ tsp	monosodium glutamate
	few drops sesame oil
	dash pepper

Seasoning B

1 tsp	sugar
½ tsp	monosodium glutamate
½ tsp	dark soy sauce
20 g (¾ oz)	black beans, mashed
125 ml (4 fl oz)	chicken stock
	dash salt
	few drops sesame oil

Thickening — mix together

1 tsp	cornstarch
1 tbsp	water

Preparation

Cut bitter melon into 1.5cm (½″) slices, seed and wash thoroughly. Cover with boiling water, add the soda and boil for 2-3 minutes. (This will brighten the colour of the melon skin). Drain, rinse in cold water, drain and leave to cool. Dry well and dust inside each melon ring with cornstarch.

Wash shrimp and pound in a mortar or with the side of a cleaver on a chopping board to make a smooth paste. Combine with seasoning A ingredients, mixing well. Stuff a little of the mixture into the centre of each melon ring, smoothing the tops. Wipe the melon rings to remove any traces of stuffing. Mix seasoning B ingredients and set aside.

Cooking

Heat the wok until it smokes, add the oil and when very hot lower heat slightly. Put in the melon rings and fry for 2-3 minutes. Turn to other side and fry for 2 minutes longer. Remove and place on a serving dish.

Add sliced garlic to the pan and stir-fry briefly, adding a little more oil if the pan is dry. Add seasoning B and the thickening and cook, stirring, on high heat until the sauce thickens. Pour over the melon rings and serve.

206

Below left: Spicy Beancurd with Ground Pork — *recipe on page 208;* 'Family Meal' Beancurd — *recipe on page 208.*
Below right: Braised Marrow with Conpoy Sauce — *recipe on page 204.* Deep-Fried Bamboo Shoots, Salted Cabbage and Conpoy — *recipe on page 209;*

'Family Meal' Beancurd
Chia Ch'ang Tou Fu 家常豆腐
Serves 6-8

4 squares	soft beancurd
1	green capsicum, 2.5cm (1″) squares
1	leek, 4cm (1½″) diagonal slices
1	red chilli, thinly sliced
1 clove	garlic, finely chopped
45 g (1½ oz)	dried black mushrooms, soaked and sliced
30 g (1 oz)	canned bamboo shoots, thinly sliced
45 g (1½ oz)	lean pork, thinly sliced
1 tsp	hot bean paste
1 tsp	dark soy sauce
4 tbsp	cooked oil
Sauce	
¼ tsp	sugar
½ tsp	monosodium glutamate
1 tsp	dark soy sauce
1 tsp	Shao Hsing wine
125 ml (4 fl oz)	chicken stock
Thickening — mix together	
2 tsp	cornstarch
1½ tbsp	water

Preparation
Cut beancurd into triangular quarters, soak in cold water for 1 minute, then drain. Mix sauce ingredients and set aside.

Cooking
Heat the wok, add 3 tbsp oil and when smoking, reduce heat slightly and fry beancurd on all sides until golden. Drain and set aside. Reheat the wok and add remaining oil. Stir-fry mushrooms, bamboo shoots and pork with hot bean paste for 1 minute. Add chilli, garlic, capsicum and leek and stir-fry for 1 minute longer. Return the beancurd and pour in the sauce. Bring to the boil, add thickening and stir over moderate heat until sauce thickens. Sprinkle in soy sauce, heat briefly and serve.

"Shih (salted, darkened soya beans) is very popular in a vast area of China; especially among the rustic population leading a very simple life ... It was almost the only relish they can afford to enjoy."

Shih Sheng-han

"From soybeans a good crop can easily be secured even in adverse years, therefore it is quite natural for the ancient people to grow soy as a provision against famine."

Fan Sheng-chih

Spicy Beancurd with Ground Pork
Ma P'o Tou Fu 麻婆豆腐

Serves 6-8

4	squares soft beancurd
125 g (4 oz)	lean pork, coarsely minced
1	leek, 2.5cm (1″) diagonal slices
1 tsp	scallion, minced
2 cloves	garlic, minced
3 tbsp	cooked oil
	few drops sesame oil
Seasoning	
½ tsp	salt
⅓ tsp	monosodium glutamate
¼ tsp	dark soy sauce
1 tsp	hot bean paste
100 ml (3 fl oz)	chicken stock
Thickening — mix together	
1 tsp	cornstarch
1 tbsp	water

Preparation
Cut beancurd into 2.5cm (1″) cubes. Soak in cold water for 1 minute, then drain. Mix seasoning ingredients and set aside.

Cooking
Heat the wok and add 2 tbsp cooked oil. When smoking, reduce heat slightly and fry leek for 1 minute. Remove and set aside. Add pork with remaining oil, scallion and garlic and stir-fry for 1 minute. Return leek and add the seasoning and bring to the boil.

Add the cubed beancurd, lower heat and simmer, covered, for 2½-3 minutes. Add thickening and stir gently until thickened. Sprinkle on sesame oil and serve.

Note: Ma P'o Tou Fu is one of the most well known Szechwan dishes, believed to have been created by a woman by the name of Chen some 400 years ago.

This dish may also be made with beef.

Deep-Fried Bamboo Shoots, Salted Cabbage and Conpoy

Kan Shao Erh Sung Tung Sun 干燒二鬆冬筍
Serves 6-8

185 g (6 oz)	canned bamboo shoots, drained
125 g (4 oz)	Shanghai salted cabbage, soaked
45 g (1½ oz)	conpoy, soaked
315 ml (10 fl oz)	chicken stock
	oil for deep-frying

Seasoning A

½ tsp	sugar
1 tsp	monosodium glutamate
1 tbsp	Shao Hsing wine

Seasoning B

½ tsp	sugar
½ tsp	monosodium glutamate

Preparation and Cooking

Cut bamboo shoots into 5cm x 1.5cm (2″ x ½″) pieces. Boil salted vegetables in water for 10 minutes. Drain and cut into 2cm (¾″) pieces. Steam conpoy over rapidly boiling water until tender. Bring chicken stock to the boil and add bamboo shoots and salt vegetable. Boil for 10 minutes, adding seasoning A ingredients after first minute. Drain well and leave to dry.

Heat the wok, add oil and when very hot deep-fry salt vegetable for about 1 minute. Remove and drain well. Add bamboo shoots and deep-fry until golden, about 4 minutes. Remove, drain and place with the salted vegetable. Flake conpoy with the fingers and place in a wire mesh strainer. Lower into the hot oil and deep-fry until crisp, about 2 minutes.

Mix conpoy, salted cabbage and bamboo shoots together in a serving dish. Sprinkle on seasoning B ingredients and serve.

When you boil beans

By burning their own stalks

The beans will weep

Even in the Pot.

Verily they grew

From the same root —

Why should they hasten

To burn their brothers?

Ts'ao Chih.

Braised Chinese Cabbage with Chestnuts

Li Tzu Shao Pai Ts'ai 栗子燒白菜
Serves 6-8

500 g (1 lb)	Chinese white cabbage
125 g (4 oz)	chestnut kernels, boiled to soften
½ tsp	ginger, minced
½ tsp	scallion, minced
250 ml (8 fl oz)	chicken stock
2 tbsp	cooked oil
	pinch bicarbonate of soda
	oil for deep-frying

Seasoning A

½ tsp	sugar
½ tsp	salt
¼ tsp	monsodium glutamate
1 tbsp	light soy sauce

Seasoning B

1 tsp	sugar
¼ tsp	salt
¼ tsp	monosodium glatamate
1 tsp	dark soy sauce
1 tbsp	Shao Hsing wine
75 ml (2½ fl oz)	chicken stock

Thickening — mix together

2 tsp	cornstarch
1 tbsp	water

Preparation

Wash cabbage, discard any damaged leaves and cut into 8cm (3″) pieces. Cut thick stems in halves, lengthways. Blanch in boiling water with a pinch of bicarbonate of soda for 2 minutes, remove and drain very well. Mix seasoning A and seasoning B ingredients and set aside.

Cooking

Heat the wok, add deep frying oil and when very hot deep-fry cabbage until it turns golden, about 1 minute. Drain, and set aside. Add chestnuts to the oil and deep-fry for 2-3 minutes until deep golden in colour. Drain and discard oil.

Return cabbage and chestnuts to the wok and add chicken stock and seasoning A. Cover and simmer on moderate heat for 10 minutes. Drain and discard stock. Set cabbage and chestnuts aside. Wipe out wok, reheat and add cooked oil and stir-fry ginger and scallion for ½ minute. Add seasoning B and the thickening and return cabbage and chestnuts. Cook, stirring, on moderate heat until sauce boils and thickens. Transfer to a serving dish. Serve.

Note: Tientsin cabbage could be used in place of Chinese white cabbage.

Braised Chinese Cabbage with Chestnuts — *recipe on page 209.*

Braised Beancurd with Mushrooms
Hung Shao Tung Ku Tou Fu 紅燒冬菰豆腐
Serves 6-8

250 g (8 oz)	dried beancurd cubes
45 g (1½ oz)	dried black mushrooms, soaked
60 g (2 oz)	broccoli, broken into florets
3 tbsp	cooked oil
	few drops sesame oil

Sauce

½ tsp	sugar
½ tsp	monsodium glutamate
1 tbsp	dark soy sauce
200 ml (6 fl oz)	chicken stock

Thickening — mix together

1 tbsp	cornstarch
2 tbsp	water

Preparation
Drain mushrooms and remove stems. Steam for 10 minutes over moderately high heat. Blanch broccoli in boiling water for 1 minute. Drain well. Mix the sauce ingredients and set aside.

Cooking
Heat the wok, add the oil and fry the beancurd cubes on all sides until slightly crisp on the surface and beginning to change colour. Add sauce ingredients, reduce heat and simmer for 3 minutes. Add the mushrooms and broccoli and cook for a further 3 minutes. Add in the thickening and cook until the sauce thickens. Sprinkle on sesame oil and serve.

Asparagus and Bamboo Fungus in Cream Sauce
Nai Yu T'ao Erh Sun 奶油套二筍
Serves 6

12 stalks	fresh asparagus
12 pieces	bamboo fungus
200 ml (8 fl oz)	superior stock
2 tbsp	evaporated milk
2 tsp	rendered chicken fat
1 tbsp	diced ham

Seasoning

¼ tsp	salt
¼ tsp	monosodium glutamate

Thickening — mix together

1 tbsp	cornstarch
2 tbsp	water

Preparation
Soak bamboo fungus in warm water until thoroughly softened. Drain and rinse in cold water.

Resoak in boiling water for 15 minutes before using. Trim hard ends of asparagus and scrape off any rough skin.

Insert a stalk of asparagus into the centre of each piece of bamboo fungus.

Cooking
Place the asparagus-stuffed bamboo fungus in a saucepan and cover with the chicken stock. Bring to the boil, reduce heat and simmer until the asparagus is tender, about 20 minutes. Remove, drain and reserve the stock, cut the stalks in halves and arrange on a serving plate.

Add the seasoning ingredients to the stock with thickening and return to the boil. Cook until thickened. Reduce heat, add the evaporated milk with chicken fat and heat through. Pour over the vegetables and sprinkle with minced ham. Serve.

Stewed Cabbage in Cream Sauce
Nai Yu P'a Chin Ts'ai 奶油扒津菜
Serves 6-8

375 g (12 oz)	Tientsin cabbage
½ tsp	ginger, minced
½ tsp	scallion, minced
150 ml (5 fl oz)	chicken stock
2½ tsp	rendered chicken fat
2 tbsp	evaporated milk
1 tbsp	cooked oil

Seasoning

½ tsp	sugar
¼ tsp	salt
¼ tsp	monosodium glutamate
1 tbsp	Shao Hsing wine

Thickening — mix together

2 tsp	cornstarch
1½ tbsp	water

Preparation
Wash cabbage, trim ends of stalks and any damaged leaves and cut into strips about 10cm x 1.5cm (4" x ½"). Place in a lightly oiled dish and steam over high heat for 15 minutes. Drain and set aside.

Cooking
Heat the wok, add oil and stir-fry ginger and scallion for ½ minute. Add stock and seasoning ingredients and bring to the boil. Add cabbage, lower heat and stew for 4-5 minutes. Add thickening and boil until the sauce thickens, then stir in rendered chicken fat and evaporated milk. Heat through and transfer to a serving dish. Serve.

Braised Mushrooms with Vegetables
Hsien Ku P'a Shih Ts'ai 鮮菇扒時菜
Serves 6-8

185 g (6 oz)	fresh straw mushrooms
250 g (8 oz)	flowering white or Chinese white cabbage
100 ml (3 fl oz)	superior stock
¾ tsp	salt
2 tbsp	cooked oil

Seasoning

1 tsp	sugar
¼ tsp	salt
1 tsp	monosodium glutamate
1 tsp	dark soy sauce
2 tbsp	oyster sauce
2 tbsp	cooked oil

Thickening — mix together

1 tsp	cornstarch
1 tbsp	water

Preparation
Trim root ends of mushrooms and wash well. Place in a pan of cold water and bring to boil. Cook for 1 minute, then drain. Trim flowers and thick lower stems of the cabbage and blanch in boiling water with 2 tsp oil added for 1 minute. Remove and drain. Mix seasoning ingredients and set aside.

Cooking
Heat the wok, add the remaining oil and salt and stir-fry the cabbage for 1 minute on high heat. Drain and arrange in the centre of a serving plate. Reheat the wok, add seasoning, superior stock and mushrooms and bring to the boil. Add thickening and stir until the sauce coats the mushrooms. Remove from heat and pour onto the vegetables. Serve.

Stir-Fried Bamboo Shoots with Shrimp Caviar
Hsia Tzu Tung Sun 蝦子冬筍
Serves 6-8

500 g (1 lb) can	winter bamboo shoots, drained
30 g (1 oz)	dried shrimp caviar (roe), soaked
125 g (4 oz)	flowering white cabbage
50 ml (1½ fl oz)	chicken stock
3 tbsp	cooked oil

Seasoning

1 tsp	sugar
¾ tsp	salt
¾ tsp	monosodium glutamate
1 tsp	dark soy sauce
2 tbsp	oyster sauce

Thickening — mix together

½ tsp	cornstarch
2 tsp	water

Preparation
Boil bamboo shoots in enough water to cover, for 2 minutes. Remove, drain and cut into wedges. Trim off flowers and thick lower stems of cabbage and drop into the same pot, with 1 tbsp cooked oil added, to blanch for 1½ minutes. Remove, drain and arrange around the rim of a serving plate. Mix seasoning ingredients and set aside.

Cooking
Heat the wok, add remaining oil and, when very hot, reduce heat slightly and stir-fry drained shrimp caviar for a few seconds. Add the bamboo shoots with seasoning and stir-fry for 2 minutes, then add chicken stock and thickening and stir on moderately high heat until the sauce thickens. Pile bamboo shoots in the centre of the plate and serve.

Agriculture

In the sixth month we eat wild plums and
    cherries,
In the seventh month we boil mallows and
    beans.
In the eighth month we dry the dates,
In the tenth month we take the rice
To make with it the spring wine,
So that we may be granted long life.
In the seventh month we eat melons,
In the eighth month we cut the gourds,
In the ninth month we take the seeding
    hemp,
We gather bitter herbs, we cut the ailanto
    for firewood,
That our husbandmen may eat.

The Book of Songs

Cheng Tu Vegetarian Stew

Cheng Tu Shang Su Hui 成都上素會

Serves 6-8

75 g (2½ oz)	carrots, cube-cut
250 g (8 oz)	young Chinese white cabbage
75 g (2½ oz)	canned bamboo shoots, sliced
30 g (1 oz)	dried black mushrooms, soaked
60 g (2 oz)	fresh straw mushrooms, halved
60 g (2 oz)	canned button mushrooms, drained
7 g (¼ oz)	dried cloud ear fungus, soaked
7 g (¼ oz)	dried white fungus, soaked
60 g (2 oz)	young broad beans
2 medium	tomatoes
6 stalks	canned asparagus, drained
1 tbsp	rendered chicken fat
4 tbsp	cooked oil
	pinch bicarbonate of soda

Seasoning

½ tsp	salt
½ tsp	monosodium glutamate
1 tsp	Shao Hsing wine
150 ml (5 fl oz)	chicken stock

Thickening — mix together

2 tsp	cornstarch
1 tbsp	water

Preparation

Boil carrots until cooked, then drain, place in cold water and set aside. Wash cabbage, discard outer and any damaged leaves and boil with a pinch of bicarbonate of soda for 1½ minutes. Drain, splash with cold water to brighten colour, and set aside. Boil bamboo shoots for ½ minute in slightly salted water, drain and set aside. Add black and straw mushrooms to the pot and boil for 1 minute. drain. Soak cloud ear and white fungus in boiling water to soften. Drop tomatoes into boiling water, lift out and peel off skin, then cut into quarters. Boil broad beans until the skins loosen, drain and rub off skins, then boil again until tender. Drain and set aside. Mix seasoning ingredients.

Cooking

Heat the wok, add the cooked oil and when very hot reduce heat slightly and stir-fry carrot, cabbage, bamboo shoots, mushrooms and beans for 1 minute. Add drained fungus, tomatoes and the seasoning, cover and simmer until all ingredients are tender, about 1 minute. Add thickening and stir until the sauce becomes clear. Add asparagus and heat through briefly. Transfer to a serving plate.

Wipe out the wok, heat chicken fat until very hot and pour over the vegetables. Serve.

Note: A colourful dish usually served after aromatic or strong tasting dishes.

Beancurd Stuffed with Shrimp Paste
Pai Hua Niang Tou Fu 百花釀豆腐
Serves 6-8

5 cubes	fresh soft beancurd
125 g (4 oz)	shrimp meat
185 g (6 oz)	flowering white cabbage
	cornstarch
1 tbsp	cooked oil

Seasoning

½ tsp	salt
¼ tsp	monosodium glutamate
2 tsp	cornstarch
	dash white pepper

Sauce

2 tsp	dark soy sauce
1 tbsp	light soy sauce
3 tbsp	chicken stock
1 tbsp	cooked oil

Thickening — mix together

½ tsp	cornstarch
2 tsp	water

Preparation

Pound shrimp meat in a mortar or with the side of a cleaver on a chopping board to make a smooth paste. Mix with the seasoning ingredients and work until smooth.

Cut each piece of beancurd into four triangular pieces and cut a slit in the widest side of each section. Sprinkle inside the slit with cornstarch, then stuff with a portion of the shrimp paste, flattening the filling on the outer surface. Trim flowers and thick lower stems of cabbage, wash and drain.

Cooking

Place beancurd on an oiled plate and steam for 4-5 minutes over moderately high heat. Blanch vegetables in boiling water with 1 tbsp cooked oil added, for 1½ minutes. Drain and place around the rim of a serving dish. Heat sauce ingredients to boiling. Add thickening and cook until clear. Place steamed beancurd in the centre of the dish and pour on the hot sauce. Serve.

Beancurd Stuffed with Shrimp Paste.

Stir-Fried Eggs with Shredded Meat, Cloud Ear Fungus and Vegetables.

Stir-Fried Eggs with Shredded Meat, Cloud Ear Fungus and Vegetables
Mu Hsu Jou 木須肉
Serves 6-8

4	eggs
90 g (3 oz)	lean pork, shredded
45 g (1½ oz)	dried cloud ear fungus, soaked
185 g (6 oz)	Chinese white cabbage
1	scallion, 1.5cm (½") pieces
1-2 sprigs	Chinese parsley, chopped (optional)
4 tbsp	cooked oil
Seasoning A	
½ tsp	salt
½ tsp	dark soy sauce
1 tsp	cornstarch
Seasoning B	
½ tsp	salt
½ tsp	monosodium glutamate
2 tsp	dark soy sauce
½ tsp	Shao Hsing wine

Preparation
Lightly beat eggs. Marinate pork with the seasoning A ingredients for 10 minutes. Drain cloud ear fungus and cut larger pieces in halves. Wash cabbage discarding outer or damaged leaves and chop coarsely.

Cooking
Heat the wok, add 2 tbsp oil and pour in the beaten egg. Stir-fry for 4 minutes on moderate heat. Remove and set aside. Reheat the wok, add remaining oil and stir-fry scallion with pork and cloud ear fungus for 1 minute. Remove. Add cabbage and stir-fry for 1 minute, then cover and cook on moderate heat, turning occasionally, until tender, about 5 minutes. Return the egg, pork scallion and cloud ears and add parsley, if used. Add the seasoning B ingredients and stir-fry for ½-1 minute, then transfer to a serving plate. Serve.

Fried Eggs Whampoa
Ch'ao Huang P'u Tan 炒黃埔蛋
Serves 6-8

12	eggs
1¾ tsp	salt
6 tbsp	cooked oil

Preparation
Break eggs into a bowl, add salt and beat lightly.

Cooking
Heat the wok and add 2 tbsp oil. When very hot, reduce heat slightly and pour in eggs. Stir-fry for a few seconds, then pour another 2 tbsp oil around the edge of the eggs. Continue to stir fry, then add the remaining 2 tbsp oil in the same way and stir-fry until the egg has just set.

Transfer to a serving plate and decorate with sprigs of parsley. Serve.

Being a daughter-in-law is difficult:
However early I rise, I am said to be late.
With undried tears I go into the kitchen.
In the kitchen there is a small melon.
Mother-in-law says to baste it,
Sister-in-law says to steam it,
Yet neither basting nor steaming suits my lord's taste.

Traditional Cantonese Rhyme

Tea Eggs
Ch'a Yeh Tan 茶葉蛋
Serves 12

12	eggs
3 tbsp	black tea leaves
Seasoning	
2 pc	cinnamon bark, about 4cm (1½")
3	anise stars
½ tsp	monosodium glutamate
2 tsp	dark soy sauce
2½ tbsp	light soy sauce

Preparation and Cooking
Place eggs in cold water to cover and boil until hard, about 10 minutes. Drain and rinse with cold water.

Tap the shells gently all over to completely marble the shells with tiny cracks.

Bring enough water to cover eggs to the boil, add tea leaves with seasonings. Put in the eggs and simmer on moderate heat with the liquid just boiling, for at least 1 hour. Drain and cool before serving.

217

Miscellaneous

Clams in Egg Custard
Ke Li Cheng Tan 蛤蜊蒸蛋
Serves 6-8

375 g (12 oz)	clams, in shells
8	eggs
315 ml (10 fl oz)	boiling water
315 ml (10 fl oz)	water or chicken stock
2 tsp	cooked oil

Seasoning:

1 tsp	salt
¼ tsp	monosodium glutamate
1 tsp	Shao Hsing wine
	dash white pepper

Preparation and Cooking
Scrub clams under running water. Place in a pot of boiling water and cook until the shells are half opened. Shake pan while cooking to help open shells. Prise open with a knife and wash with cold water.

Beat eggs in a bowl, add seasoning ingredients and the boiled water and water or chicken stock. Add the cooked clams and set the bowl in a steamer. Cover and cook over high heat for 15 minutes.

Sprinkle the cooked oil over the custard. Serve.

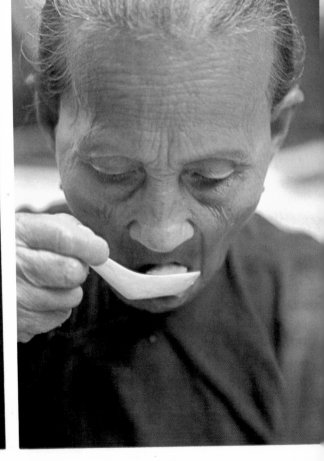

Braised Bird's Nest with Pigeons' Eggs — *recipe on page 222.*

Clams in Egg Custard.

Fish Dressed as Crab
Sai P'ang Hsieh 賽螃蟹
Serves 6-8

8	egg whites
125 g (4 oz)	fillet of dace, or other white fish
45 g (1½ oz)	conpoy, soaked until soft
45 g (1½ oz)	cooked crabmeat (optional)
½ tsp	ginger, minced
½ tsp	scallion, minced
2 tsp	Chinese parsley, finely chopped
3	lettuce leaves
1	egg yolk
3 tbsp	oil

Seasoning A

½ tsp	salt
1 tsp	monosodium glutamate
1 tbsp	Shao Hsing wine
1 tsp	black vinegar
1 tbsp	chicken stock
1½ tsp	cornstarch

Seasoning B

1 tsp	sugar
¼ tsp	salt
½ tsp	monosodium glutamate
1 tsp	light soy sauce
2 tsp	Shao Hsing wine
1 tsp	red vinegar
2 tbsp	chicken stock
¾ tsp	cornstarch

Preparation

Lightly beat egg whites. Cut fish into slivers and add to the egg with shredded conpoy and crabmeat and seasoning A ingredients. Mix seasoning B ingredients and set aside.

Cooking

Heat the wok, add 1 tbsp oil and fry ginger and scallion briefly. Add remaining oil and pour in the egg mixture, adding Chinese parsley, and stir-fry on moderate heat until the egg begins to set, about 1 minute. Cover and cook on moderate to low heat, stirring frequently, for another 2 minutes. Pour in seasoning B and stir-fry until the egg is firm and there is a thin sauce in the pan.

Spoon the egg mixture over the lettuce leaves in a shallow serving dish, make a shallow well in the centre and drop in the egg yolk.

Note: This is an inexpensive substitute for stir-fried crab and has the taste and texture of the real thing.

The egg yolk should be stirred into the 'crab' mixture before eating and gives the appearance of crab coral in the dish.

"Don't eat with your ears. By this I mean do not aim at having extraordinary, out-of-the-way foods just to astonish your guests. For that is to eat with the ears, not with the mouth."

Yuen Mai

Stir-Fried Frog's Legs
Ch'ao T'ien Chi Tui 炒田雞腿

Serves 6-8

440 g (14 oz)	prepared frog's legs
5-6 slices	ginger, flower-cut
5-6 slices	carrot, flower-cut
1 clove	garlic, finely chopped
2	scallions, 4cm (1½") strips
3 tbsp	cooked oil
	oil for deep-frying

Seasoning

½ tsp	salt
½ tsp	monosodium glutamate
1 tbsp	cornstarch
1 tbsp	cooked oil

Sauce:

½ tsp	sugar
½ tsp	salt
½ tsp	monosodium glutamate
60 ml (2 fl oz)	chicken stock

Thickening — mix together

1 tsp	cornstarch
1 tbsp	water

Preparation

Skin frog's legs, cut off feet and divide at the pelvic joint, Cut each into two, de-boning if preferred.

Mix the seasoning ingredients and pour over the frog's legs. Leave to marinate for 10 minutes. Mix the sauce ingredients and set aside.

Cooking

Heat the wok, add oil and stir-fry ginger, carrot, garlic and scallion for ½ minute. Add frog's legs and stir-fry for ½ minute longer, then pour in the sauce and cook until frog's legs are tender, about 2 minutes. Add thickening and stir until the sauce thickens and becomes clear. Serve.

Steamed Fish and Beancurd Cake
Lao Shao P'ing An 老少平安
Serves 6-8

185 g (6 oz)	fillet of dace (or other soft white fish)
6 squares	soft beancurd, diced
20 g (¾ oz)	roast pork, diced
20 g (¾ oz)	dried shrimps, soaked
1	scallion, chopped

Seasoning

½ tsp	salt
¾ tsp	monosodium glutamate
1½ tbsp	cornstarch
	dash white pepper

Sauce

2 tsp	sugar
½ tsp	monosodium glutamate
1 tbsp	dark soy sauce
1 tbsp	light soy sauce
2 tbsp	cooked oil

Preparation
Finely chop the fish, discarding any bones and pound to a smooth paste. Drain the dried shrimps and chop finely. Work into the fish paste with seasonings, roast pork and half the chopped scallion and when well blended, add in the beancurd. Transfer to a lightly oiled shallow dish and spread evenly.

Mix sauce ingredients stirring until sugar dissolves and pour into a small bowl.

Cooking
Place the dish in a steamer, cover and steam over moderate heat for 10-15 minutes. Remove and scatter on remaining scallion and add several sprigs of Chinese parsley. Pour sauce over the dish or serve separately.

Steamed Fish and Beancurd Cake.

Firepot, Shanghai Style
Shang Hai Huo Kwo 上海火鍋
Serves 12

625 g (1¼ lb)	Tientsin cabbage
90 g (3 oz)	dried bean thread vermicelli, soaked
90 g (3 oz)	dried beche-de-mer, soaked, cleaned and sliced (*1)
250 g (8 oz)	chicken fillet, sliced
185 g (6 oz)	fresh shrimps, peeled
155 g (5 oz)	pork tripe, boiled (*2)
60 g (2 oz)	chicken liver, sliced and parboiled
12 slices	egg roll stuffed with minced pork (*3)
12	pork meatballs, boiled (*4)
12	fish balls, boiled (*5)
12	thin slices Yunnan ham

Stock

1½ lit (48 fl oz)	superior stock
1½ tsp	salt
½ tsp	monosodium glutamate
1 tbsp	Shao Hsing wine
1 tbsp	melted lard
	dash white pepper

Dip

1 tsp	monosodium glutamate
4 tbsp	light soy sauce
4 tbsp	scallion, minced
2 tbsp	Chinese parsley, finely chopped
1 tbsp	chive shoots, finely chopped (optional)
12	eggs

Preparation

Wash cabbage, separate leaves and cut in halves. Mix dip ingredients, except the eggs and pour into 12 small bowls. Place the eggs in a serving dish (these may be broken, beaten lightly and used as an additional dip).

Place hot charcoal in a fire-pot funnel and set on the table. (A large fondue pot or saucepan over a portable cooking ring will suffice). Pour stock into the fire-pot, add seasonings and bring to the boil.

Arrange the ingredients in the fire-pot with cabbage first and vermicelli on top, then group the other ingredients in the fire-pot. Simmer until done. Serve directly from the fire-pot, dipping the food into the sauce and beaten egg before eating.

Note: *1 For method of preparing beche-de-mer, see page 185

*2 For method of preparing pork tripe, see page 196

*3 For method of making egg roll with minced pork, see next page

*4 For method of making pork meatballs, see next page

*5 For method of making fish meatballs, see next page

Braised Bird's Nest with Pigeons' Eggs
Kuan Yen Ko Tan 官燕鴿蛋
Serves 6-8

90 g (3 oz)	bird's nests
8	pigeons' eggs
2 tbsp	cooked oil
	oil for deep-frying

Seasoning A

1 tsp	salt
1 tsp	monosodium glutamate
2 tbsp	Samshu wine
900 ml (30 fl oz)	chicken stock

Seasoning B

¼ tsp	salt
1 tsp	monosodium glutamate
100 ml (3 fl oz)	chicken stock

Thickening — mix together

1 tsp	cornstarch
2 tsp	water

Preparation

Soak bird's nests in boiled water for 4 hours, changing water two or three times. Pick out any feathers. Drain well. Boil pigeons' eggs until hard cooked, drain and remove shells. Mix the seasoning A ingredients.

Cooking

Heat the wok, add cooked oil and when hot pour in seasoning A and bring to the boil. Add bird's nests, boil for 5 minutes. Drain and place in the centre of a serving plate.

Drain wok, wipe out and add deep-frying oil. When very hot, reduce heat slightly and deep-fry pigeons' eggs until the skin bubbles. Drain and arrange around the bird's nest.

Discard most of the oil (retain only about 1 tablespoon), and reheat the wok. Add seasoning B ingredients with thickening and bring to the boil. Cook until the sauce clears. Pour over the bird's nest. Serve.

Pork/Fish Meatballs
Chu Jou Wan/Yu Tan 肉丸，魚蛋

500 g (1 lb)	lean boneless pork or fish fillets
30 g (1 oz)	pork fat, steamed for 10 minutes
¼ tsp	sugar
½ tsp	monosodium glutamate
1 tsp	salt
1 tsp	ginger wine
1	egg white
1 tbsp	cornstarch
	few drops sesame oil
	dash white pepper

Very finely mince or chop the pork, or chop the fish until it becomes a sticky paste. Very finely chop the pork fat. Mix pork fat and all the remaining ingredients with pork or fish, then lift and drop the mixture forcefully back into the basin. Do this constantly for about 1 minute until the mixture becomes a smooth, sticky paste. To make balls, take the paste in one hand and squeeze a portion out between thumb and forefinger. Scrape the ball off with a spoon and drop into a saucepan of cold water. Bring to the boil and cook until the balls rise to the surface. Remove and drain. Refrigerate or store in a plastic bag in the freezer until needed.

Note: A simple soup can be made with these meatballs, using the basic chicken stock, see page 278. Add a little fresh vegetable and boil for a few minutes.

Pork Sausage
Cha T'i 扎蹄

750 g (1½ lb)	semi fat pork, boneless
625 g (1¼ lb)	pork skin, shaved
3 slices	ginger
2	scallions
1 tbsp	sugar
2 tsp	salt
1 tsp	monosodium glutamate
6 tbsp	light soy sauce
2 tbsp	Shao Hsing wine
1	anise star
2 lit (64 fl oz)	hot water

Scrape any fat from the pork skin and wash very well. Blanch pork and pork skin in boiling water for 5 minutes. Remove, drain and cover with the hot water. Add all ingredients and bring to the boil. Cover and simmer for 1½ hours until the liquid is well reduced and the pork very tender. Remove meat and break into bite-size slivers.

Lift out the pork skin, drain and use to line a 23cm (9″) rectangular baking tin. Pile the pork into the tin on top of the skin. Bring the reserved liquid back to the boil and simmer until reduced to about 625 ml (20 fl oz) strain over the pork and chill until firmly set. Remove from the tin and upturn. Cut in halves, then slice thinly.

"I always say that chicken, pork, fish and duck are the original geniuses of the board, each with a flavour of its own, each with its distinctive style; whereas sea-slug and swallows-nest (despite their costliness) are commonplace fellows with no character — in fact, mere hangers-on."

Yuan Mei

Egg Roll with Minced Meat
Shui Jou Tan Chuan 碎肉蛋卷

5	eggs
250 g (8 oz)	lean pork, finely minced
60 g (2 oz)	fresh shrimp meat, pounded smooth
2	dried black mushrooms, soaked and chopped
1 tsp	sugar
1 tsp	salt
½ tsp	monosodium glutamate
1 tbsp	cornstarch
2 tbsp	water
1 tsp	sesame oil
1 tbsp	cooked oil
	dash white pepper

Lightly beat the eggs and set aside. Mix the remaining ingredients except cooked oil and work well with the fingers to make a smooth sticky paste. Heat the wok and add the oil. Pour in the egg mixture and turn the pan over high heat to make a large, very thin omelette. Cook until just firm, then flip over and cook the other side until lightly coloured. Lift out and leave to cool. Spread with the meat and roll up into a long sausage shape. Place the roll on an oiled plate and set in a steamer. Steam over high heat for 10 minutes. Remove and leave to cool. Cut into 2cm (¾″) slices to serve.

Cantonese Hot Pot

Cantonese Hot Pot
Yueh Shih Huo Kwo 粤式火鍋
Serves 12

185 g (6 oz)	lean beef, very thinly sliced
185 g (6 oz)	lean mutton, very thinly sliced
250 g (8 oz)	chicken or pork fillet, very thinly sliced
125 g (4 oz)	pork liver, thinly sliced
125 g (4 oz)	pork kidney, thinly sliced
185 g (6 oz)	pork tripe, 5cm (2") squares*
185 g (6 oz)	white fish fillets, thinly sliced
4 squares	soft beancurd
250 g (8 oz)	Tientsin cabbage
250 g (8 oz)	spinach or watercress
185 g (6 oz)	lettuce
90 g (3 oz)	boiled peanuts
125 g (4 oz)	bean thread vermicelli, soaked
125 g (4 oz)	scallion, 10cm (4") pieces

Stock

3 slices	ginger
2	scallions
2 tsp	salt
½ tsp	white pepper
1½ lit (48 fl oz)	chicken stock
8 tbsp	cooked oil
12	eggs

Dip

12 tbsp	light soy sauce
1 tbsp	ginger, finely minced
2 tbsp	scallion, finely chopped
2 tbsp	Chinese parsley, coarsely chopped
5-6 tbsp	cooked oil

Preparation

To make the dip, bring soy sauce and oil just to the boil. Add ginger and scallion and leave to cool. Pour into 12 individual sauce dishes and add chopped parsley.

Blanch liver and kidney in boiling water for 2 minutes. Drain well and soak in cold water for 1 minute. Drain. Prepare tripe and boil until tender. Soak beancurd in cold water for 1 minute, drain and cut into 2cm (¾") cubes.

Wash vegetables, remove ends of stems and cut larger leaves in halves. Shake out excess water. Drain vermicelli and place in a serving dish. Arrange the meat, fish, vegetables, nuts and vermicelli on serving plates and take to the table with the sauces.

Break an egg into each bowl and beat lightly.

Cooking

Bring the stock ingredients to boil in a large pot over a portable cooker placed in the centre of the table. Cook at the table, boiling the ingredients in the stock until just cooked through. Cook vermicelli last and serve with the soup.

Note: *For method of preparing pork tripe, see page 196.

A variety of other ingredients and seasonal vegetables can be cooked in the Cantonese Hot Pot. Try fish, shrimp or chicken meat balls, large prawns, slices of fresh or dried squid, chicken livers, fresh bean sprouts, Chinese white cabbage or flowering white cabbage.

Fried Milk, Ta Liang Style
Ta Liang Ch'ao Niu Nai 大良炒牛奶
Serves 6-8

275 ml (10 fl oz)	fresh milk
10-12	egg whites
3 tbsp	lard, melted
1½ tbsp	cornstarch
30 g (1 oz)	olive beans (pine kernels)
30 g (1 oz)	rice vermicelli
4 tbsp	cooked oil
	oil for deep-frying

Seasoning

½ tsp	sugar
2 tsp	salt
1 tsp	monosodium glutamate
2 tsp	cooked oil
	dash white pepper

Preparation

Mix milk, egg whites, lard, cornstarch and seasoning ingredients lightly together.

Heat the wok, add oil and when very hot deep-fry the pine kernels for 1 minute, or until golden. Remove, drain and set aside. Reheat the oil and add broken rice vermicelli. Fry until the noodles expand and float to the surface, about 20 seconds. Remove, drain well and arrange on a serving plate.

Pour off the oil. Add 2 tbsp cooked oil and heat the wok. Pour in the egg and milk mixture and stir-fry on moderate heat until just set, about 4 minutes adding remaining 2 tbsp oil during cooking. Pour over the noodles and garnish with the fried pine kernels and chopped Chinese parsley. Serve.

Sieve the flour into a mixing bowl and make a well in the centre. Add the egg and salt and mix in, then gradually add the water, mixing well, to make a stiff dough. Remove from the bowl and knead for several minutes to make a smooth, pliable dough. Wrap in plastic wrap and set aside for at least 4 hours, or overnight. Roll out on a well floured board to about 1cm (¼″) thick, then cut into 18 pieces. Cover the remainder of the dough while rolling each square out as thinly as possible, into pieces roughly 15cm (6″) square.

Use in the same way as commercial spring roll wrappers, using a dab of flour and water paste to glue the flaps down. Fry the prepared spring rolls in moderately hot oil until crisp and golden. Drain well and serve immediately.

Spring Roll Wrappers

Chun Chuan P'i 春卷皮

The paper-thin, opaque spring roll wrappers sold commercially can be made at home, though it does require considerable skill.

Make a soft batter using two parts flour to one part water, with a pinch of salt. Cover and leave for 1 hour until slightly bubbly. Heat a heavy cast-iron frying pan or griddle and rub hard with a lightly oiled cloth.

Take a handful of the batter and smear it across the pan, to make a thin round sheet of about 15cm (6″) diameter. Cook on moderate heat until the wrapper can be peeled off — the upper side should be dry in just a few seconds. Lift off and stack. Cover with a damp cloth until needed.

Alternatively, use the following recipe to make thicker, tasty wrappers.

Makes about 18

185 g (6 oz)	all-purpose flour
1	duck egg or large chicken egg
40 ml (1½ fl oz)	water
1 tsp	salt

Wonton Wrappers

Yun Tun P'i 雲吞皮
Makes about 48

125 g (4 oz)	high gluten flour
60 g (2 oz)	mixed beaten egg and water

Preparation
Sieve the flour into a mixing bowl and make a well in the centre. Gradually add the egg and water mixture and work until well mixed. The dough should be quite hard and fairly dry. Remove from the bowl and knead firmly for 5 minutes. Cover with a piece of plastic wrap and set aside for 4-5 hours, in a warm place. Knead again briefly, then roll into a ball, press flat and roll out using a lightly floured rolling pin on a lightly floured large flat surface. Continue to roll out until the wrapper is almost transparent, and is large enough to cut out about 48 8cm (3″) round or square wrappers.

Dust with cornstarch and stack together. Wrap well in plastic wrap and store in the refrigerator for up to 24 hours, until needed.

Dumpling Wrappers
Chiao Tze P'i 餃子皮
Makes about 48

315 g (10 oz)   all-purpose flour
200 ml (6 fl oz)   cold water

Preparation
Sieve the flour into a mixing bowl and make a well in the centre. Gradually add the cold water and mix in well to make a firm but not dry dough. Remove from the bowl and knead for 3-4 minutes, then wrap in a piece of plastic wrap and set aside for ½ hour.

Roll out as thinly as possible — the wrappers should be nearly transparent. Cut into 15 cm (6″) squares.

These wrappers will dry out if not used within a few hours of making.

Crispy Rice Crackers
Kwo Pa 鍋巴

If glutinous rice crackers cannot be purchased, they can be simply made by scraping the crusty layer of rice from the bottom of the rice-cooking pan, and drying it in the oven.

Alternatively, the following is a recipe along the traditional method.

250 g (8 oz)   glutinous white rice

Wash rice well and pour into a saucepan. Add cold water to 5 cm (2″) above the rice and bring to the boil. Reduce heat, cover and cook until the liquid is absorbed and then place the saucepan in the oven and continue cooking at very low heat until the rice is completely dried out. It will stick to the pan. Pull up and cut into 4 cm (1½″) squares. Store in an airtight plastic bag or box.

Vegetarian Goose
Su Ngo 素鵝

20   dried beancurd skins (about 41 cm/16″ in diameter)
1½ tbsp   sugar
½ tsp   salt
1 tsp   monosodium glutamate
3 tbsp   light soy sauce
1 tbsp   dark soy sauce
275 ml (9 fl oz)   boiling water
1½ tbsp   sesame oil
5 tbsp   cooked oil

Wipe the beancurd skins with a damp cloth. Mix the remaining ingredients, except cooked oil, stirring until the sugar is completely dissolved. Spread one beancurd skin with about 1 tbsp of the sauce, top with another skin and spread this with the sauce. Keep working in this way until half of the beancurd skins are used up. Roll into a loaf and flatten slightly. Wrap in a piece of thin clean cloth and place on a plate in a steamer. Repeat the process with remaining beancurd skins, wrap and place in the steamer. Pour on any remaining liquid so that the rolls are very well saturated. Steam over high heat for 10 minutes, then leave to cool slightly. Remove from the steamer and unwrap. Leave to cool completely. Heat the cooked oil and fry the rolls on all sides. Remove and drain well.

227

Rice

Assorted Meat Congee
San Chi Ti Chou 三及第粥
Serves 6-8

440 g (14 oz)	rice
185 g (6 oz)	pork tripe*
125 g (4 oz)	pork liver
125 g (4 oz)	pork kidney
125 g (4 oz)	white fish fillets
3 slices	ginger, shredded
2	scallions, chopped

Seasoning:

1½ tbsp	salt
1 tsp	sesame oil
	dash white pepper

Preparation
Wash rice well, place in a large saucepan and add 4 lit (128 fl oz) chicken stock. Add chopped, cleaned pork tripe and bring to the boil. Reduce heat to low, partially cover the pot and simmer for at least 1½ hours, until the rice has become a soft pulp.

Thinly slice liver and kidney and blanch in boiling water for 1 minute. Drain well and add to the congee and boil for 5 minutes, then add thinly sliced fish fillets, ginger, half the scallion and seasoning ingredients and cook for a further 10-15 minutes.

Pour into large soup bowls and garnish with remaining scallion. Serve.

Note: *For method of preparing pork tripe, see page 196.

Yang Chow Fried Rice
Yang Chou Ch'ao Fan 揚州炒飯
Serves 6-8

500 g (1 lb)	cooked white rice*
125 g (4 oz)	fresh shrimp meat, chopped
90 g (3 oz)	frozen or cooked peas
125 g (4 oz)	roast pork or cooked ham, diced
2	scallions, chopped
2	eggs, beaten
4 tbsp	cooked oil

Seasoning

2½ tsp	salt
1 tsp	monosodium glutamate

Note: *Spread rice on a tray to partially dry before using.

Preparation
Blanch shrimp and frozen peas separately in boiling water, drain well. Mix the seasoning ingredients with rice.

Cooking
Heat the wok, add ½ tbsp oil and fry the beaten egg, stirring constantly, until cooked and broken into small lumps. Remove and set aside. Add remaining oil and fry shrimp, peas, roast pork or ham and scallions for 1½ minutes. Add rice and stir-fry 3 minutes longer. Serve.

Note: *Fried rice is best made with rice cooked at least one day in advance.

Vegetable Rice
Ts'ai Fan 菜飯
Serves 6-8

750 g (1½ lb)	rice
625 g (1¼ lb)	Chinese white cabbage
3 tbsp	cooked oil

Seasoning

1½ tsp	salt
½ tsp	monosodium glutamate

Preparation
Wash rice and drain very well. Wash cabbage, discard any damaged leaves and cut into 2.5cm (1") pieces.

Cooking
Heat the wok, add oil and stir-fry cabbage for 1 minute.

Place rice in a pot with cold water to 3cm (1¼") above the level of the rice. Cover and bring to the boil, then reduce heat and simmer until water is level with the rice. Sprinkle on seasonings and arrange vegetables on top of the rice. Cover the pot, reduce heat to very low and cook until the rice is tender and dry, about 20 minutes. Stir vegetables evenly into the rice and raise heat for a few seconds. Serve.

"In the Peking dialect, to have a job is to have *chiao ku* ("the grains to chew") and to have lost a job is to have *ta p'o le fan wan* ("broken the rice bowl")".

Cooking White Rice
Pai Fan 白飯

While there are endless individual methods for cooking perfect rice, we have found that the following method generally has good results and is one of the least complicated.

Allow about 60g (2 oz) rice per person. Rinse with cold water until the water runs clear, then drain well and pour into a glazed earthenware pot. Add cold water to cover rice to one finger joint, about 2.5cm (1″) above the rice. Cover and place on fierce heat until the pot begins to steam, then reduce heat to the lowest possible regulation. If the control will not regulate to very low, place the pot on an asbestos mat over the heat. Keep covered tightly during cooking, which will take around 18 minutes. The rice will be cooked through and each grain separate, but will retain a certain stickiness which is ideal for eating with chopsticks. Remove from the heat and keep covered until needed.

Yang Chow Fried Rice

Chicken Rice Pot
Pao Tzu Chi Chiu Fan　保仔鷄球飯
Serves 6-8

750 g (1½ lb)	rice
½	chicken (about 750 g/1½ lb)
6	dried mushrooms, soaked
6 slices	ginger, flower-cut
2	scallions, 2.5cm (1″) lengths

Seasoning

½ tsp	sugar
1½ tsp	salt
1 tsp	monosodium glutamate
2 tsp	light soy sauce
4 tsp	cornstarch
2 tbsp	cooked oil

Preparation
Wash and debone chicken and cut into 2.5cm (1″) pieces. Mix seasoning ingredients, pour over chicken and marinate for 15 minutes. Cut mushrooms into 3 pieces each. Wash and drain rice very well.

Cooking
Pour rice into a pot and add water to 4cm (1½″) above the level of the rice. Bring to the boil, reduce heat slightly, and boil for 3-4 minutes to reduce the liquid to the level of the rice. Stir so that rice does not stick to the pot.

Scatter chicken pieces, mushrooms and ginger over the rice, re-cover pot and reduce heat to very low. Cook for 15 minutes, then add scallions and continue to cook until rice is very tender and slightly dry, about 2 more minutes. Stir vegetables and chicken into the rice and serve immediately.

"Don't eat birds with beaks closed."

Fried Rice Noodles with Beef; Assorted Meat Congee — *recipe on page 228.*

Fried Rice Noodles with Beef
Kan Ch'ao Niu Ho 乾炒牛河
Serves 6-8

500 g (1 lb)	fresh rice sheet noodles*
185 g (6 oz)	lean beef, thinly sliced
75 g (2½ oz)	silver sprouts
2-3 slices	ginger, shredded
2	scallions, shredded
5 tbsp	cooked oil

Seasoning A

½ tsp	salt
½ tsp	monosodium glutamate
2 tsp	light soy sauce
1 tbsp	cornstarch
2 tbsp	water
2 tbsp	cooked oil

Seasoning B

1 tsp	sugar
½ tsp	monosodium glutamate
2 tbsp	dark soy sauce
2 tbsp	light soy sauce

Preparation
Mix beef with the seasoning A ingredients and marinate for 20 minutes. Rinse silver sprouts in cold water and drain very well.

Mix the seasoning B ingredients and set aside.

Cooking
Heat the wok, add oil and when very hot stir-fry ginger and scallion briefly. Remove. Add beef to the pan and stir-fry until it changes colour, about 1 minute. Place with the ginger and scallion. Add sprouts to the pan and fry for 1 minute. Return beef, scallion and ginger and stir-fry for ½ minute. Lift out and set aside.

Add noodles to the pan, with a little more oil if needed, and stir-fry for 1 minute. Add in the seasoning B ingredients and stir well. Return the beef and sprouts mixture and stir to mix thoroughly with the noodles.

Transfer to a serving plate. Serve.

Note: *If fresh rice sheet noodles are unavailable use about ¼ the weight of dried rice sheet noodles. Boil in slightly salted water until tender, then drain and rinse with cold water.

"He who aims to be a man of complete virtue in his food does not seek to gratify his appetite."

Confucius

Stir-Fried Shanghai Noodles.

Stir-Fried Shanghai Noodles
Shang Hai T'su Ch'ao Mien　上海粗炒麵
Serves 6-8

750 g (1½ lb)	fresh thick Shanghai noodles
250 g (8 oz)	Tientsin cabbage
90 g (3 oz)	lean pork, shredded
375 g (12 fl oz)	chicken stock
½ tsp	sesame oil
¼ tsp	white pepper
5 tbsp	cooked oil

Seasoning

½ tsp	monosodium glutamate
3 tbsp	dark soy sauce

Preparation
Wash cabbage, shake out excess water and chop coarsely. Blanch in boiling water for ½ minute. Drain well, splash with cold water and drain again. Set aside.

Cooking
Heat the wok, add 3 tbsp oil and when very hot stir-fry meat with cabbage for 1½ minutes. Remove and set aside. Add noodles to the pan and stir-fry until lightly coloured, about 1 minute, then add stock, cover and simmer for 5 minutes. Add the pork and cabbage and the seasoning ingredients and stir-fry until the sauce is completely evaporated. Add remaining oil and stir in lightly. Transfer to a serving plate, sprinkle on sesame oil and pepper and serve hot.

I sent out invitations

To summon guests,

I collected together

All my friends.

Loud talk

And simple feasting:

Discussion of philosophy,

Investigation of subtleties.

Tongues loosened

And minds at one.

Hearts refreshed

By discharge of emotion!

Sui Ch'eng-kung

Noodles With Braised Eel
Shan Hu Mien　鱔糊麵
Makes 6-8 servings

500 g (1 lb)	thin Shanghai noodles
1½ kg (3 lb)	live eels
4 slices	ginger, minced
2	scallions, minced
6-8 cloves	garlic, sliced
2 tsp	sesame oil
5-6 tbsp	cooked oil
	white pepper

Seasoning

2 tsp	sugar
¼ tsp	monosodium glutamate
3 tbsp	dark soy sauce
2 tsp	black vinegar
100 ml (3 fl oz)	water
1 tbsp	cornstarch
	dash white pepper

Sauce

1 tsp	salt
½ tsp	monosodium glutamate
1 tbsp	light soy sauce
2 tbsp	cooked oil
1 lit (32 fl oz)	chicken stock

Preparation
To clean, fillet and prepare eel for cooking, see recipe page 185.

Marinate with the seasoning ingredients and set aside.

Cooking
Heat the wok, add 4-5 tbsp oil and stir-fry garlic for 1 minute. Remove and set aside. Add ginger and scallion to the pan and stir-fry briefly, then add the eel and stir-fry for 2½ minutes. Remove, drain and arrange on a serving dish. Make a small hollow in the centre and put in the garlic. Reheat the wok, heat remaining oil with sesame oil and pour over the eel. Season generously with white pepper.

Drop noodles into a pot of boiling water and bring back to the boil. Add several tablespoons cold water, reboil and cook for 3-4 minutes until noodles are just tender. Drain and divide between 6-8 large soup bowls.

Bring sauce ingredients to a rapid boil, reduce heat and simmer for 1 minute. Pour over the noodles. Serve the bowls of noodles with the plate of eel.

  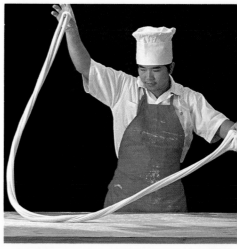

Szechwan Noodles
Tan Tan Mien 担担麵
Makes 6-8 servings

750 g (1½ lb)	soft, fresh egg based noodles, or
375 g (¾ lb)	dried egg noodles
60 g (2 oz)	preserved vegetables with chilli (preferably turnip)
30 g (1 oz)	dried shrimp, soaked
60 g (2 oz)	roasted peanuts, chopped
30 g (1 oz)	scallion, finely chopped
2 tsp	white sesame seeds
1 tbsp	cooked oil
	oil for deep-frying

Sauce

2 tbsp	sugar
1 tsp	monosodium glutamate
2 tbsp	dark soy sauce
3 tbsp	light soy sauce
1 tbsp	black vinegar
2 tbsp	chilli sauce (or to taste)
2 tbsp	sesame or peanut paste
1 tbsp	sesame oil
2 lit (64 fl oz)	chicken stock

Preparation
Finely dice preserved vegetables and dried shrimp. Mix sauce ingredients and set aside.

Cooking
Heat the wok, add deep-frying oil and when very hot fry dried shrimps briefly, then drain. Discard the oil and fry sesame seeds in the dry pan until crackling, remove and set aside.

Drop noodles into a pot of boiling water and when boiling again lower heat and splash in 3-4 tbsp cold water and boil for 5 minutes. (If using dried noodles, boil until just tender.) Drain and divide between 6-8 bowls.

Wipe out the wok and pour in the sauce, bring to the boil, then add the chopped vegetables, shrimps, peanuts and scallion and boil for 2 minutes. Pour over the noodles and sprinkle on sesame seeds. Serve.

Note: Thin Shanghai noodles could be used.

Pork Chop Noodles in Soup
P'ai Ku Mien 排骨麵
Makes 6-8 servings

500 g (1 lb)	thin Shanghai noodles
6-8	pork chops (about 155 g/5 oz each)
1	scallion, finely chopped
	oil for deep-frying

Seasoning

2 tsp	sugar
1 tsp	salt
½ tsp	monosodium glutamate
2 tbsp	light soy sauce
2 tsp	Shao Hsing wine
1 tsp	black vinegar
1 tsp	curry or chilli oil
2 cloves	garlic crushed
2	egg whites, beaten
	dash white pepper

Soup

1 tsp	salt
½ tsp	monosodium glutamate
1 tbsp	dark soy sauce
1¼ lit (40 fl oz)	chicken stock

½ tsp	sesame oil
	dash white pepper

Preparation
Drop noodles into a pot of boiling water, bring back to the boil. Add several tablespoons cold water, reboil and cook for 3-4 minutes until noodles are just tender. Drain and divide between 6-8 large soup bowls.

Trim pork chops. Mix the seasoning ingredients, pour over the chops and leave to marinate for 20 minutes.

Cooking
Heat the wok, add oil and when very hot reduce heat to moderate. Deep-fry the pork chops, several at a time, until cooked through and deep brown, about 7 minutes. Remove, drain and place one on each bowl of noodles. Discard most of the oil, reheat the wok, add the soup ingredients and bring to the boil, simmer for 3 minutes. Pour over the noodles and pork chops. Serve.

Szechwan Noodles; Dumplings with Red Chilli Sauce — *recipe on page 255.*

Pork Chop Noodles in Soup

Noodles with Pork and Vegetables in Soup
Tai Lu Mien 大鹵麵
Serves 6-8

250 g (8 oz)	thick Shanghai noodles
90 g (3 oz)	broccoli heads, quartered
90 g (3 oz)	canned bamboo shoots, shredded
90 g (3 oz)	dried beche-de-mer, soaked and shredded*
60 g (2 oz)	dried black mushrooms, soaked and shredded
90 g (3 oz)	lean pork, shredded
90 g (3 oz)	fresh shrimps peeled and diced
1	egg, beaten
4 tbsp	cooked oil
Soup	
½ tsp	salt
¼ tsp	monosodium glutamate
625 ml (20 fl oz)	chicken stock or water
2 tbsp	cooked oil

* For method of preparing beche-de-mer, see page 185.

Preparation and Cooking
Drop noodles into a pot of boiling water and bring back to the boil. Add several tablespoons cold water and continue to boil for about 2 minutes, or until noodles are tender. Drain well and place in a serving bowl. Blanch broccoli in boiling water for ½ minute. Drain. Heat the wok, add oil and stir-fry bamboo shoots, beche-de-mer, mushrooms and broccoli for 1½ minutes. Remove, and drain well. Add pork and shrimp to the pan and stir-fry until cooked, about 1½ minutes. Remove, and drain. Drain off oil and pour the soup ingredients into the pan and bring to the boil. Simmer for 5 minutes, then add meat and vegetables and heat through. Remove from the heat and pour in beaten egg and leave to set in threads in the soup. Return to the heat and bring back to the boil, then pour over the noodles. Serve.

"When feasting with a man of superior rank and character, the guest first tastes the dishes and then stops. He should not bolt the food, nor swill down the liquor. He should take small and frequent mouthfuls. While chewing quickly, he should not make faces with his mouth."

"Good meat results in good soup."

Chinese Proverb

Fried Noodles with Mixed Meat and Vegetables
San Ssu Ch'ao Mien 三絲炒麵
Serves 6-8

155 g (5 oz)	thin Shanghai noodles
45 g (1½ oz)	chicken fillet, shredded
75 g (2½ oz)	lean pork, shredded
45 g (1½ oz)	canned bamboo shoot, shredded
45 g (1½ oz)	broccoli heads, quartered
15 g (½ oz)	Yunnan ham, shredded
1 tbsp	cooked oil
	oil for shallow-frying
Seasoning A	
½ tsp	cornstarch
	pinch of salt
	pinch of monosodium glutamate
Seasoning B	
¼ tsp	salt
¼ tsp	monosodium glutamate
¼ tsp	Shao Hsing wine
200 ml (6 fl oz)	chicken stock
Thickening — mix together	
2 tsp	cornstarch
1 tbsp	water

Preparation and Cooking
Mix pork and chicken with the seasoning A ingredients and marinate for 15 minutes. Drop noodles into a pot of boiling water and when it begins to boil again, untangle the noodle cakes, remove and drain. Rinse under cold running water until cool. Drain well, then spread on a tray to partially dry. Heat the wok, add shallow oil and heat to smoking. Add the noodles and stir in the hot oil until golden brown. Turn once. Drain away the oil and continue to fry the noodles, on both sides, until lightly brown and crisp. Remove, drain well and place on a serving plate.

Reheat the wok, add cooked oil and stir-fry chicken, pork and bamboo shoots until the meat changes colour, about 1 minute. Remove and set aside. Stir-fry broccoli for 1 minute, then return meat and bamboo shoots and add the seasoning B ingredients and stir-fry briefly.

Add the thickening, cover and cook until sauce thickens, stirring occasionally. Pour over the noodles and garnish with shredded ham. Serve.

Fried Noodles with Mixed Meat and Vegetables.

Two Sides Browned Noodles with Pork and Vegetables
Liang Mien Huang 兩面黃
Serves 6-8

625 g (1¼ lb)	hand-made noodles
90 g (3 oz)	lean pork, shredded
185 g (6 oz)	Tientsin cabbage, coarsely shredded
½ tsp	ginger, minced
½ tsp	scallion, minced
4 tbsp	cooked oil

Seasoning

¼ tsp	salt
¼ tsp	monsodium glutamate
1 tsp	dark soy sauce
1 tbsp	light soy sauce
1 tsp	Shao Hsing wine
3 tbsp	chicken stock
1 tsp	cornstarch
	few drops sesame oil

Preparation and Cooking

Mix seasoning ingredients and set aside. Drop noodles into a pot of boiling water and bring back to the boil. Add several tablespoons cold water, and boil for 3-4 minutes. Drain and rinse in cold water.

Heat wok, add 3 tbsp oil and fry noodles on one side until lightly coloured, then turn and cook other side. Turn the noodle cake several times until well coloured on both sides, and slightly crisp on the edges. Place on a serving plate and set aside. Reheat the wok, add remaining oil and lightly stir-fry ginger and scallion. Add pork and cabbage and stir-fry for 3-4 minutes. Add seasoning and cook for 1½ minutes. Pour over the noodles and garnish with a little shredded scallion. Serve.

Noodles with Minced Beef and Celery Hearts
Chin Wang Niu Jou Mien 芹王牛肉麵
Makes 6-8 servings

750 g (1½ lb)	soft, fresh egg based noodles, or
375 g (¾ lb)	dried egg noodles
185 g (6 oz)	lean beef, minced
185 g (6 oz)	Chinese celery hearts, finely chopped
2	scallions, minced
1 clove	garlic, minced
1 tbsp	hot bean paste
2 tbsp	cooked oil

Sauce

1 tsp	dark soy sauce
2 tsp	light soy sauce
1½ lit (48 fl oz)	chicken stock

Seasoning

1 tsp	monosodium glutamate
2 tsp	dark soy sauce
1½ tsp	light soy sauce
2 tsp	Shao Hsing wine
1-2 tsp	chilli oil

Preparation and Cooking

Drop noodles into a large pot of boiling water, reduce heat very slightly and return to the boil. Add in 3 tbsp cold water and continue to boil for 5 minutes. (If cooking dried noodles, boil in the same way until just tender). Drain and divide between 6-8 bowls.

Bring chicken stock to the boil and add remaining sauce ingredients. Pour over the noodles.

Heat the wok, add oil and when smoking, stir-fry beef with garlic for 1 minute. Add hot bean paste and fry briefly, then add in the seasoning ingredients with celery and scallion and stir-fry for 2 minutes. Pour a portion of the sauce and ingredients over each bowl of noodles and serve.

"The old legend that Marco Polo brought pasta from China (including spaghetti derived from *mien* and ravioli from *chiao tzu*) is probably wrong; at least some sorts of pasta were clearly known well before that. Egg noodles seem definitely Chinese, and the rest may well be, but there is little evidence. Small, thin-skinned, meat-filled dumplings virtually identical to *hun t'un* and *chiao tzu* are found widely in Asia: Russian pelemeni, Jewish kreplachs and Tibetan *mo mo*, with especially important and elaborate versions in Afghanistan and neighbouring areas. China might have got them, and Italy too, indirectly, from central Asia."

Food in Chinese Culture, Chapter 8
E.N. Anderson, Jr and Marja L. Anderson

On the seventh day of the seventh month pick seven ounces of lotus flowers; on the eighth day of the eighth month gather eight ounces of lotus-root; on the ninth day of the ninth month collect nine ounces of lotus-seeds. Dry in the shade and eat the mixture and you will never grow old.

Imperial Cookery Book of the Mongol Dynasty — Yin Shan Cheng Yao

Lotus Root Pudding
Kuei Hua T'ang Lien Ou 桂花糖蓮藕
Serves 6-8

750 g (1½ lb)	lotus roots, (5cm/2" in diameter)
60 g (2 oz)	glutinous rice
75 g (2½ oz)	sugar
45 g (1½ oz)	candied lotus seeds (optional)

Sauce:

75 g (2½ oz)	sugar
250 ml (8 fl oz)	water
1 tbsp	cornstarch

Preparation
Soak glutinous rice in cold water to cover for 2 hours, adding more water as it is absorbed. Wash the lotus roots, cut a 2cm (¾") piece from each end and set aside, Wash well, and drain.

Drain excess water from rice and stuff the rice into the hollows of the lotus roots. Replace the ends and secure in place with toothpicks. Mix the sauce ingredients in a small saucepan.

Cooking
Place lotus roots in a pan of boiling water to cover, and simmer until tender enough to easily pierce with a skewer. Remove and leave to cool.

Peel and cut into 1cm (¼") slices. Arrange in a lightly greased bowl, working in a circular fashion. Sprinkle on the sugar, cover with a piece of greaseproof paper and steam over high heat for about 1 hour.

Remove from the heat and invert the pudding into a serving plate, pile the candied lotus seeds on top. Bring the sauce to the boil and cook quickly until it thickens. Pour over the pudding just before serving.

Note: Sweet preserved Osmanthus flowers may be added to the sauce before cooking.

Sweet Pea Paste
Su Tou T'ien Ni 酥豆甜泥

1 can	green peas (about 440 g/14 oz)
5 tbsp	sugar
5 tbsp	cooked oil

Preparation
Drain peas and place in a metal sieve. Push through into a basin. Run the water through the sieve, then strain off excess water.

Cooking
Heat the wok, add oil and stir-fry the pea paste, adding sugar a little at a time. Cook until the liquid has evaporated leaving a thick dryish paste. Spread on a serving plate and serve.

Note: Dried red beans, pre-soaked and cooked until soft, may also be cooked in this way.

"When I eat sugarcane, I start from the less sweet end so that I may gradually enter the region of bliss."

Ku Kai-chih

White Fungus Sweet Soup
Ping T'ang Yin Erh 冰糖銀耳
Serves 6-8

30 g (1 oz)	dried white fungus
280 g (9 oz)	rock sugar
1½ lit (48 fl oz)	water

Preparation
Soak white fungus in cold water for 1 hour, then drain and cover with hot water. Soak until softened, about 20 minutes, then drain and pick off any hard parts.

Cooking
Dissolve sugar in water over moderate heat. Add the white fungus and simmer gently, covered, for 1¼-1½ hours. Remove and serve hot, or leave to cool and add a little iced water before serving.

Note: If keeping, drain fungus and store separately in a plastic container. Chill or reheat before serving. Drained, chilled canned fruit may be added.

239

Minced Date Cake.

Minced Date Cake
Tsao Ni Kwo Ping 棗泥鍋餅
Serves 6-8

Pastry

125 g (4 oz)	flour
1	egg
200 ml (6 fl oz)	water
2 tbsp	cooked oil
	oil for deep-frying

Filling

185 g (6 oz)	dried red dates
30 g (1 oz)	slab sugar
2 tbsp	lard

Preparation

Sieve flour into a bowl, make a hollow in the centre and add the egg. Work into the flour, then add water a little at a time, to make a smooth batter. Set aside.

Place dates in a saucepan with water to cover by about 5cm (2"). Boil until completely softened, drain well, reserving liquid, and leave to cool. Mash dates through a sieve, discarding skin and seeds. Pour just enough of the water through to make a smooth very thick paste.

Cooking

Heat the wok and add lard. When melted crush the sugar and add to the wok. Stir on moderate heat until the sugar is completely dissolved and then add the date mixture and cook until the liquid evaporates leaving a thick, dry paste. Leave to cool a little.

Wipe out a large wok or pan with an oiled cloth. Pour in the batter and turn the pan to make a large very thin pancake. Cook on moderate heat until the underside is firm, then turn and cook other side. Remove and cool.

Spread paste along the centre of the pastry and fold into a rectangular parcel to encase the paste. Seal edges with a flour and water paste. Clean the wok, reheat and add 2 tbsp oil. Fry the cake on both sides until slightly crisp and lightly coloured. Lift out. Add deep-frying oil and when very hot put in the cake to deep-fry for about ¾-1 minute, until crisp and bubbling on the surface. Lift out and leave to cool slightly, then cut into slices to serve.

"Turn the pie, toast the pie,

The pie with filling fried in oil.
Turn it over and let us see."

Anon

Eight-Treasure Rice
Pa Pao Fan 八寶飯
Serves 6-8

220 g (7 oz)	glutinous rice
8-10	dried lotus seeds, boiled
3	red maraschino cherries, sliced
3	green maraschino cherries, sliced
6	preserved red dates, sliced
2-3 slices	candied melon
20	raisins, soaked
90 g (3 oz)	sweet red bean paste*
2 tbsp	lard, softened

Sauce

90 g (3 oz)	sugar
200 ml (6 fl oz)	water
2-3 tbsp	liquid from red cherries
2 tsp	cornstarch

Preparation

Soak rice for 3 hours in cold water, then drain and place on a damp cloth. Set in a steamer and steam over high heat for 15 minutes, sprinkling with several tablespoons of cold water every 2-3 minutes.

Grease the inside of a 15cm (6") bowl with a little of the lard. Arrange lotus seeds, red and green cherries in a pattern in the centre, then working outward in a circular fashion arrange the remaining fruits. Mix rice with the remaining lard and half the sugar (see sauce ingredients) and divide into two portions. Place one portion over the fruit arrangement, making a hollow in the centre. Put the red bean paste in this hollow and cover with remaining rice.

Cooking

Cover the bowl with a cloth and set in a steamer over gently boiling water. Cover and steam for 1 hour.

Boil sauce ingredients together until slightly thickened.

Loosen the cooked rice pudding around the edges and turn out of the inverted bowl into a shallow serving plate. Pour on the hot sauce and serve.

Note: *For preparation of sweet red bean paste, see page 278.

241

Sweet Almond Milk — *recipe on page 244.*

Sweet Almond Milk
Hsing Jen Ch'a 杏仁茶
Serves 6-8

250 g (8 oz)	almonds
315 g (10 oz)	sugar
1 lit (32 fl oz)	water

Thickening — mix together

5 tbsp	rice powder
150 ml (5 fl oz)	water

Preparation
Soak almonds in boiling water until skins loosen. Drain and peel. Grind or blend, adding the water a little at a time, until very smooth. Strain through a piece of fine clean cloth into a saucepan.

Cooking
Bring to the boil. Add the sugar a little at a time, stirring until dissolved. Slowly add the rice powder paste and stir until the mixture thickens slightly. Bring to the boil, then remove from the heat. Serve.

Golden Puffs with Sweet Red Bean Paste
Kao Li Tou Sha 高力豆沙
Serves 12

8	egg whites
1 tbsp	flour
1 tbsp	cornstarch
90 g (3 oz)	sweet red bean paste*
	cornstarch
	sugar
	oil for deep-frying

Preparation
Divide the red bean paste into 12 pieces and roll each into a ball. Coat lightly with cornstarch and set aside. Whip the egg whites until fairly stiff, then add in the flour and cornstarch and whip again until the mixture stands in firm peaks.

Cooking
Heat the wok, add the oil and when very hot reduce heat slightly. Dip the red bean paste balls, one at a time, into the egg white, to coat thickly, making balls of at least 5cm (2") diameter.

Carefully place, several at a time, in the hot oil and deep-fry until golden, about 2½ minutes. Lift out, drain and arrange on a serving plate. Sprinkle with sugar. Serve immediately.

*For method of preparing sweet red bean paste, see page 278.

Note: Sweet lotus seed paste may be used as an alternative filling.

Candied Apple
Pa Ssu P'ing Kuo 拔絲蘋果
Serves 6-8

3	green apples
45 g (1½ oz)	all-purpose flour
2½ tbsp	cornstarch
1	egg white, beaten
1 tbsp	white sesame seeds
	oil for deep-frying

Toffee

90 g (3 oz)	sugar
1 tbsp	lard
30 ml (1 fl oz)	water

Preparation
Peel and core apples. Cut into 1.5cm (½") slices and roll in flour. Mix remaining flour with cornstarch and egg white, adding a little water to make a thick batter. Stir well.

Cooking
Heat the wok, add oil and when very hot, deep-fry the apple for 1½-2 minutes, until golden. Remove, drain and set aside. Pour off the oil, reheat the wok and add sugar and lard. Stir until the sugar melts, then pour in water and simmer until the syrup begins to colour. Reduce heat and cook until the toffee is a light golden colour. Add the apple and stir until well coated with the toffee. Remove to an oiled serving plate. Sprinkle on sesame seeds. Dip each piece of toffied apple into a bowl of iced water to harden the toffee before eating.

Fried honey-cakes of rice flour and malt-sugar sweetmeats;

Jadelike wine, honey-flavoured, fills the winged cups;

Ice-cooled liquor, strained of impurities, clear wine, cool and refreshing;

Here are laid out the patterned ladles, and here is sparkling wine.

Ch'u ts'e

Sweet Taro Cream — *recipe on page 246.*

Eight-Treasure Rice —
recipe on page 241

Sweet Taro Cream
Yu Ni 芋泥
Serves 6-8

750 g (1½ lb)	taro
280 g (9 oz)	sugar
150 ml (5 fl oz)	coconut milk
150 ml (5 fl oz)	fresh milk
1 lit (32 fl oz)	water
6 tbsp	cornstarch

Preparation
Peel and wash taro. Cut into 1.5cm (½″) slices and steam for 15 minutes, or until well softened. Cut into small pieces. Place in a blender with about one-third of the water and blend to a smooth puree.

Cooking
Bring remaining water to the boil, add taro puree and sugar and boil until the sugar melts and the liquid is smooth. Blend again if slightly lumpy. Mix cornstarch with a little cold water and add to the soup, stirring continually until the soup begins to thicken. Add coconut milk and fresh milk and heat through. Serve hot.

Buns & Pastries

Bottom picture, from left: Steamed Open Dumplings — *recipe on page 253;* Shrimp Dumplings — *recipe on page 252;* Wonton in Soup — *recipe on page 255;* Cantonese Spring Rolls — *recipe on page 252.*

Steamed Bread
Man Tou 饅頭
Makes about 24

600 g (19 oz)	all-purpose flour
60 g (2 oz)	sugar
365 ml (11½ fl oz)	warm water
1 tbsp	dried yeast
2 tbsp	lard, melted
	pinch lye (optional)

Preparation
Sieve flour into a bowl. Dissolve sugar in warm water, then add yeast and stir until dissolved. Leave in a warm place for 10 minutes until foamy. Pour into the flour and add melted lard. Add in lye, if used. Mix together, then remove from the bowl and knead for about 3 minutes until smooth and elastic.

Roll out into a long sausage shape and divide into about 24 parts. Flatten into thick circular shapes and press a chopstick in the centre of each to make a waist. Fold in halves and pinch at the fold to form open sided buns. Stick a little plain paper under each. Let rise for 10 minutes, until springy to the touch.

Cooking
Arrange in a bamboo steaming basket, set in a steamer over rapidly boiling water and steam for 10-12 minutes. Serve.

Lotus Leaf Buns
Ho Yeh Pao 荷葉包
Makes 24

1 tbsp	cooked oil

Dough
For ingredients see recipe for Steamed Bread, above.

Preparation
Prepare a full quantity of dough and roll into a thick sausage shape. Cut into 24 pieces and flatten each piece with the fingers to about 1cm (¼") thick. Brush one side with oil and fold each in halves. Press the back of a knife along the top of each bun marking across the fold.

Cooking
Arrange in a bamboo steaming basket and set in a steamer over rapidly boiling water. Cover and steam over high heat for 8-10 minutes. The buns are done when the dough is smooth and dry. Serve with Camphor and Tea Smoked Duck.

Roast Pork Buns
Char Shau Pao 叉燒包
Makes 24

Dough
For ingredients see recipe for Steamed Bread, left.

Filling

315 g (10 oz)	roast pork, diced
1 slice	ginger
1	scallion
1 tbsp	cooked oil

Seasoning

2 tsp	sugar
¼ tsp	salt
½ tsp	monosodium glutamate
1 tsp	dark soy sauce
2 tsp	light soy sauce
1 tbsp	oyster sauce
125 ml (4 fl oz)	chicken stock
1 tsp	sesame oil
	dash white pepper
	dash red colouring

Thickening — mix together

1 tbsp	cornstarch
1 tbsp	water

Preparation
Prepare a full quantity of the dough and roll into a long sausage shape. Cover with a cloth.

Mix the seasoning ingredients together and set aside.

Cooking
Heat the wok, add oil and stir fry the diced pork with ginger and scallion for 1 minute on high heat, then discard the ginger and scallion. Add the seasoning and thickening and cook until the sauce becomes very thick. Remove from the heat and leave to cool completely. Divide the dough into 24 pieces and flatten each with the fingers. Place a spoonful of the filling in the centre of each piece of dough and work the dough around the filling. Pinch the edges firmly together and stick a small square of plain paper under the buns. Leave to rise for 10 minutes.

Arrange in a bamboo steaming basket and set in a steamer over rapidly boiling water. Cover and steam for about 12 minutes. Leave plenty of space between the buns as they will expand during cooking. Do not remove the lid during cooking, or the buns will not split open on top as they should. Serve hot in the basket or transfer to a serving plate.

Pork and Vegetable Buns

Ts'ai Jou Pao 菜肉包

Makes 24

Dough

For ingredients see recipe for Steamed Bread, left.

Filling

500 g (1 lb)	Chinese white cabbage
250 g (8 oz)	semi-fat pork, diced
2	scallions, finely chopped
3 tbsp	cooked oil

Seasoning

1 tsp	sugar
2 tsp	salt
½ tsp	monosodium glutamate
1 tsp	cornstarch
1 tsp	sesame oil
	dash white pepper

Prepartion

Wash cabbage and drain well. Chop coarsely and blanch briefly in boiling water. Remove and drain, then wrap in a piece of clean, thin cloth. Squeeze hard to remove excess liquid. Mix pork, cabbage and scallion with the seasoning ingredients and leave to marinate for 20 minutes.

Prepare a full quantity of the dough and roll into a long sausage shape. Divide into about 24 pieces and flatten each with the fingers. Place a large spoonful of the filling in the centre of each piece of dough and pull the dough up around the filling. Pleat the edges of the dough together, working in a circular fashion around the edges. Leave a small hole in the centre. Stick small squares of plain paper underneath. Leave to rise for 10 minutes.

Cooking

Arrange in a bamboo steaming basket and set in a steamer over rapidly boiling water. Cover and steam over high heat for 12 minutes. Serve hot in the basket or transfer to a serving plate.

Silver Thread Rolls with Ham

Huo Tui Yin Ssu Chuen 火腿銀絲卷

Makes about 24

| 60 g (2 oz) | Yunnan Ham, finely minced |

Dough

For ingredients see recipe for Steamed Bread, left.

Preparation

Prepare a full quantity of the dough and divide into two pieces. Roll each out thin and roll up like a Swiss Roll. Cut across the roll into noodle-like shreds. Divide into twelve lots and wrap each bundle of dough shreds around a chopstick to form into a ball shape. Stick a piece of plain paper under each and sprinkle a little chopped ham on top. When all are done, arrange in bamboo steaming baskets and let rise for 10 minutes until springy to the touch.

Cooking

Set on a steamer over rapidly boiling water to steam for 10-12 minutes. Serve.

Flower Rolls

Hua Chuen 花卷

Makes 12

| 1 tbsp | cooked oil |

Dough

For ingredients see recipe for Steamed Bread, left.

Preparation

Prepare a full quantity of the dough and roll out to about 1cm (¼") thick. Spread with oil and sprinkle lightly with all purpose flour. Roll up into a long sausage shape. Pull the roll to make it about 23cm (18") long and cut into 12 pieces. Press a floured chopstick across the centre of each roll and bend around the chopstick to make a double-flower. Pinch the folds and stick a small square of plain paper underneath.

Cooking

Arrange in a bamboo steaming basket and set in a steamer over rapidly boiling water. Cover and steam over high heat for 10 minutes. The rolls are done when the dough is smooth and dry.

"Even at night, people who carry dishes on a frame slung on a shoulder pole offer various foods, mostly *ping*. They sing out along the side of the road. People in the capital consider this perfectly common-place, but if a rustic from some distant place should be confronted with it, he would think it extraordinary."

Kuan P'u Nai Te Weng
(Translated by Michael Freeman)

Scallion Pancakes — *recipe on page 252.*

Scallion Pancakes
Ts'ung Yu Ping 葱油餅
Makes 12

220 g (7 oz)	all-purpose flour
150 ml (5 fl oz)	cold water
1 tbsp	melted lard
2 tbsp	scallion, chopped
1 tsp	salt
2 tsp	sesame oil
	oil for shallow frying

Preparation
Sieve flour into a mixing bowl, and pour in the cold water. Quickly work into the flour, adding just a little more water if the dough is dry and hard. It should be soft and workable. Knead for 3 minutes, then cover with a damp cloth and leave for 15 minutes. Cut into 12 pieces. Roll each out into a rectangle about 1cm (¼″) thick and brush with melted lard. Scatter on chopped scallion and add salt and sesame oil. Roll up lengthways to encase the scallion. Twist into a spiral shapes. Flatten each piece with the fingers or by using a rolling pin on a floured board.

Cooking
Heat the wok or a large frying pan and add about 2cm (¾″) oil. Fry pancakes two at a time, for 3-3½ minutes. Cover the pan during half the cooking, and shake the pan occasionally to make the pancakes puff up slightly. Remove, drain and keep warm while the remainder of the pancakes are cooked. Serve hot.

Cantonese Spring Rolls
Ch'un Chuan 春卷
Makes 12

12 sheets	spring roll wrappers.*
125 g (4 oz)	lean pork or chicken fillet, shredded
90 g (3 oz)	canned bamboo shoots, shredded
2	dried black mushrooms, soaked and shredded
1½ tsp	chive shoots, chopped
1½ tsp	cornstarch
2 tbsp	cooked oil
	oil for deep-frying

Seasoning

1 tsp	sugar
¼ tsp	salt
½ tsp	monosodium glutamate
½ tsp	dark soy sauce
2 tsp	light soy sauce
2 tbsp	chicken stock
1 tbsp	cooked oil
	few drops sesame oil
	dash white pepper

Preparation
Sprinkle cornstarch on meat and leave for a few minutes. Heat the wok, add oil and when very hot stir-fry the meat, bamboo shoots and mushrooms for 1 minute. Add seasoning ingredients, well mixed, and stir-fry until the liquid has evaporated. Mix in chopped chive shoots, remove from the pan and spread on a plate to cool before using.

Place a portion of the filling diagonally across the centre of each wrapper. Fold in two sides to cover the filling, then fold the lower flap over and roll up. Seal the end flap with water or a flour and water paste.

Cooking
Heat the wok, add deep-frying oil and heat to very hot. Deep-fry the spring rolls several at a time to a deep golden colour, about 1½ minutes. Do not turn more than twice. Drain and serve.

*If spring roll wrappers are unobtainable, see page 226 for recipe.

Shrimp Dumplings
Hsia Chiao 蝦餃
Makes about 24

Pastry

125 g (4 oz)	'Tang' flour
2 tsp	cornstarch
150 ml (5 fl oz)	water
¼ tsp	lard

Filling

155 g (5 oz)	fresh shrimp meat, chopped
60 g (2 oz)	canned bamboo shoots, very finely diced

Seasoning

½ tsp	sugar
½ tsp.	salt
½ tsp	monosodium glutamate
1 tsp	cornstarch
	few drops sesame oil
	dash white pepper

Preparation
Mix shrimp and bamboo shoots with the seasoning ingredients and work well with the fingers until the mixture is firm and slightly sticky. Chill for ½ hour before using.

Bring the water to a rapid boil and quickly add in 'Tang' flour mixed with cornstarch. Stir with a wooden spoon until the flour is well mixed and becomes transparent. Cover for 5 minutes, then lift out and knead well, working in the lard. The dough should be smooth and shiny. Roll out into a long sausage shape. Cover with a cloth. Pull off small pieces, about 1½ tsp, and shape into thin round wrappers on a dry board. (Using a blunt pastry cleaver press down on the pastry and turn in a circular motion about three times right, three times left.) Peel from the board with the cleaver.

Place a spoonful of filling, a little off-centre on the wrappers. Fold the larger part over and form into several small pleats, pinching with the fingers. Press against the flat side to seal and press into crescent shapes.

Cooking
Arrange the dumplings in a greased bamboo steaming basket and set in a steamer over rapidly boiling water. Cover and steam for 4-5 minutes. Serve.

Steamed Open Dumplings
Shao Mai 燒賣
Makes 24

24	wonton wrappers, 8cm (3″) rounds*
155 g (5 oz)	semi-fat pork
125 g (4 oz)	fresh shrimp meat
3	dried black mushrooms, soaked
Seasoning	
1 tsp	sugar
½ tsp	salt
¼ tsp	monosodium glutamate
½ tsp	dark soy sauce
2 tsp	light soy sauce
1 tbsp	cornstarch
	few drops sesame oil
	dash white pepper

Preparation
Wash and very finely dice pork and shrimp meat. Drain and very finely dice mushrooms. Mix with the seasoning ingredients. Chill for ½ hour before using. Make a circular shape with the fore-finger and thumb of left hand. Place a wonton wrapper over the fingers and place a spoonful of filling in centre of the wrapper. Push into the circle of the fingers, producing an open ended dumpling with the sides of the wrapper gathered up around the filling. Flatten the bases and place in a lightly greased bamboo steaming basket.

Cooking
Set basket in a steamer over rapidly boiling water and steam for 10 minutes. Serve.

*If wonton wrappers are unobtainable, see page 226 for recipe.

Mandarin Pancakes
Po Ping 薄餅

Makes 12

250 g (8 oz)	all purpose flour
100 ml (3 fl oz)	boiling water
75 ml (2½ fl oz)	cold water

Preparation
Sieve the flour into a mixing bowl and make a well in the centre. Pour in the boiling water and mix in the flour, then add the cold water a little at a time, working with a wooden spoon, until the dough is smooth and just soft enough to work, but is not sticky. Knead for 5 minutes, then cover with a damp cloth and leave for 20 minutes.

Roll into a long sausage shape and cut into 12 pieces. Flatten each piece with the fingers. Roll out on a floured board until very thin.

Cooking
Heat a heavy frying pan until hot and cook the pancakes one side, then the other, until lightly coloured with flecks of brown over the surfaces. The pan should be hot enough to cook both sides in about ¾ minute. Remove, fold into a triangular shape and wrap in a cloth until needed.

"If they have no powered means of refrigeration, the (modern) northern Chinese make use of the cold of their winter ... *chiao tzu* (meat dumplings) are put in an unheated, empty room, or ... in the open air. They are promptly frozen. Then, instead of busying themselves with cooking for the holiday meals, the women simply toss the needed number of dumplings into boiling water."

Food in Chinese Culture, Chapter 7
Vera Y.N. Hsu and Francis L.K. Hsu

Dumplings with Red Chilli Sauce
Hung Yu Ch'ao Shou 紅油炒手
Serves 6-8

Dumplings

48 pc	dumpling wrappers (about 12.5 cm (5″) square)*
440 g (14 oz)	semi-fat pork, finely minced
2-3	scallions, minced
2-3 slices	ginger, minced
1	egg, beaten

Seasoning

1 tsp	sugar
1 tsp	salt
½ tsp	monosodium glutamate
½ tsp	Shao Hsing wine
150 ml (5 fl oz)	water
1	egg
	few drops sesame oil
	dash white pepper

Sauce

1 tbsp	sugar
1 tsp	monosodium glutmate
4 tbsp	dark soy sauce
2-3	red chillies, seeded and minced
4-6 cloves	garlic, minced
200 ml (6 fl oz)	chicken stock

Preparation

Mix pork with scallion, ginger and the seasoning ingredients and work well with the fingers until the mixture is a smooth paste. Lift from the bowl and slap the mixture forcefully back into the bowl continually for about 1 minute, to make the paste very smooth and firm. Chill for ½ hour before using. Place a spoonful of the mixture in the centre of each wonton wrapper, brush beaten egg around the filling and wrap the filling, squeezing gently, to form a ball shape in the centre of the wrapper, with the edges loose in a tail shape.

Cooking

In a large pot bring about 8 cm (3″) water to the boil, reduce heat slightly and put in the wontons. Boil for about 2 minutes, until they float to the surface. Remove and drain.

Divide between 6-8 bowls.

Bring the sauce ingredients to a rapid boil and pour over the wontons. Serve.

*For method of making dumpling wrappers, see page 227.

Wonton in Soup
Yun Tun 雲吞
Serves 6-8

Wonton

48	wonton wrappers (about 10 cm (4″) square)*
375 g (12 oz)	fresh shrimp meat, chopped
60 g (2 oz)	chive shoots, shredded
1	egg, beaten

Seasoning

1 tsp	sugar
½ tsp	salt
½ tsp	monosodium glutamate
	few drops sesame oil
	dash white pepper

Soup

1½ lit (48 fl oz)	chicken stock
1 tsp	salt
½ tsp	monsodium glutamate
2 tsp	light soy sauce
¼ tsp	sesame oil
	dash white pepper

Preparation

Mix shrimp meat with seasoning ingredients and chill for ½ hour before using.

Place a spoonful of the mixture in the centre of each wonton wrapper, brush beaten egg around the filling and wrap the filling, squeezing gently, to form a ball shape in the centre of the wrapper with the edges loose in a tail shape.

Cooking

In a large pot bring about 8 cm (3″) water to the boil, reduce heat slightly and put in the wontons. Boil for about 2 minutes, until the wontons float to the surface. Remove and drain. Place half the shredded chive shoots into 6-8 bowls and top with several wontons.

Bring the soup ingredients to a rapid boil, add remaining chive shoots and boil for 1 minute. Pour over the wonton. Serve.

Note: *If wonton wrappers are unobtainable, see page 226 for recipe.

255

Fried Meat Dumplings
Kwo Tieh 窩貼
Makes about 36

Pastry

250 g (8 oz)	all-purpose flour
200 ml (6 fl oz)	boiling water
	pinch of salt

Filling

375 g (12 oz)	semi-fat pork, finely minced
125 g (4 oz)	Chinese white cabbage or canned bamboo shoots, very finely chopped
30 g (1 oz)	chive choots, finely chopped
60 ml (2 fl oz)	chicken stock
4 tbsp	cooked oil

Seasoning

1 tsp	sugar
1 tsp	salt
½ tsp	monosodium glutamate
1 tsp	light soy sauce
1 tsp	Shao Hsing wine
30 ml (1 fl oz)	water
1 tsp	sesame oil
1 tbsp	cooked oil

Preparation

Place finely chopped cabbage in a fine, clean cloth and squeeze hard to remove excess liquid. Mix pork, cabbage or bamboo shoots and chives in a bowl. Add seasonings and work well with the fingers until the mixture is a smooth paste. Lift from the bowl and slap the mixture forcefully back into the bowl continually for about 1 minute to make the paste very smooth and firm. Chill for ½ hour before using.

Sieve the flour into a bowl. Bring water to the boil and when bubbling rapidly, pour onto the flour and mix quickly to a thick dough. Cover and set aside for 30 minutes. Knead for about 3 minutes until smooth and springy, then roll into a long sausage shape and cut into two pieces. Cover one piece with a cloth. Divide the other into 18 pieces and roll out each into a round wrapper about 7cm (2¾″) in diameter. Place a spoonful of the mixture a little off the centre of each wrapper. Fold the pastry around the filling and pleat one side, pressing against the other unpleated side to seal, making a crescent shaped dumpling. Prepare the remaining pastry and make into dumplings.

Cooking

Heat a large flat bottomed pan and add 2½ tbsp oil. Put in dumplings with seams upwards, and fry on moderately high heat for about 1 minute until golden and crisp underneath. Drain off any excess oil, add the chicken stock, cover and simmer for 3-4 minutes, until cooked through. Drain off any remaining liquid. Place a flat plate over the pan and invert dumplings, stuck together, onto it. Reheat the pan, add remaining oil and return the dumplings, seam sides downwards. Fry for about 1 minute, until lightly golden underneath. Lift onto a serving plate and serve hot.

Steamed Meat Dumplings

Ching Chiao Tze 蒸餃子
Makes about 48

Pastry

Refer to the previous recipe, Fried Meat Dumplings.

Filling

See also previous recipe.

Preparation

Prepare the filling, following the instructions given in the previous recipe.

Chill for ½ hour before using.

Prepare a full quantity of the pastry and cut into two pieces. Cover one with a cloth and divide the other into 24 parts. Roll out into thin round wrappers, about 6cm (2½″) in diameter.

Place a spoonful of the filling in each wrapper, a little off-centre. Fold the pastry around the filling and pleat one side, pressing against the unpleated side to seal. This will make crescent shaped dumplings.

Prepare the remaining pastry and make into dumplings, as above.

Cooking

Line a bamboo steaming basket with a clean, thin cloth or use several blanched cabbage leaves.

Place the dumplings in the steamer, leaving a little space between each.

Cover and steam over high heat for 10 minutes. Serve hot with a dip of ginger slivers in vinegar, see page 277.

Four Happiness Dumplings

Szu Hsi Chiao 四喜餃
Makes 36

Pastry

For method of preparing pastry, see previous page.

Filling

45 g (1½ oz)	chive shoots, minced
155 g (5 oz)	semi-fat pork, finely minced
2	egg, beaten
2	dried black mushrooms, soaked and minced
1 medium	carrot, boiled and minced
60 g (2 oz)	green peas, cooked and chopped
	a little cooked oil

Seasoning

½ tsp	sugar
½ tsp	salt
½ tsp	monosodium glutamate
1 tsp	light soy sauce
2 tbsp	cornstarch
	few drops sesame oil
	dash white pepper

Preparation

Mix the pork and chive shoots with the seasoning ingredients and work well with the fingers until the mixture is a smooth paste. Lift from the bowl and slap forcefully back into the bowl continually for about 1 minute to make the paste very smooth and firm. Chill for ½ hour before using.

Prepare a full quantity of the pastry and roll out into a long sausage shape. Cover with a cloth. Break off small pieces and roll out into very thin wrappers about 8cm (3″) in diameter. Place a spoonful of the meat mixture in the centre of each wrapper and pull the pastry up around the filling.

Pinch the edges of the pastry to form four points, then curl over to form four separate compartments, in a four leaf clover shape. Place a small portion of the mushroom, carrot and peas each in one section of every dumpling. Heat the wok, wipe out with an oiled cloth and pour in the beaten egg. Turn the pan so the omelette spreads thinly across the pan. Cook both sides, then remove and leave to cool briefly. Chop very finely and insert a little chopped egg into the remaining empty sections of the dumplings.

Cooking

Arrange in a lightly oiled steamer and cook over high heat for 10 minutes. Remove and serve hot.

Steamed Red Bean Paste Buns
Tou Sha Pao 豆沙包
Makes 24

Dough
For method of preparing sweet dough, see Steamed Bread, page 248.
Filling
315 g (10 oz)   sweet red bean paste

Preparation
Prepare a full quantity of dough and roll out into a long sausage shape. Divide into 24 parts and flatten each with the fingers. Divide the filling into 24 parts and roll each into a ball. Place a ball of filling in the centre of each piece of dough and pull the dough up around it to completely encase; pleat the open edges in a circular fashion leaving a small hole surrounded with the pleated dough. Stick a piece of plain paper over the pleats.

Cooking
Arrange in a bamboo steaming basket and set in a steamer over rapidly boiling water. Cover and steam over high heat for 10 minutes. The buns are cooked when the dough is soft and springy.

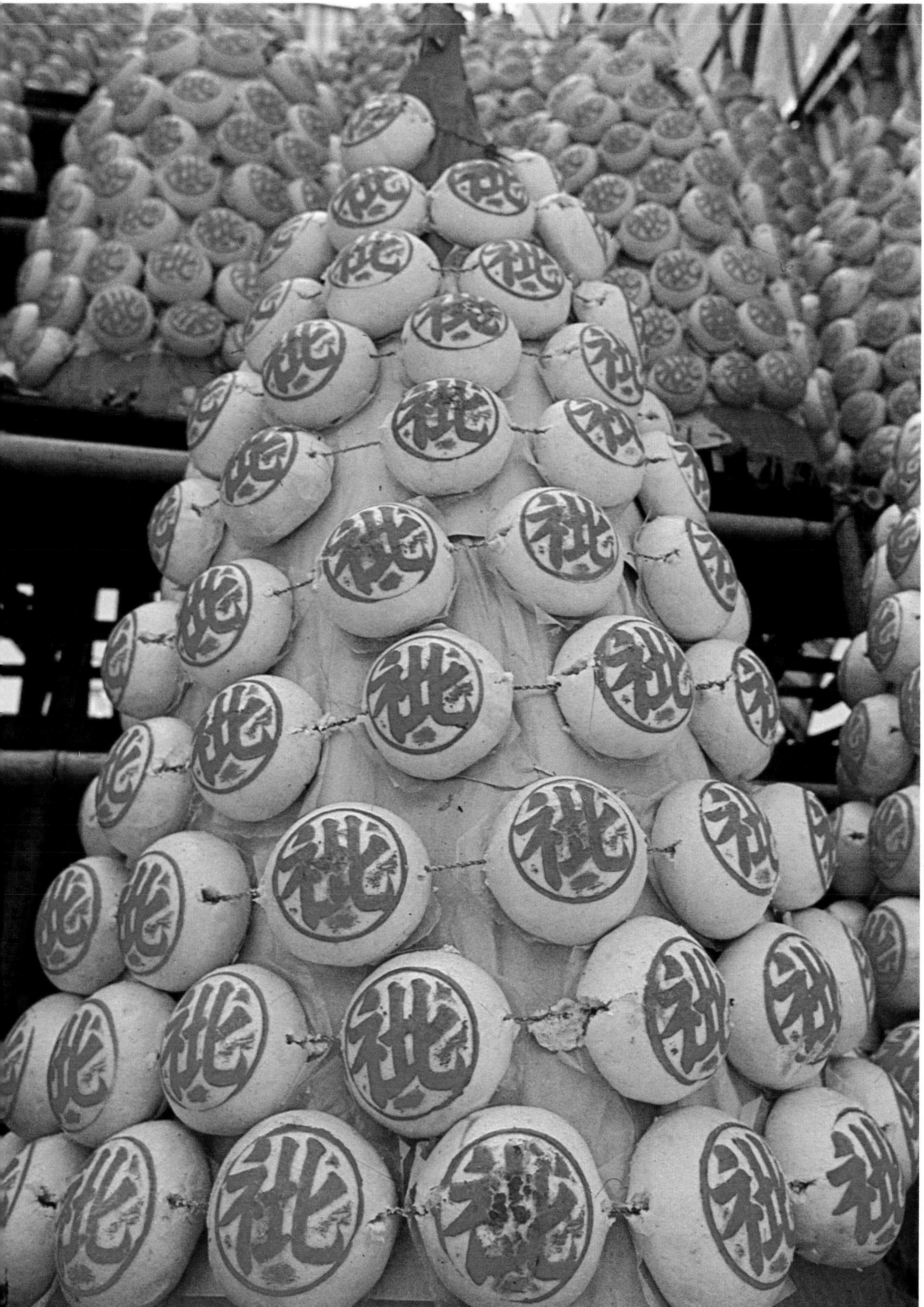

Special Occasions

The Imperial Banquet

If what we read is correct, the Emperors of China probably never indulged in what has come down to us as the Imperial Banquet. More likely, it was wealthy officials, anxious to impress their relatives, who developed the tradition of holding ever more elaborate meals, lasting several days and incorporating the most rare foods, lavishly prepared, served with every embellishment of pomp and circumstance.

The Emperor's kitchens were more impressive for the scale on which they operated, rather than for the quality of the food that they produced. Most of the hundreds of retainers employed in the kitchens of the Emperor were appointed for political, rather than culinary or gastronomic, reasons.

As with their counterparts in other parts of the world, Chinese cooks with outstanding talent were usually reluctant to divulge their secrets. Tricks of the trade were sometimes passed down from one generation to the next, but they were rarely committed to paper. In any event, few of these cooks were able to read or write, and they chose to work by instinct and accumulated knowledge, not to precise directions. Apprenticeship to a master cook was hard and lasted, until not very long ago, for between seven and ten years — or more.

Interesting accounts have been given of an experiment made during the early 1950s in China. Some of the last of the imperial cooks were summoned from retirement and asked to pass on something of their knowledge and skill in the interests of preserving the national heritage. Many of these men were in their seventies and eighties, and had difficulty in recalling the finer details of their art after so many years without practice. But enough material was gathered by the research team to set up a number of eating establishments in Pei Hai (North Sea) Park, in Peking, specialising in dishes 'after the style of the Imperial Kitchen'.

In Hong Kong in recent decades, occasional attempts have been made to revive the idea of the great feast, for the benefit local gourmets or visiting celebrities. T Mandarin Hotel has held several such ba quets over the years, and we quote from introduction to the menu for the last su event in 1970.

"It should not be supposed that a Chin Emperor ever partook of what became kno as an Imperial Banquet — none is recorded ever having spent the necessary three days unrestrained feasting. The Imperial Banqu are of later date and derive most proba from the vast culinary experience gair during the imperial tours when hundreds the finest ingredients that could be discove in the whole of the south and other parts the land were brought together to please Emperor. The tradition of supreme cooki given a head start in those times, continu and was utilised by the wealthy who wished entertain important friends and relatio whether for business or any other reason".

Reproduced on the following pages are parts of menu presented to the people who attended Imperial Banquet served by The Mandarin Hotel, H Kong, in 1970.

Working on the banquet was Chef Lau Cheong, joined The Mandarin Hotel in 1970 as an assistan Chef Leung Sze. Now 46 years old, he was rece promoted to the position of Head Chef of the ho Man Wah Restaurant on Chef Leung Sze's retireme

Lau Cheong is a veteran of two Imperial Banqu something which is quite a testimony to any Chin chef's expertise. What is more, the 1970 Impe Banquet was an acid test of Lau Cheong's organisatic abilities. Most of the necessary food had to be bou well beforehand — an exercise that spanned all of th months — as much of it was anything but rea available. In fact, many of the dishes would be e more difficult to prepare today, particularly The Ei Treasures: monkey, leopard, leopard's embryo, phoe marrow, bear's paw, dragon's liver, elephant's trunk deer.

In the event, the preparations — leading up to actual cooking — took about ten days ... and wer complex that no fewer than 11 assistants were invol

260

The Imperial Banquet

OFFERINGS

THE CARP AT THE DRAGON GATE	FRESH FRUIT PORTRAITS
TWO PHOENIX FACING A LANTERN	FOUR DECORATIVE FRUITS
THE CEREMONY OF INVESTITURE	FOUR FRESH FRUITS GROWN IN WATER
THE THREE HOLY MEN	FOUR FRUITS IN SEASON
THE EIGHT IMMORTALS OF TAOISM	FOUR PRESERVED FRUITS
THE FIVE AUSPICIOUS ANIMALS	FOUR DRIED FRUITS
	FOUR HONEYED FRUITS
	FOUR CRYSTALZED FRUITS
	ALMOND & MELON-SEED

品供

杏仁瓜子　四糖果　四蜜果　四乾果　四京果　四生果　四水果　四省果　四時果　生果像　五瑞獸　八大仙　禽禄雙封　雙鳳朝陽　鯉躍龍門

The Offerings

The offerings are displayed on a table in front of the altar. Among them the pastry figures represent various ideas from Chinese folklore and mythology. But there is more to some of them than simply that.

The Carp at the Dragon Gate means by analogy that any ordinary person has the opportunity of rising to the most exalted position in the State.

The Three Deities are Blessings, Wealth and Longevity.

The Eight Immortals are wise men and women who, having performed meritorious deeds in life became immortals intervening on behalf of the living when asked to do so. Two of them are female.

The Five Auspicious Animals are the Dragon, the Phoenix, the Deer, the Lion, and the mythical Ch'i-lin which resembles the Western concept of a Unicorn.

FIRST REPAST
度弐筵

PRELUDE
— · —

TWO KINDS OF CHINESE DELICACIES
SLICED NOODLES IN SOUP

THE LUNCHEON
— · —

COLD MEAT PLATE PEACOCK PATTERN
FINEST BIRD'S NESTS IN CLEAR SOUP
SLICED CONCH SAUTÉ
BRAISED BEAR PAWS
BARBECUED DUCK
YELLOW FUNGUS AND PIGEON EGGS IN SOUP
BRAISED TURTLE

TWO KINDS OF CHOICE SAVOURIES
WUN-TUN SOUP WITH SLICED GAROUPA

SECOND REPAST
度弐筵

THE DINNER
— · —

SCALLOP SAUTÉ WITH MUSHROOMS
BRAISED BIRD'S NESTS WITH SHARK'S FIN
"BUDDHA'S HAND" STYLE
— · —

STEWED SNOW FROG WITH CRAB CORAL IN SOU
SLICED STURGEON SAUTÉ
STEAMED CHICKEN STUFFED WITH MINCED SHRIM
BARBECUED WHOLE SUCKLING PIG
DOUBLE BOILED WILD DUCK SOUP WITH DEER'S TA
BRAISED BÊCHE-DE-MER WITH YUNNAN HAM
HOT AND SOUR SOUP
CRISP RICE AND BEAN CURD YANGCHOW STYI

TWO KINDS OF PASTRIES
PURÉE OF WATERCHESTNUT

THIRD REPAST
度叁筵

PRELUDE
— · —
TWO KINDS OF SWEET DELICACIES
DOUBLE BOILED FRESH MILK WITH GINGER SAUCE

THE LUNCHEON
— · —
COLD MEAT PLATE BUTTERFLY PATTERN
DOUBLE BOILED WHITE CRANE SOUP WITH CORDYCEPS
BRAISED WILD CAT
FROG'S LEGS SAUTÉ WITH VEGETABLES
BAKED LEG OF PORK MANCHURIAN STYLE
FISH LIPS IN CLEAR SOUP
STEAMED FRESHWATER FISH

TWO KINDS OF CHOICE SAVOURIES
LONGEVITY NOODLES IN SOUP

FOURTH REPAST
度四筵

THE DINNER
— · —
SLICED WOOD PIGEON SAUTÉ WITH CHINESE HAM
STUFFED CHICKEN WINGS WITH CRAB CLAWS

BRAISED SHARK'S FIN
SLICED ABALONE
SLICED SPOTTED DEER SAUTÉ
BARBECUED CHICKEN
CHICKEN KIDNEY WITH SNOW FUNGUS IN SOUP
FRESH PERCH SAUTÉ
ASSORTED MEATS IN SPICED SOUP

TWO KINDS OF PASTRIES
PURÉE OF RED BEAN WITH LOTUS SEED

FIFTH REPAST
度五筵

PRELUDE
— · —
TWO KINDS OF CHINESE DELICACIES
RICE NOODLES WITH CRAB MEAT IN SOUP

THE LUNCHEON
— · —
COLD MEAT PLATE PHEASANT PATTERN
STEWED PARTRIDGE IN SOUP
BRAISED SEA BEAR
LOBSTER SAUTÉ WITH CHICKEN LIVER
ROAST RICE BIRDS
BIRD'S TONGUES WITH VEGETABLES IN SOUP
FROG'S LEGS AND CHICKEN WINGS SAUTÉ

TWO KINDS OF CHOICE PASTRIES
FISH DUMPLINGS IN SOUP

SIXTH REPAST
度陸筵

THE DINNER
— · —
FRESHWATER SHRIMP SAUTÉ
SLICED PIGEON SAUTÉ WITH FRIED MILK
— · —
CHICKEN STUFFED WITH SHARK'S FIN IN CLEAR SOUP
SPECIAL STEAMED FISH
BONED QUAILS SAUTÉ WITH BAMBOO SHOOTS
ROAST SPICED CHICKEN
FROG'S BELLY WITH MINCED SHRIMP IN SOUP
BRAISED YELLOW MUSHROOMS WITH COCKSCOMB
WOOD FUNGUS IN SPICED SOUP
VEGETABLES AND PRESERVED EGGS

TWO KINDS OF PASTRIES
DUMPLINGS IN ALMOND CREAM

Abalone in Oyster Sauce
Hao Yu Yuan Chih Pao Yu 蠔油原隻鮑魚
Serves 12

12	dried abalone (about 250 g/8 oz)
1 kg (2 lb)	leaf mustard
250 g (8 oz)	lean pork, sliced
2-3 slices	ginger
2	scallions
250 ml (8 fl oz)	chicken stock
2 tbsp	cooked oil

Seasoning A

½ tsp	salt
½ tsp	monosodium glutamate
1 tsp	dark soy sauce
1 tbsp	Shao Hsing wine
1 pc	dried tangerine peel

Seasoning B

1 tsp	sugar
½ tsp	salt
½ tsp	monosodium glutamate
2 tsp	dark soy sauce
1 tbsp	Shao Hsing wine
3 tbsp	oyster sauce
1 tsp	sesame oil
	dash white pepper

Thickening — mix together

1 tbsp	cornstarch
1 tbsp	water

Preparation and Cooking

Soak dried abalone in cold water for 6 hours, drain and cover with boiling water. Simmer for about 4 hours, then drain and scrub with a soft brush to clean thoroughly.

Return to the pot, cover with more boiling water and add pork, ginger, scallion and the seasoning A ingredients. Cover and bring back to the boil. Reduce heat and simmer until the abalone is tender, about 6 hours, adding more water as needed to keep the abalone just covered. Remove from the heat and drain well. Trim off the uneven edges. Discard pork, ginger, scallion and peel. Trim leaf mustard, discarding leaves and keeping only about 10cm (4″) of the stems.

Heat the wok, add cooked oil and chicken stock and bring to the boil. Add the leaf mustard stems and bring to the boil. Simmer for 1 minute, drain and arrange around the rim of a serving plate. Keep warm. Add abalone to the pan with the seasoning B ingredients and bring to the boil. Reduce heat and simmer for 5 minutes. Add thickening and stir until the sauce thickens and becomes clear.

Arrange the abalone on the serving plate and pour on the sauce. Serve.

Water Spinach with Pigeons' Eggs
Chu Chieh Miao Ko Tan 竹節苗鴿蛋
Serves 12

2 kg (4 lb)	water spinach
12	pigeons' eggs
1 tsp	light soy sauce
2 tbsp	cornstarch
1 tbsp	cooked oil
2 tbsp	oil
	oil for deep-frying

Seasoning A

½ tsp	salt
100 ml (3 fl oz)	chicken stock
	few drops sesame oil

Seasoning B

1 tbsp	oyster sauce
¾ tsp	cornstarch
2 tsp	water

Preparation
Remove stems from water spinach and rinse very well (weight will reduce to about 500 g/ 1 lb).

Boil pigeons' eggs until hard cooked, cool, then remove shells. Sprinkle with soy sauce and coat thickly with cornstarch. Set aside. Blanch water spinach in boiling water with cooked oil for 1 minute. Remove and drain well. Mix seasoning B ingredients.

Cooking
Heat the wok, add 2 tbsp oil, then pour in seasoning A ingredients and bring to the boil. Add water spinach, reduce heat and stir on moderate heat for 2½ minutes. Drain vegetables, reserving the liquid and arrange on a serving plate.

Clean the wok, add deep-frying oil and heat until almost smoking. Deep-fry eggs for 2 minutes. Drain and arrange on the vegetables. Discard the oil and add reserved liquid to the wok with the seasoning B ingredients. Bring to the boil, then pour over the spinach and eggs. Serve.

Braised Seasonal Vegetables with Yunnan Ham
Tsui P'ien San Pao Su 腿片三寶蔬
Serves 12

750 g (1½ lb)	fresh bamboo shoots
375 g (12 oz)	fresh broccoli
315 g (10 oz)	fresh straw mushrooms
90 g (3 oz)	Yunnan ham, thinly sliced
315 ml (10 fl oz)	chicken or superior stock
6 tbsp	cooked oil
	few drops ginger juice
	few drops Shao Hsing wine

Seasoning

1 tsp	salt
	few drops sesame oil
	dash pepper

Sauce

2 tsp	dark soy sauce
1½ tbsp	oyster sauce
125 ml (48 fl oz)	chicken or superior stock
2 tbsp	cooked oil

Preparation
Peel bamboo shoots, remove hard stems and discard everything but the soft central cores. Angle-cut into bite-size pieces. Cook in boiling water for 25 minutes, drain. Remove thick broccoli stems and cut large heads into pieces. Add to the same water and boil for ½ minute. Drain well. Trim root ends of mushrooms and simmer in another pot of boiling water for 1½-2 minutes. Drain well.

Cooking
Steam sliced ham until softened. Set aside.

Heat the wok, add the oil and stir-fry bamboo shoots with broccoli for 1 minute. Remove and drain. Reheat the wok and stir-fry the mushrooms for ½ minute, remove and drain. Pour off the oil and return mushrooms with half the chicken or superior stock, ginger juice and wine and simmer for 1 minute. Remove and set aside.

Return broccoli and bamboo shoots to the wok with remaining stock and simmer for 1 minute, then return mushrooms, add seasoning ingredients and heat to boil. Remove from the heat, drain well and arrange on a serving plate.

Cut ham into 4cm x 1.5cm (1½" x ½") slices and overlap on top of the vegetables. Mix sauce ingredients in the wok and bring to the boil. Pour over the dish and serve at once.

265

Braised Shark's Fin.

Steamed Sea Bream
Ch'ing Cheng Hsien Li Yu 清蒸鮮鱲魚
Serves 12

1	whole sea bream, bass or garoupa (about 750 g/1½ lb)
45 g (1½ oz)	cooked ham, thinly sliced
45 g (1½ oz)	canned button mushrooms, thinly sliced horizontally
10 slices	ginger, flower-cut
3	scallions, shredded
6 tbsp	superior stock
1 tsp	salt
2 tbsp	cooked oil
Seasoning	
½ tsp	salt
½ tsp	sesame oil
Thickening — mix together	
1 tsp	cornstarch
2 tsp	water

Preparation

Scale, gut and thoroughly wash the fish. Drain well. Make diagonal slits at 2cm (¾″) intervals across both sides of the fish. Rub with salt and place fish on an oiled plate. Cut the ham into small pieces, about the size of mushroom slices and insert ham, mushroom and ginger slices alternately in the slits in the fish. Place half of the scallion around the fish. Pour 1 tbsp oil and 2 tbsp stock over the fish.

Cooking

Set in a steamer over rapidly boiling water, cover and steam for 12-15 minutes, until cooked through.

Remove and set aside, discarding scallion. Heat the wok, add remaining stock and seasoning and bring to the boil. Add thickening and stir until the sauce becomes clear. Pour over the fish. Heat remaining oil in the wok and pour over the fish and surround with Chinese parsley sprigs and remaining scallion. Serve.

Glazed Chicken with Four Treasures
Szu Pao P'ien P'i Chi 四寶片皮雞
Serves 12

1	chicken (about 2 kg/4 lb)
1 lit (32 fl oz)	Lu Shui sauce*

Glaze

3 tbsp	maltose
2 tsp	red vinegar
1 tsp	cornstarch
1 tbsp	water

Four-Treasure Garnish

3 slices	white bread, halved with crusts removed
6	raw shrimps
60 g (2 oz)	Yunnan ham, thinly sliced
60 g (2 oz)	roasted chicken liver, sliced
45 g (1½ oz)	roast pork, cut into 6 pieces
45 g (1½ oz)	chicken liver pate

Seasoning A

¼ tsp	salt
¼ tsp	custard powder
¼ tsp	cornstarch
	few drops sesame oil

Seasoning B

2	egg yolks
¼ tsp	cornstarch

Preparation

Clean and thoroughly wash the chicken, drain and wipe dry. Bring Lu Shui sauce to the boil in a saucepan large enough to hold the chicken. Add the chicken, reduce heat and simmer for 15-20 minutes. Remove and drain well. Wipe dry. Thoroughly mix glaze ingredients and brush thickly over the chicken. Hang to dry for up to 6 hours. Peel and de-vein shrimps and slit almost in halves. Press flat. Brush the seasoning A ingredients over the bread pieces and press a shrimp on top of each. Set aside. Coat the ham and chicken liver slices with the mixed seasoning B ingredients and set aside. Spread the pate thickly over the roast pork slices.

Cooking

Heat the wok, add deep-frying oil and when very hot, deep-fry the ham and liver slices for about ½ minute. Remove, drain well and place in the centre of the serving dish. Reheat the oil and deep-fry the shrimps on toast for 2 minutes. Remove and set aside.

Reheat the oil again and when very hot put in the chicken to fry until skin is very crispy and golden brown. Remove, leave to cool slightly, then carefully separate the skin and de-bone the meat. Cut the meat into bite-size pieces and arrange on the serving plate over the ham and chicken livers. Cut the skin into bite-size pieces and arrange over the meat. Arrange the roast pork and shrimp toast around the edge of the plate and garnish with tomato flowers, parsley sprigs, and, if desired, cubes of pineapple and potato crisps.

*For method of making Lu Shui sauce, see page 159.

Braised Shark's Fin
Hung Shao Tai Pao Chih 紅燒大鮑翅
Serves 12

275 g (12 oz)	dried Ngar Ghan Au Shark's Fin
45 g (1½ oz)	Yunnan ham, shredded
125g (4 oz)	silver sprouts
250 ml (8 fl oz)	chicken stock

Seasoning

1 tbsp	Shao Hsing wine
1 tbsp	ginger juice
1 tbsp	cooked oil

Sauce

½ tsp	salt
1 tsp	monosodium glutamate
2 tsp	dark soy sauce
250 ml (8 fl oz)	chicken stock
2 tbsp	cooked oil

Thickening — mix together

3 tbsp	cornstarch
3 tbsp	water

Preparation

Soak shark's fin in cold water for 2 hours, then bring to the boil and boil for 1 hour on low heat. Drain and cover with more cold water. Repeat the soaking and boiling process three or four times until the fins are softened. Scrub with a brush to clean thoroughly and rinse well in cold water. Pin the shark's fin on a rack to hold in shape. Place in a dish which will fit in a steamer.

Cooking

Sprinkle shark's fin with the seasoning ingredients and pour on the stock. Steam over moderately high heat for 1½ hours. Bring the sauce ingredients to the boil. Add thickening and boil until thickened and clear. Remove the shark's fin from the steamer and detach from the rack. Place on a serving plate and pour on the boiling sauce.

Blanch silver sprouts in boiling water for 1 minute. Drain well and scatter over the shark's fin with the shredded ham, or serve separately with a dish of red vinegar.

267

Double-Boiled Winter Melon Soup
Yuan Tun Tung Kua Chung 原燉冬瓜盅
Serves 12

½	winter melon (about 6 kg/12 lb)
125 g (4 oz)	lean pork, diced
125 g (4 oz)	chicken, diced
30 g (1 oz)	Yunnan ham, finely diced
60 g (2 oz)	angled luffa, peeled and diced
30 g (1 oz)	fresh straw mushrooooms, sliced
60 g (2 oz)	dried duck, soaked and diced
20	dried lotus seeds, boiled
45 g (1½ oz)	fresh shrimps, peeled and diced
60 g (2 oz)	crabmeat, cooked
1 tbsp	minced ham
20	'Yinh Hsieng Hua' buds
1½ lit (48 fl oz)	chicken stock
Seasoning	
2 tsp	salt
1 tsp	monosodium glutamate

Preparation
Decorate the rim of the melon with a zig-zag cut all round. Scoop out seeds and rinse out the melon with boiling water. Drain well. Blanch pork, chicken, Yunnan ham, angled luffa, straw mushrooms and the dried duck in boiling water for 5 minutes. Place in the melon with lotus seeds and add chicken stock and seasoning. Stand upright in a perforated metal or bamboo container in a steamer over boiling water.

Cooking
Cover and simmer over gently boiling water for 4 hours. Add shrimps and crabmeat and simmer for a further 15 minutes. Carefully transfer the melon to a serving container which will hold it upright — or serve in the container in which is was cooked. Stud the zig-zag edge with the 'Yinh Hsieng Hua' buds and sprinkle with minced ham. Serve.

White Fungus in Chilled Watermelon
Tung Hsueh Erh Hsi Kua Chung 凍雪耳西瓜盅
Serves 12

1	watermelon, (about 3½ kg/7 lb)
30 g (1 oz)	dried white fungus, soaked
125 g (4 oz)	rock sugar
500 ml (16 fl oz)	water

Preparation and Cooking
Drain white fungus, pick out any hard parts and discard. Bring water to boil, adding sugar and simmer until sugar is completely dissolved. Add white fungus and cook for 5 minutes.

Remove the top quarter of the melon, then decorate the rim of the larger piece with a scalloped or zig-zag design using a sharp knife. Scoop out the seeds and discard, then cut out the meat and cut into small dice. Return to the melon shell. Scoop the meat from the remaining portion of melon and pass through a juice extractor to obtain a clear pink liquid.

Pour into the shell. Add the fungus and syrup and mix with the watermelon dice. Chill well before serving.

Stir-Fried Rice with Chicken, Shrimp and Mushrooms in Lotus Leaf
Hsien Chi Li Ho Yeh Fan 鮮雞粒荷葉飯
Serves 12

625 g (1¼ lb)	cooked rice (about 280 g/9 oz raw)
185 g (6 oz)	chicken fillet, diced
125 g (4 oz)	boneless roast duck, diced
125 g (4 oz)	fresh shrimp meat, diced
90 g (3 oz)	fresh straw mushrooms, trimmed and sliced
1½ tsp	salt
1 stalk	Chinese parsley, chopped
5 tbsp	cooked oil
1	fresh lotus leaf
Seasoning	
1 tsp	salt
½ tsp	monosodium glutamate
1 tbsp	cornstarch
Omelette	
2	eggs, beaten
1 tsp	oil
	pinch of salt

Preparation
Marinate chicken and shrimp meat with seasoning ingredients for 2 minutes. Blanch straw mushrooms in boiling water for 1 minute. Drain, wash the lotus leaf, wipe dry and brush with oil on the inside.

Cooking
Heat the wok, add 2 tsp oil and pour in beaten eggs. Turn the pan to make a large, thin omelette. Cook on moderate heat until lightly coloured, then turn and cook other side until firm. Remove and leave to cool, then cut into small dice. Reheat the wok, add 3 tbsp oil and stir-fry chicken, duck and shrimp for ½-1 minute. Remove and set aside. Add mushrooms and stir-fry for 1 minute, then add the remaining oil and stir-fry rice until lightly coloured.

Return the chicken, duck and shrimp and add the salt. Stir on moderate heat for 1½ minutes. Add the cooked egg and chopped parsley and mix well. Place the lotus leaf in a dish and pile on the fried rice. Fold into a parcel and invert to hold the edges closed. Place in a steamer over rapidly boiling water. Cover and steam for 15 minutes. Unfold the leaf and serve hot.

Fried Meat Dumplings Dipped in Soup
Shang T'ang Chien Fen Kao 上湯煎粉果
Serves 12

Pastry

125 g (4 oz)	rice powder
30 g (1 oz)	'Tang' flour
150 ml (5 fl oz)	boiling water
	pinch of salt

Filling

75 g (2½ oz)	semi-fat pork, diced
75 g (2½ oz)	fresh shrimp meat, diced
75 g (2½ oz)	soaked black mushrooms, diced
60 g (2 oz)	canned bamboo shoots, diced
2 tsp	Chinese parsley, finely chopped
3 tbsp	cooked oil
	oil for shallow frying

Seasoning

1 tsp	sugar
½ tsp	salt
1 tsp	light soy sauce
1 tsp	cornstarch
	few drops sesame oil

Soup

½ tsp	salt
1 tsp	light soy sauce
1½ lit (48 fl oz)	chicken stock

Preparation
Mix the pork, shrimp, mushrooms, bamboo shoots and parsley with the seasoning ingredients. Stir-fry on moderate heat for 2 minutes. Remove and leave to cool, then chill for ½ hour before using. Bring water to boil. Add rice powder, salt and Tang flour and stir very quickly until the flour is well mixed and becomes transparent. Cover and leave for 5 minutes, then knead to a smooth pliable pastry. Divide into 24 portions. Using an oiled pastry cleaver press down on the pastry and turn in a circular motion about three times right, three times left, to make a thin round wrapper about 8cm (3″) in diameter. Peel from the board with the cleaver. Place a spoonful of the filling in the centre of each wrapper and fold over to make a half circle. Pinch the edges together.

Cooking
Heat the wok, add shallow oil and when very hot reduce heat slightly. Add the dumplings and fry on one side until golden, about 1½ minutes, turn and fry other side until golden. Drain and arrange on a serving plate.

Bring soup ingredients to the boil and pour into several small bowls. Serve with the dumplings.

"I am very fond of a little wine with my meals but I do not like elaborate food, or too many dishes at a time."

Shen Fu

Pork Shoulder with 'Fat Choy' — *recipe on page 276;* Sauteed Clams with Hoisin Sauce — *recipe on page 273.*

Lotus Seed Tea with Eggs; 'Long Life' Buns.

Sauteed Clams with Hoisin Sauce
Fa Ts'ai Tai Hsien 發財大蜆
Serves 12

2½ kg (5 lb)	fresh clams
2 tsp	garlic, minced
2 tbsp	scallion, minced
4-5 tbsp	cooked oil

Seasoning:

1¼ tsp	sugar
1 tsp	salt
1 tbsp	black vinegar
2 tbsp	hoisin sauce

Preparation
Wash the clams thoroughly. Cook in boiling water until they open, shaking the pan occasionally, Drain and set aside. Mix the seasoning ingredients.

Cooking
Heat the wok, add the oil and when it is very hot add the garlic and scallion and cook briefly. Add the clams and seasonings and stir-fry for 2-3 minutes. Serve.

'Long Life' Buns
Shou Pao 壽包
Makes 24

600 g (19 oz)	all purpose flour
2 tbsp	baking powder
60 g (2 oz)	sugar
345 ml (11 fl oz)	warm water
	red food colouring powder

Filling

| 315 g (10 oz) | lotus seed paste |

Preparation
Sieve flour and baking powder into a bowl and add sugar. Add warm water a little at a time, working well into the flour. Do not use all the water if dough begins to become sticky. Knead until smooth and soft. Divide in halves and roll each out into a long sausage shape. Cut each into 12 pieces.

Flatten each piece with the fingers.

Roll the lotus seed paste into a sausage and cut into 24 pieces. Roll each into a ball and coat with a little cornflour. Place a lotus seed paste ball on a piece of dough and work the dough around the filling, pinching the edges to seal well. Mould into a peach shape, with a point at one end. Prepare all the buns and stick small pieces of plain paper underneath.

Cooking
Arrange in a bamboo steaming basket and set in a steamer over rapidly boiling water. Cover and steam for about 6 minutes. Leave plenty of space between the buns as they will expand to about double the size during cooking.

Remove from the steamer and press the back of a knife along each bun to make an indentation similar to that of a peach. Rub a little red food colouring mixed with water near the tips of each 'peach'. Serve hot or cold.

Lotus Seed Tea with Eggs
Lien Tzu Chi Tan Ch'a 蓮子雞蛋茶
Serves 12

185 g (6 oz)	dried white lotus seeds, soaked
125 g (4 oz)	sugar
12	eggs

'Tea'

| 315 g (10 oz) | sugar |
| 2 lit (64 fl oz) | water |

Preparation and Cooking
Drain lotus seeds, place in a saucepan with cold water to about 5cm (2") above the seeds. Add sugar and bring to the boil, stirring until sugar dissolves. Reduce heat and simmer until the seeds are softened, about 20 minutes. Drain. Boil eggs until hard-boiled, remove shells and set aside.

Boil the water, add sugar and stir until dissolved. Add lotus seeds and bring back to the boil. Add in eggs and leave to simmer for 2 minutes. Serve hot.

Bitter, salt, sour, hot and sweet: there are dishes of all flavours,

Ribs of the fatted ox cooked tender and succulent;

Sour and bitter blended in the soup of Wu:

Stewed turtle and roast kid, served up with yam sauce;

Geese cooked in sour sauce, casseroled duck, fried flesh of the great crane;

Braised chicken, seethed tortoise, high-seasoned, but not to spoil the taste;

Ch'u Tzu

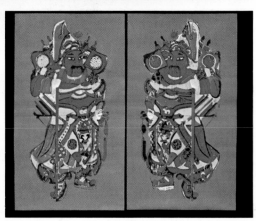

Feeding the Hungry Ghosts

No month in the Chinese lunar calendar is not marked by several festivals; and each of these is duly celebrated either by every Chinese person, or by those Chinese people for whom it has a particular relevance: because it has to do with their regional background, for example, or because it is in honour of a god who traditionally watches over some aspect of their domestic or working lives.

In almost every case, food plays as significant a part in these celebrations as it does in every other aspect of Chinese life.

There are foods that are exchanged as gifts, offered to visitors or served at banquets in the belief that they will convey good fortune, happiness, long life or prosperity to those who eat them. Again, there are foods that are sacrificed at grave sides, shrines and altars to recently-departed relatives and friends, long-departed ancestors, the divinities who control the welfare of the living, or the 'hungry ghosts' (whose festival is held on the 15th

day of the Seventh Moon) — all of this being a homage to the inhabitants of another world who rely on the inhabitants of this world to feed and clothe them, and to furnish their everyday needs.

桔砂珠

Pork Shoulder with 'Fat Choy'
Fa Ts'ai Yuan T'i 發財元蹄

Serves 12

1½ kg (3 lb)	pork shoulder
45 g (1½ oz)	fa ts'ai*
750 g (1½ lb)	Chinese lettuce
1½ tbsp	dark soy sauce
1 tsp	salt
3 tbsp	cooked oil
	oil for deep-frying

Seasoning

2½ tbsp	sugar
2 tsp	salt
3	anise stars
1 tsp	monosodium glutamate
3 tbsp	preserved beancurd
315 ml (10 fl oz)	chicken stock

Thickening — mix together

2 tsp	cornstarch
2 tbsp	water

Thickening — mix together

Cut pork shoulder into chunks, place in a saucepan, cover with water and boil until it begins to soften, about 45 minutes. Soak fa ts'ai in cold water to soften. Drain pork and rub with dark soy sauce, then leave to dry out a little. Heat wok, add deep-frying oil and when very hot, reduce heat slightly. Deep-fry pork for several minutes, until the skin bubbles and is lightly coloured. Remove from the oil, drain and rinse in hot water to remove excess oil. Place in a dish and add the seasoning. Set over a steamer, cover and steam over rapidly boiling water for ½ hour. Drain, reserving sauce. Arrange pork pieces on a serving plate.

Wash lettuce, then stir-fry with the cooked oil and salt for ¾ minute. Arrange around the pork.

Drain fa ts'ai, add to the wok with the reserved sauce and bring to the boil. Add thickening and stir until clear. Pour sauce over the pork and serve.

Note: *Fa Ts'ai is a type of gelatinous seaweed, almost black in colour and resembling human hair.
It is a Cantonese custom to serve Fa Ts'ai (or Fat Choy, in the Cantonese dialect) at Chinese New Year, as the words form part of the New Year greeting, "Kung Hei Fat Choy". It is said to bring prosperity and good fortune.

Pork Knuckles with Ginger in Sweet Vinegar Sauce
T'ien Ting T'ien Tsu Chu Chio Chiang
添丁甜醋豬脚羌

Note: It is a Cantonese custom that after a baby is born the family will cook this dish for the confined mother to share with friends and relatives who visit her, within the first month from the birth. The name implies 'A gift from the stork.'

Serves 8

1½ kg (3 lb)	pork knuckles
1 kg (2 lb)	ginger

Sauce

1 lit (32 fl oz)	sweet vinegar
500 ml (16 fl oz)	white vinegar
250 g (8 oz)	sugar
1 tbsp	salt

Preparation and Cooking

Have the butcher trim the knuckles well. Shave and cut each in halves. Place in a large pot of boiling water and boil for about ½ hour. Peel ginger, cut into large pieces and crush slightly, then add to the pot after the knuckles have boiled for about 20 minutes. Drain pork, reserving ginger with the knuckles.

Pour the sauce ingredients into a large casserole or earthenware pot and bring to the boil, stirring constantly. Add the knuckles and ginger and bring to the boil again. Cover and simmer until the knuckles are very soft, about 1½ hours. Stir frequently. Remove from the heat and leave for 24 hours before serving for maximum flavour. Reheat before serving.

Note: Because of the preservative qualities of the sauce, refrigeration is unnecessary for up to 24 hours in a moderate climate.

Garlic Dip
Suan Yung Ts'u　蒜蓉醋

| 2 tbsp | white vinegar |
| 1 tbsp | garlic, finely chopped |

Mix the two ingredients together and leave for several hours before using.

Ginger Juice
Chiang Chik　羌汁

| 2 tbsp | ginger |
| 2 tsp | water |

Peel and finely mince ginger and place in a piece of muslin. Squeeze tightly to extract as much juice as possible. Pour the water over the ginger pith and squeeze again until dry.

Ginger Wine
Chiang Chik Chiu　羌汁酒

| 8 slices | ginger |
| 4 tbsp | Shao Hsing wine |

Place the ginger and wine in a screw top jar and leave for several days before using.

Ginger and Scallion Dip
Chiang Chung Yu　羌葱油

4 slices	ginger
2	scallions, white parts only
1 tsp	salt
6 tbsp	cooked oil

Finely shred ginger and scallion. Add salt. Heat the oil until hazy and pour over the ginger and scallion. Stir, then leave to cool before using.

Spicy Salt Dip
Huai Yen　淮鹽

| 4 tbsp | salt |
| 1½ tsp | five-spices powder |

Heat salt in a dry pan, stirring constantly, until beginning to colour. Remove from the heat and leave to cool slightly, then mix in finely ground five-spices powder and stir well. When cool transfer to a jar with a screw top lid to store.

Pepper Salt Dip
Chiao Yen　椒鹽

| 4 tbsp | salt |
| 1 tbsp | brown peppercorns |

Toast the peppercorns in a dry pan until very fragrant, about 1 minute, stirring constantly. Remove, pour into a mortar and pound to a fine powder. Heat salt in the dry pan, stirring constantly, until beginning to colour. Remove from the heat and leave to cool slightly, then mix in the powdered pepper. When cool transfer to a jar with a screw top lid to store.

Red Vinegar Dip
Hung Ts'u　紅醋

Chinese red rice vinegar, used unadulterated, as a dip.

Ginger Slivers in Vinegar
Chiang Ts'u　羌醋

4 slices	ginger, shredded
1 tsp	sugar
2 tbsp	white vinegar

Heat the vinegar gently, adding sugar. Stir until dissolved. Pour over the ginger and leave for several hours before using.

Five-Spices Bouquet
Wu Hsiang　五香

5 g (⅙ oz)	brown peppercorns
5 g (⅙ oz)	fennel seeds
5 g (⅙ oz)	cinnamomum cassia (cinnamon bark)
5 g (⅙ oz)	star anise
5 g (⅙ oz)	clove

Tie the spices in a small square of muslin so they can easily be retrieved from the dish before serving.

Five-Spices Powder
Wu Hsiang Fen　五香粉

Grind the same spices used in preparing a Five-Spices Bouquet, to a fine powder. Store in screw top jar.

Superior Stock
Shang T'ang 上湯

1 large	boiler chicken (about 2½ kg/5 lb)
30 g (1 oz)	Yunnan ham, 2.5cm (1″) cubes
5 slices	ginger
2	scallions
2 lit (64 fl oz)	water
	salt
	white pepper

Clean and thoroughly wash the chicken. Place in a large saucepan with the ham and water and bring to the boil. Reduce heat and simmer for 1½ hours. Add ginger, scallion and seasonings and simmer for a further 1½-2 hours. Skim the stock every 15 minutes, but do not remove all of the fat, as this gives the stock much of its flavour. Strain and discard all solid ingredients.

Chicken Stock
Chi Shang T'ang 鷄上湯

1 kg (2 lb)	chicken trimmings (bones, wings, legs, necks)
5 slices	ginger
2	scallions
2 lit (64 fl oz)	water
	salt
	white pepper

Wash the chicken trimmings and place in a saucepan with the water. Bring to the boil, skim, then cover and boil for 1 hour on moderate heat. Add the ginger, scallion and seasonings and simmer for 15 minutes, but do not remove all of the fat, as this gives the stock much of its flavour. Strain and discard all solid ingredients.

Substitute Wine Lees Paste
Hung Mi Tsao Chiang 紅米糟醬

2 tsp	sugar
1 tbsp	soya bean paste
2 tbsp	Shao Hsing wine
1 tsp	preserved beancurd

Mix the ingredients and leave for several hours before using. Store in a screw-top jar.

Sweet Bean Paste Dip
Tien Tou Chiang 甜豆醬

4 tbsp	sugar
4 tbsp	sweet bean paste
2 tbsp	sesame oil
125 ml (4 fl oz)	water

Mix sugar, bean paste and water well.

Heat the pan, add sesame oil and heat until very warm. Add the mixed ingredients and stir on high heat until the sugar is completely dissolved, and the sauce thickened. Cool before using.

Rendered Chicken Fat
Chi Yu 鷄油

Place fresh chicken fat from the inside of a chicken, in a double boiler over boiling water. Cover and cook until all the oil is extracted, about 1 hour, depending on the amount of fat. Strain and store in a screw top jar in the refrigerator.

Sweet Red Bean Paste
Hung Tou Sha Hsien 紅豆沙餡

Boil small red beans in plenty of water, until completely soft. Drain and mash or pass through a sieve to make a thick puree. Place in the wok over moderate heat and slowly blend in sugar and vegetable oil or lard until the paste is sweet, smooth and shiny. Can be kept in the refrigerator for several months.

Sweet and Sour Sauce
Tien Suan Chiang 甜酸醬

4 tbsp	sugar
¼ tsp	salt
½ tsp	light soy sauce
4 tbsp	red vinegar
1 tsp	ginger, minced
2 tsp	leek, finely chopped
100 ml (3 fl oz)	water
1 tbsp	cornstarch
2 tsp	cooked oil
	few drops red food colouring

Mix all the ingredients together in the wok and bring to the boil. Cook until the sauce is smooth and clear.

Chapter 6

Eating & Drinking

*Insights into the approach of
the Chinese to eating at home and
'eating out' ... and to drinking
with Chinese food.*

Eating at Home

Chinese cooking at home remains a personal mixture of science and artistry. In many families, the cook is the wife of the head of the family. Sometimes the mother-in-law superintends the kitchen, even if she does not actually prepare everything herself. Wealthy families tend to regard an outstanding professional cook as a conveted status symbol, on a level with a Rolls Royce or a rare *objet d'art.* Tales of paragon poaching in the acquisition of the best cook of the moment circulate from time to time, invoking mingled gasps of amazement and sighs of envy.

In time gone by, meal-time was hedged around by many social barricades. Male family members were waited on by their womenfolk, and it was unheard of for both sexes to eat together. For the poor, space was precious and it was rarely feasible for all to sit around the same table. Today, there can be few Chinese families, however, who do not meet at mealtime, at least once a day.

Given the nature of a Chinese meal, served in communal portions for all to help themselves, a round table is the only sensible arrangement. All are thus placed equally when it comes to reaching for food; seating can be more readily adjusted to accommodate extra diners as required.

Each diner has chopsticks, a rice bowl, a small plate or saucer (for bones) and a porcelain spoon possibly to partner the extra soup bowl. Chopstick rests may be supplied, but only on more pretentious occasions; and the same goes for individual serving spoons. A tea bowl will probably be lined up at each plate, although the tea may not be served until after the meal.

The basic principle wherever Chinese food is eaten, remains the same — one dish per head. Extra numbers mean extra variety, rather than larger quantities of a particular dish. Everyone at the table is given a bowl of plain steamed rice. More rice is placed on, or near, the table to provide further helpings.

A typical lunch or dinner for eight or ten people might include four meat dishes, two vegetable dishes, one fish dish and a soup. (Soup is considered important as an aid to washing down rice, and is therefore served well after the beginning of a meal). Dessert, with the exception of fruit, is relatively rare.

Bear in mind that most dishes include a number of different ingredients, so one would expect to find meat and vegetables mixed together in several of the dishes.

Eating patterns vary from one family to another, but, until recently, most people began the day with steaming hot congee (a rice gruel). Accompanying it might be salt fish, salty peanuts, vegetables, minced pork or preserved egg. Finely sliced fish cooks well in the hot congee, and so does a beaten raw egg. Fried dough-sticks — the Cantonese name for which translates as 'fried ghost' — serve to provide oil and a welcome addition of protein.

For convenience many Hong Kong families are switching to toasted or plain bread these days for breakfast. The morning meal is most likely eaten at home, although, like every other kind of meal and in-between snack, it can be found in restaurants.

"The rice is opened; please come in!"

The summons of a Chinese host and hostess, urging their guests to enter the dining room.

---

1. Soup Bowl
2. Rice Bowl
3. Saucer
4. Shark's Fin Bowl
5. Chopsticks
6. Porcelain Soup Spoon
7. Tea Pot
8. Round Serving Platter
9. Soup Serving Spoon
10. Covered Soup Bowl
11. Oval Cold Dish Platter
12. Deep Serving Plate
13. Small Serving Platter
14. Condiment Dish
15. Bone Plate
16. Soy Sauce Dish
17. Tea Cup

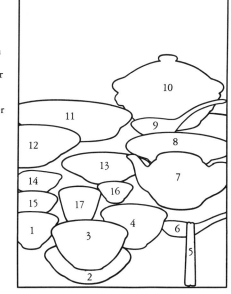

Elaborate Family Menu

Serves 4-6 persons

Roast 'Gold Coin' Pork

Stewed Lamb with Dry Beancurd

Steamed Garoupa with Ham and Vegetables

Sauteed Squid with Celery

Double-Boiled Chicken with White Fungus in Soup

Celebration Family Dinner

Serves 8-10 persons

Barbecued Pork

Braised Bird's Nest with Pigeons' Eggs

Prawn Cutlets

Chicken with Ham and Green Vegetables

Sliced Duck with Winter Bamboo Shoots

Eight-Treasure Beancurd Soup

Braised Mushrooms with Vegetables

Yang Chow Fried Rice

Cantonese-Style Family Meal

Serves 4-6 persons

Braised Shin of Beef with 'Cloud Ears' and 'Golden Needles'

Diced Pork with Walnuts

Steamed Fish and Beancurd Cake

Chicken Meatballs Garnished with Glutinous Rice

Sliced Pork Liver and Matrimony Vine Soup

White Rice

Southern-Style Family Dinner
Serves 8-10 persons

'White-Cut' Chicken with Ginger and Scallion Dip

Beef Balls, Kweilin Style

Fried Milk, Ta Liang Style

Sauteed Prawns with Chinese Broccoli

Diced Pork with Walnuts

Fried Stuffed Dace

Stir-Fried Seasonal Vegetables

Pork Tripe and Gingko Nut Soup

White Rice

Sweet Almond Milk

Simple Southern-Style Menu
Serves 4-6 persons

Steamed Chicken on Lotus Leaf

Braised Marrow with Conpoy Sauce

Fried Eggs Whampoa

Fried Salted Fish

Sliced Pork Liver and Matrimony Vine Soup

White Rice

Vegetarian Family Meal
Serves 4-6 persons

Vegetarian Goose

Cheng Tu Vegetarian Stew

Braised Mushrooms with Vegetables

Mushrooms with Crispy Rice Crackers in Soup

White Rice

Simple Northern-Style Menu
Serves 4-6 persons

Spiced Pork Spare Ribs

Smoked Chicken, Peiping Style

Steamed Bread

Sliced Fish in Wine Sauce

Braised Beancurd with Mushrooms

Chicken Blood in Soup

Cantonese-Style Festival Menu
Serves 6-8 persons

Paper-Wrapped Chicken, Wu Chou Style

Sauteed Sliced Beef with Oyster Sauce

Fried Crispy Pomfret

Steamed Meat Cake with Salted Fish

Braised Mushrooms with Vegetables

Eight-Treasure Beancurd Soup

White Rice

Sweet Almond Milk

Northern-Style Family Meal
Serves 4-6 persons

Deep-Fried Eel, Wu Hsi Style

Fish Dressed as Crab

Spicy Beancurd with Ground Pork

Stir-Fried Diced Chicken with Bean Paste

Yellow Fish in Soup

Vegetable Rice

"Each *hu-ping* (deep-fried puff pastries) shop had three to five men to prepare and mix the dough and man the braziers. From the fifth watch (7.00 a.m. to 9.00 a.m.), their voices could be heard far and wide."

Meng Yuan-lao

Top picture, from right: Steamed Pork with Salted Cabbage — *recipe on page 103;* Fried Crispy Pomfret — *recipe on page 168;* Braised Mushrooms with Vegetables — *recipe on page 213;* Stir-Fried Beef with Onion and Angled Luffa — *recipe on page 119;* White Rice — *method on page 229.*

Eating Out

In Hong Kong, at least, eating out covers every kind of food in every type of restaurant, served with every degree of style — or lack of

it. 'Five-star' establishments can produce an Imperial Banquet costing several thousands of dollars, lasting for a few days and lingering in the memory for a lifetime. Modest pavement food-stalls (*ta pai tang* 大牌檔) have their own specialities. While Northern Chinese tend to eat three major meals a day — morning, noon and evening — with fewer snacks, Southern Chinese have a different way of life. The morning and evening meals are relatively fixed institutions, but lunch may well be a very different kind of repast; and it may be eaten mid-morning or mid-afternoon. Such snacks are collectively termed by the Cantonese as *dim sum* (or *tien hsin* in the national language romanization), served in a tea house which often has much the same function as the neighbourly public house in an English context.

The dumplings and pastries served in a tea house must be subtle enough to compete with the fine teas enjoyed by connoisseurs.

Pictured at right, clockwise from top right: Sliced Duck with Winter Bamboo Shoots — *recipe on page 153;* Sauteed Prawns with Chinese Broccoli — *recipe on page 169;* Fried Eggs Whampoa — *recipe on page 217.*

The atmosphere is leisurely, with friends meeting regularly at the same table in the same establishment, year after year. Businessmen still keep 'office hours' in a favourite tea house, where professional middle-men can be sure of locating them.

By no means everything eaten at home originates in the family kitchen. Take-aways and home catering services have several centuries of respectable tradition. And a study in themselves are the mobile kitchens — kitchens on wheels — supplying congee or noodles in soup, dumplings in season, freshly

steamed peanuts, roasted chestnuts, grilled salt fish or satay, or deep-fried prawns or beancurd, to be consumed on the spot or carried home. And for dessert, peeled pear, fresh orange or sugar cane juice and coconut 'milk shake' are produced on the spot.

Chinese Restaurants

Limitations of space or skill at home make eating out a matter of routine for many people in Hong Kong and even, so we are told, in modern China. The restaurant chef is blessed with more space than his home counterpart and is probably something of a specialist. Indeed, most Chinese eating establishments, humble or grand, attain a certain degree of fame for their ways with one or another type of food. Regional specialities are equally important, and a single superb recipe may be a restaurant's passport to fame.

Entertaining in restaurants is part of the life-style for many Chinese. Meal vouchers can be a welcome gift, like a book token: the recipient need not feel obliged to invite the donor to the feast when it takes place.

A host may well decide to treat friends to a meal in a restaurant which specialises in food from his own home region: or the restaurant may be selected for its skill with a seasonal delicacy. Devotees rightly claim that only a Shanghai restaurant, for instance, can truly serve Shanghai crabs.

Decor is rarely a deciding factor in selecting a restaurant. Indeed some of the best Chinese restaurants seem to take perverse pride in their utilitarian surroundings, plastic table tops and bright lights. The proprietor, rightly, argues that food will always bring fame and fortune, but too much money spent on the decorating of an establishment can give rise to suspicion.

Banquets, for ten or tens of dozens of people — to celebrate a wedding or the birthday of a senior member of the family — almost invariably take place in a restaurant. The usual procedure is for the organiser to visit the establishment some weeks ahead to book tables. The high points of the meal will be determined by the price agreed. If shark's fin soup or some rarer delicacy like turtle is to be the climax, then the other dishes will have to be selected to provide proper relief. Each dish should be memorable in itself, while still leaving the main dish at the pinnacle.

"There is no need of combining the five tastes extremely well or harmonizing the different sweet odours. And efforts should not be made to procure rare delicacies from far countries."

Extract from the Laws of Eating and Drinking of the Ancient Sage-Kings.

In the past, the formalities of banquet organisation contained many pitfalls for the unwary. Even the seat of honour varied according to traditions of China's various regions. Today, much of the ritual etiquette has been forgotten, but there are still some aspects of a formal banquet which catch the newcomer by surprise. Play things by ear, and be every-ready to jump to your feet to take part in a toast — to the host, to other guests, or even to the next course in the meal. Do not feel tempted to linger after the meal is finished. A few polite words of thanks and farewell to your host are all that is required.

Many small Chinese restaurants cater largely to regular customers, to the extent of storing private bottles of liquor (almost inevitably five-star Cognac) for them. Informality is the keynote, with the kitchen the most serious area of the place. You will probably be greeted by the sound of quick-frying and rhythmic stirring and chopping from that quarter. Your host may not look at the menu. Instead, he will have a lengthy session with the waiter as a prelude to ordering. Moreover, no-one would be particularly surprised if he entered the kitchen to ensure that everything was being prepared as required. No doubt the remarkable standard of cooking in all types of Chinese restaurants owes much to generations of cooks and gourmets having worked harmoniously together.

Seafood Dinner
Serves 6-8 persons

Steamed Prawns

Deep-Fried Rice Birds

Braised Crabs in Ginger Sauce

Deep-Fried Oysters

Steamed Sea Bream

Beancurd Stuffed with Shrimp Paste

Stir-Fried Seasonal Vegetables

Chinese Parsley and Sliced Fish Soup

Yang Chow Fried Rice

Sweet Almond Milk

Elaborate Northern-Style Menu
Serves 8-10 persons

Drunken Chicken

Prawn Cutlets

Shark's Fin and Chicken in Soup

Camphor and Tea Smoked Duck

Braised Carp Tails

Steamed Bread

Fish Lips with Crispy Rice Crackers

Braised Lamb

Cheng Tu Vegetarian Stew

Candied Apple

Szechwan-Style Festival Menu
Serves 8-10 persons

Cold Seasoned Beef

Tangerine Peel Chicken

Crispy Rice Crackers with Seafood and Vegetables

Crispy Yellow River Carp

Fried Spiced Duck

'Family Meal' Beancurd

Bitter Melon Rings Stuffed with Shrimp Paste

Hot and Sour Soup

Szechwan Noodles

Dumplings with Red Chilli Sauce

Lotus Root Pudding

Cantonese-Style Formal Dinner
Serves 12 persons

Asparagus and Bamboo Fungus in Cream Sauce

Stuffed Crab Claws

Shark's Fin in Brown Sauce

Braised Duck with Lo Han Vegetables

Steamed Garoupa with Ham and Vegetables

Double-Boiled Pigeons with Mushrooms

Sliced Pork Liver and Matrimony Vine Soup

Salt-Baked Chicken

Yang Chow Fried Rice

Two Sides Browned Noodles with Pork and Vegetables

Sweet Almond Milk

Steamed Red Bean Paste Buns

Cantonese-Style Banquet
Serves 12 persons

Cold Meat Combination

Braised Seasonal Vegetables with Yunnan Ham

Water Spinach with Pigeons' Eggs

Braised Shark's Fin

Glazed Chicken with Four Treasures

Abalone in Oyster Sauce

Double-Boiled Winter Melon Soup

Steamed Sea Bream

Stir-Fried Rice with Chicken, Shrimp and Mushrooms in Lotus Leaf

Fried Meat Dumplings dipped in Soup

White Fungus in Chilled Watermelon

Simple Northern-Style Menu
Serves 4-6 persons

Tangerine Peel Beef

Shredded Pork with Preserved Vegetables

Poached Chicken with Hot Sesame Sauce

Sliced Fish in Wine Sauce

Hot and Sour Soup

White Rice

Hakka-Style Dinner
Serves 6-8 persons

Salt-Baked Chicken

Deep-Fried Pork Intestines

Steamed Pork with Salted Cabbage

Fried Milk, Ta Liang Style

Bitter Melon Rings Stuffed with Shrimp Paste

Braised Mushrooms with Vegetables

Pork Tripe and Gingko Nut Soup

White Rice

Simple Northern-Style Menu
Serves 4-6 persons

Shantung Chicken

Sesame Beef

Beancurd with Shredded Pork in Soup

Deep-Fried Bamboo Shoots, Salted Cabbage and
    Conpoy

Pork Meatballs in Casserole

Fried Noodles with Mixed Meat and Vegetables

Pancake Dinner
Serves 6-8 persons

Stir-Fried Eggs with Shredded Meat, Cloud Ear
    Fungus and Vegetables

Peiping Shredded Pork

Stir-Fried Beef with Scallions

Fried Fresh Prawns

Mandarin Pancakes

Stewed Cabbage in Cream Sauce

Braised Fish with Beancurd and Vegetables

Chiu Chow-Style Dinner
Serves 6-8 persons

'Lu Shui' Goose

Fried Shrimp Balls

Fu Yung Crab in Cabbage Rolls

Pan-Fried Oyster Cake

Fried Crispy Pomfret

Stir-Fried Seasonal Vegetables

Fish Meatballs in Soup

White Rice

Sweet Taro Cream

Shanghai-Style Banquet
Serves 12 persons

Spiced Sliced Beef

Drunken Crabs

Deep-Fried Spiced Chicken

Stir-Fried Pork Kidneys

Vegetables Braised with Chicken Fat

Fish Heads in Casserole

Spiced Pork Spare Ribs

Braised Beancurd with Mushrooms

Stir-Fried Shanghai Noodles

Steamed Meat Dumplings

Minced Date Cake

Festival Northern-Style Menu
Serves 8-10 persons

Cold Meat Combination

Fried Prawns in Hot Sauce

Fish Dressed as Crab

Steamed Duck in Wine Sauce

Silver Thread Rolls with Ham

Hilsa Herring on Hot Plate

Exotic-Tasting Chicken

Braised Chinese Cabbage with Chestnuts

Chicken Soup with Bamboo Fungus in Hot Pot

Fried Meat Dumplings

Golden Puffs with Sweet Red Bean Paste

Peking-Style Banquet
Serves 12 persons

Jellied Lamb Loaf

Salad with Agar Agar

Fried Shrimp on Croutons with Sesame Seeds

Stir-Fried Beef with Scallions

Roast Peking Duck

Hilsa Herring on Hot Plate

Braised Beche-de-Mer with Scallions

Braised Chinese Cabbage with Chestnuts

Duck Carcass Soup

Fried Meat Dumplings

Noodles with Minced Beef and Celery Hearts

Candied Apple

Szechwan-Style Banquet
Serves 12 persons

Shredded Jelly-Fish Salad

Sliced Pork with Garlic Sauce

Fried Prawns in Hot Sauce

'Bon Bon' Chicken

Beche-de-Mer with Crispy Rice Crackers

Fish Flavoured Shredded Pork

Silver Thread Rolls with Ham

Braised Fish with Beancurd and Vegetables

Stir-Fried Seasonal Vegetables

Bamboo Fungus Soup

Dumplings with Red Chilli Sauce

Eight-Treasure Rice

Drinking with Chinese Food

Tea has been part of the Chinese way of life for many thousands of years. Certainly literary references from as early as AD 270 reveal tea-drinking as an already well-established habit. The very proper mistrust of unboiled drinking water perhaps led directly or indirectly to tea drinking. After all, you cannot make tea with water that is below boiling point as the leaves refuse to settle, and your lack of due care is revealed indisputably for all to see.

Fanciful stories relate how one of the ancient sages (or was it an Emperor or a lesser deity?) accidentally allowed a few leaves of the camellia shrub in his garden to fall into his vessel of boiling water. The brew that resulted had an unexpectedly pleasant flavour, and the experiment was deliberately repeated.

Certainly tea is closely related to the camellia. So it was a lucky chance, blessed by countless millions around the world to this day, when the first leaves were infused to produce the cup which cheers but does not inebriate. As a stimulant, digestive and generally pleasant drink, tea can have few rivals.

The varieties of Chinese tea are almost endless. Each region of the country produces its own speciality, and each can of course have a unique quality — hence the subsidiary, but subtle art of blending. The original shrub, the type of local soil and the local weather can make vast differences in flavour, just as they do with grapes and the resulting grape vine.

The connoisseurs of the tea world multiplied in the regions producing the most varieties of tea — in the south, for geographical reasons.

Some tea bushes are said to grow in such inaccessible gorges that only trained monkeys can pluck the leaves. Hangchow was famous for its three trees which produced the Ta Hung P'ao leaf (大紅袍), and this 'Big Red Robe' tea is reputed to have retailed at US$5.00 per ounce as long ago as 1930. Again, certain types of tea from Fukien are still prized (and priced) like the rarest liqueurs.

All manner of shapes and sizes of tea leaf are utilized in tea production; but the 'golden rule' is that the finest-quality end-product is to be obtained from the youngest leaves and buds.

Processing after picking decides the nature of the final flavour. Smoking and fermenting add strong notes to the brew, and other substances may be added for special tastes — jasmine, chrysanthemum, rose, lychee flowers and even ginger and bergamot are common.

But, when all is said and done, tea is only flavoured water, and a certain snobbery grew up around the quality of the water boiled for the pot. Melted mountain snow from a 'vintage' year and rain water from the first day of spring were particularly treasured for special occasions. Provided the local water is not heavily chlorinated, the modern-day tea drinker though, can be assured of a satisfactory cup of tea in almost any part of the world.

With Chinese tea, as with any tea, the use of freshly-drawn water is essential. The pot should be warmed before the dry leaves are added — one spoonful per person is the usual ratio, with one or more for the pot (porcelain or eathenware is more satisfactory than metal) if you like a strong flavour. When the water is really boiling, take the pot to the water and pour it in. Do not delay or the water will lose all its oxygen and give a flat taste to the tea. If the water is really boiling as it meets the tea, it should not be necessary to use a strainer. Wait no more than a few minutes before pouring out the tea, to prevent too much tannin from building up in the pot.

"As soon as the water begins to bubble, even though it means a break in conversation or an interruption of business, use it at once, or the very soul of the hot water will be lost."

Su I

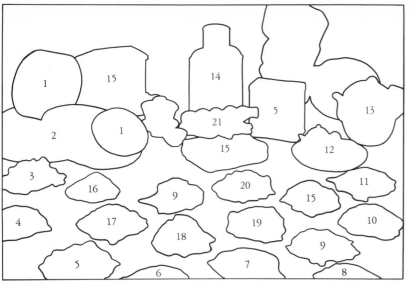

1. Ngan Ki Heung
2. Pu Erh
3. Black Tea
4. Tieh Lo Han Tea
5. Jasmine Tea
6. Rose Black Tea
7. Green Tea
8. Loong Ching Tea
9. Lu Au Tea
10. Ching Yuen
11. Shui Hsien
12. Chiu Chow teacups and pot
13. Teapot
14. Tea Container
15. Tieh Kuan Yin
16. Tea Powder
17. Oo Loong Tea
18. Lu Pao Tea
19. Pu Erh Tea
20. White Peony Tea
21. Jasmine Tea

Finally, do not hesitate to top up the pot with newly-boiled water as most Chinese teas lend themselves well to this treatment — until, or unless, their taste tells you otherwise.

Herbal teas are a study in themselves, but many of these restorative and curative brews are designed basically to refresh the drinker in hot weather. Allied to them are the familiar infusions that round off substantial Northern Chinese meals in particular. Quince, plum or

crab apple are often pulped, dried and reconstituted with hot water as a pleasant after-dinner drink, mid-way between digestive and dessert.

Alcoholic Drinks

In the Chinese languages, the general term *chiu* (酒) covers all wines and spirits, from drinks that are milder than sherry to colourless, flavourless distillations that are virtually pure alcohol.

It is difficult to get a clear picture of Chinese drinking habits in ancient times. The poets of the T'ang Dynasty (618-906), for example, were great ones for extolling the virtues of imbibing in the moonlight (though judging by their polished language, much of the labour of writing seems to have been undertaken in more sober conditions). Another indication is that more than 40 edicts have been promulgated in China during the past 2,500 years to impose a complete ban on alcohol. So, while each of these edicts was subsequently repealed, it has to be assumed that the introduction of such laws would not have been deemed necessary if consumption of alcohol had not been generally, and undesirably, high.

Perhaps all that needs to be said, then, is that a wide variety of alcoholic drinks — determined by local agriculture and climate — has long been produced throughout China.

If wine were not favoured by Heaven

No Wine Star would shine in the sky;

If wine were not loved by the Earth,

No Wine Spring would gush from her breast.

The blessing of Heaven, Earth's cordial stream

No man in his senses denies.

Li Po

The people of Kansu and Shensi were making wine from their famous grapes as long ago as in the seventh century AD. The first distillers' manual — describing how to make all types of liquor from almost every grain and fruit grown in China — was published in 1127. And European wines were among the more valued of the earliest imports from that part of the world, with Marco Polo writing of having seen and partaken of them during his stay in China in the 13th century. Beer, too, found its way into the country, and domestic breweries were established in the early 1900s under the direction of German and East European experts who passed on the technical know-how that supports the thriving brewing industry of today.

Three cups are the gateway to bliss;

A jar, and the world is all yours.

The rapture of drinking, and wine's dizzy joy,

No man who is sober deserves.

Li Po

However, spirits and other wines (or should that be wines and other spirits?) aside, the word *chiu* is most correctly translatable as 'wine distilled from rice'; and it is rice-based distillations — whether they are classified as wines or spirits — that are generally thought of as really 'typically Chinese'.

Two Chinese liquors are particularly deserving of mention, being equally well-known — albeit for rather different reasons. One is the notorious *Mao T'ai* (茅台), from Kweichow, which is the fiery millet-based wine (the undoing of so many uninitiates) drunk by Chairman Mao and President Nixon to toast each other at their first encounter. The other is *Shao Chiu* (紹酒), the finest yellow rice wine from Shaohsing, which is usually served warm (ideally, according to some experts, at blood temperature) and which goes down remarkably well, so to speak, with Westerners, who enjoy the benevolent effect that it produces when taken — in moderation, mind — on a cold evening. The best *Shao Chiu*

1. Shuang Jin Chiew
2. Huang Chiew
3. Seng Yung Yao Chiew
4. Chu Yeh Ching Chiew
5. Fen Chiew
6. Mei Kuei Lu Chiew
7. Dah Chu Chiew
8. Wu Chia Pi Chiew

9. Hu Gu Mu Gua Chiew
10. Pu Tao Chee Chiew
11. San Jin Chiew
12. Chia Fan Chiew
13. Yuk Ping Chun Chiew
14. Kuei Hua Chan Chiew
15. Lychee Chiew
16. Glutinous Rice Wine

17. Mou Tai Chiew
18. Shao-Hsing Hua Tiao Chiew
19. Wild-Grape Wine
20. China White Wine
21. Lien Hua Pai Chiew
22. Sam Shu Chiew
23. Kao Liang Chiew
24. Chin Lu Chiew

is reputedly that which has aged for anywhere between seven and as many as 15 years; and prudent parents in Shaohsing traditionally laid down a stock of this at the birth of a daughter, to form part of her dowry in later years.

The decision as to which alcoholic drink is the most pleasant accompaniment to a Chinese meal is a matter of taste ... and discretion.

Some Westerners who can afford champagne avow that there is nothing to match it. Other Westerners maintain that a medium-to-dry white wine is more than adequate. Still others drink their usual 'tipple' (whether it be whisky, vodka or somesuch) or beer.

"The man of refinement should strive to increase the number of rounds he can stand and so add to the number of his conquests and raise his prestige."

Sung Huang-fu

Much depends on where the meal is being eaten, as few Chinese restaurants offer anything like a wide selection of spirits and mixes, let alone a selection of Western wines. So diners either take along their own bottles or resign themselves to a choice of water, tea, soft drinks, Chinese wines, beer, whisky (usually) or brandy (almost always, especially in Hong Kong where the *per capita* consump-

tion of VSOP Cognac — not just brandy — is the highest of any country in the world!).

Ultimately, however, much more depends on the individual. Because, when all is said and done, only the most insensitive would allow the selection and supposed enjoyment of drinks, to go with a Chinese meal, to run more than a very poor second to the selection and genuine enjoyment of the dishes that make up the meal.

Bottoms up

Many games are mischievously resorted to by the Chinese to speed up the drinking process at all but the most formal dinner parties. There is the familiar 'stone, paper, scissors'. There is a game in which two players each show anything from one finger to all five fingers on one hand while calling out a number between one and 10 (the winner being the person who calls out the number equivalent to the total number of fingers shown). There is a variation on the 'fingers game' for more than two players which, frankly, defies description. There is a spoon-spinning game (the loser being the person in whose direction the bowl of the spoon points at the end of the spin). And there are many more — all calculated to induce a general sense of euphoria.

In every case the loser has to pay a forfeit, usually by downing the contents of his, or her, glass in one gulp. This variation of the Western 'bottoms up' practice goes by the name of *kan pei* (乾杯) or *yum sing* (飲勝) in Cantonese parlance; and it is all the more fiendish because custom dictates that a seemingly harmless series of toasts can end up in 'social warfare', with no-one's glass allowed to remain empty for longer than it takes someone to replenish it.

Glossary & Index

A listing of the ingredients called for in the recipes, showing such Western substitutes as may be used; together with an index of the recipes themselves and of the photographs of the many dishes illustrated.

Glossary

Glossary of Ingredients and Cooking Materials

The notes in this section are intended mainly for the guidance of readers in countries where the ingredients and cooking materials listed here are sufficiently 'foreign' as to be available only in specialist Chinese grocery stores in the form, of forms, indicated. In each case where a more readily available ingredient or cooking material may be substituted, its name is given.

Abalone （鮑魚）
A mollusc, the meat of which is firm and chewy in consistency. Sold (shelled) canned in liquid or dried. Canned abalone will keep indefinitely, after opening, if covered with fresh cold water and refrigerated (change the water daily). Dried abalone will keep indefinitely in dry conditions.

Agar Agar （大菜）
A gum produced from seaweed. Sold dried in flat sheets or translucent 'strings' about 30cm long. Substitute bean thread vermicelli in dishes where agar agar is used as a main ingredient.

Angled Luffa （勝瓜）
An elongated gourd with ridged, dark-green skin. Resembles a large okra and is also known as Chinese okra or Silk Squash. Substitute: bitter melon or zucchini.

Anise Star （八角）
An eight pointed star-shaped spice with a strong anise flavour. Sold in 'points' i.e. broken, whole or ground. An ingredient of Five-Spices Powder.

Bamboo Fungus （竹笙）
A lacy fungal growth gathered from bamboo plants in the Szechwan region and dried. Usually used in vegetarian cooking. Very expensive — late 1978 retail price in Hongkong, around US$750 a kilo. Bamboo Shoots are not a suitable substitute.

Bamboo Shoots/Winter Bamboo Shoots （筍／冬筍）
The shoots of the bamboo tree. Sold fresh or canned in liquid. Fresh bamboo shoots are covered with a thick layer of leaves which must be removed.

Canned bamboo shoots will keep for several weeks, after opening, if covered with fresh cold water and refrigerated (change the water daily). Winter Bamboo Shoots are of a softer, less fibrous texture, having a more delicate flavour.

Beancurd （豆腐）
A cream-coloured, jelly-like 'cake' produced from liquid extracted from soya beans and set with gypsum. Bland in flavour. Will keep for up to a week if covered with cold water and refrigerated (change the water daily). Now available in instant powdered form.

Beancurd, Dry（豆腐乾）: a firmer 'cake' produced by compressing soft beancurd to extract more liquid. Will keep for at least a week if refrigerated.

Beancurd Cubes, Fried （炸豆腐）: cubes of soft beancurd deep-fried until their surface is brown and crusty and their inside almost dry. Will keep for several weeks in dry conditions.

302

Beancurd Cubes, Preserved (辣腐乳): cubes of soft beancurd preserved in a solution of brine and wine with chillies to produce a red-coloured, strong-flavoured seasoning. Also known as Preserved Beancurd and Chinese Cheese.

Beancurd Skins, Dried (腐皮): thick, yellowish translucent sheets of dried soya bean liquid. Used as an edible wrapping. Dissolves in water after slow heating, to produce soya bean milk.

Beancurd Sticks, Dried (腐竹): yellowish strips of dried soya bean liquid. Used frequently in vegetarian cooking. Keeps indefinitely in dry conditions.

Bean Pastes (乾豉醬)

Sauces produced from soya beans and other ingredients, depending on the flavour required. Sold canned, in jars or by weight at specialist stores. Canned bean paste will keep for several months, after opening, if transferred to a screw-top jar and refrigerated. Bean paste in jars will keep for several months without refrigeration.

Hot Bean Paste (香豉辣醬): produced from soya beans with chillies and oil. Very hot and slightly salty.

Soya Bean Paste (磨豉醬): dark brown, salty paste made from ground, fermented black soya beans.

Sweet Bean Paste (甜豉醬): produced from fermented black soya beans, flour, sugar and spices. Substitute: Hoisin sauce.

Yellow Bean Paste (豆瓣醬): produced from fermented yellow soya beans (often left whole), very salty in flavour. Substitute: soya bean paste or Japanese Miso paste.

Beans Sprouts

Shoots of the mung bean (芽菜) or the soya bean (大豆芽菜) the latter being much larger and stronger-flavoured. Sold fresh or canned in liquid. Fresh bean sprouts will keep for several days if refrigerated in a perforated plastic bag. Canned bean sprouts will keep for several weeks, after opening, if covered with fresh cold water and refrigerated (change the water daily).

Before using, pick out any greying shoots, which would give a bitter taste to a dish if used.

When roots and seed pods are removed from mung bean sprouts, the result is known as Silver Sprouts (銀芽).

Bean Thread Vermicelli (see noodles)

Beche-de-Mer (海參)
Also known as the Sea Slug (an apt description), the Sea Cucumber or Sea Bear. Sold dried. Will keep indefinitely in dry conditions. For method of preparation, see page 185.

Bird's Nest (燕窩)
Edible bird's nests, see page 57.

Bitter Melon (涼瓜)
As the name implies, a bitter tasting small melon, rather resembling a wrinkled cucumber. Sometimes available canned. Cucumber or zucchini can be substituted.

Black Beans (豆豉)
Salted, fermented black soya beans. Lightly salty in flavour. Used as seasoning. Will keep indefinitely in dry conditions.

Broccoli, Chinese (芥蘭)
A bright green stem vegetable bearing small yellow clusters of flowers, resembling miniature broccoli. Sold fresh. Substitute Chinese flowering white cabbage or broccoli.

Black Vinegar (see vinegar)

Brown Peppercorns (花椒)
These bear little resemblance to black peppercorns, being of a pungent, slightly anise flavour and aroma. Should be roasted lightly in a dry pan and ground before use. Will keep indefinitely in dry conditions. Also known as Szechwan Pepper or Fagara. An ingredient of Five-Spices Powder.

Cabbage, Chinese White
There are two varieties of Chinese white cabbage *pai t'sai* (白菜) (in Cantonese, pak choy) and the more tender flowering white cabbage, *t'sai sum* (菜心) (in Cantonese, choy sum). Sold fresh. If

unavailable, substitute Tientsin cabbage, or Western cabbage.

Camphor Wood Chips （樟木屑）
Aromatic wood chips used for smoking poultry and fish, particularly in the Western provinces. Substitute pine wood or black tea leaves.

Celery, Chinese （中國芹）
Similar to Western celery, but smaller and with a more pronounced flavour.

Chao Pai Salted Fish （see fish, dried）

Chestnuts, Water （馬蹄）
The bulb-like stem of the tule or other bulrush. Crisp in texture and sweet in flavour. Sold canned in liquid or dried and ground into flour (ideal for making batter — though very expensive). Canned water chestnuts will keep for about a month, after opening, if covered with fresh water and refrigerated (change the water daily). Dried water chestnut powder will keep indefinitely in dry conditions.

Chicken Blood, Coagulated （雞血）
Fresh chicken blood set with a solidifying agent and steamed. Used in soups and stews. If unavailable, no substitute is necessary.

Chicken Fat, Rendered （鮮雞油）
Pure chicken fat used as a seasoning. For method of preparation, see page 278.

Chilli Oil （辣椒油）
A hot seasoning produced by infusing heated vegetable oil with dried chillies. Sold in bottles.

Chilli Paste （椒蒜醬）
A seasoning sauce or condiment produced from ground fresh chillies, garlic and other spices. Sold in jars.

Chilli Sauce （辣椒醬）
A seasoning agent and condiment produced from red chillies and vinegar. Very hot and slightly sour in taste. Sold in bottles.

Chinese Cheese （see beancurd cubes, preserved）

Chive Shoots （韭黃）
Chives grown under cover to prevent them from becoming dark green. Delicate, though pungent, in flavour. Sold fresh. Will keep for several days if refrigerated in a perforated plastic bag. Also known as Garlic Chives.

Chives Flowering （韭菜花）
A type of chive, having slightly thicker and more fibrous stems and bearing small fragrant white flowers. See also pages 58 and 61.

Chu Hau Sauce （柱候醬）
A thick, dryish brown seasoning paste made from beans, flour and spices. Used in stews and braised dishes.

Cinnamomum Cassia (Cinnamon Bark) （玉桂）
The coarse outer bark of the cinnamon tree. Different in texture and flavour from the smoother cinnamon quills. An ingredient of Five-Spices Powder.

Cloud Ear Fungus （see mushrooms）

Conpoy（江瑤柱）
A shell-fish related to (and often confused with) the scallop. Dried, its meat is used as a seasoning and occasionally as a main ingredient. Expensive. Will keep indefinitely in dry conditions.

Curry Oil （咖喱油）
A seasoning oil produced by infusing vegetable oil with curry powder.

Cuttlefish (Squid) （墨魚）
A mollusc resembling a small octopus. Used in dried form in soups as a seasoning. Used fresh in seafood dishes.

Dai Chu Wine (see wines)

Dates, Black Chinese (蜜棗)
Dried prunelike fruits which must be soaked to soften before use. Used for sweet fillings. Will keep indefinitely in dry conditions. Also sold crystallized.

Dates, Red Dried (紅棗)
Wrinkled red pods with a musky, sweet flavour and distinct fragrance. Will keep, in dry conditions, for many months.

Dry Beancurd (see beancurd, dry)

Duck Egg, Salted (鹹鴨蛋)
Yolks of preserved duck eggs, resembling dried apricots. Used in sweet fillings, particularly the Moon Cakes made for the Mid-Autumn festival. If soft, they should be steamed before use. Unopened, salted eggs will keep for several months. The yolks may be kept in the refrigerator, covered, for one or two days.

Duck, Dried (臘鴨)
A duck — with the bones removed — coated with seasoning and hung to dry. Then compressed to flatten. Used as a flavouring agent in soup stocks.

Fagara (see brown peppercorns)

Fa Ts'ai／Fat Choy (髮菜)
Known also as Hair Vegetable or Black Moss as in its dried state it resembles a bundle of black hair. Actually a type of seaweed. Used particularly in Chinese New Year cooking because of the auspicious connotations of the name in Cantonese, which translates as 'prosperity'.

Fennel (小茴香)
A sweet seed spice, one of the ingredients of Five-Spices Powder.

Fish, Dried (鹹魚)
Produced from all types of fish through a process of curing with salt, and sun drying. Extremely fishy and pungent in aroma and flavour. Used as a main ingredient and as a flavouring agent. One of the most popular varieties is Chao Pai (鰽白).

Fish Sauce (魚露)
A thin light-brown sauce made from salted dried fish. Used as a seasoning and occasionally as a condiment.

Five-Spices Powder (五香粉)
A strong seasoning comprising equal parts of powdered brown peppercorns (fagara), cinnamon bark (cinnamomum cassia), clove, fennel and anise star or aniseed, the spices being finely ground.

Five-Spices Bouquets, used to add flavour to stocks and the 'master sauce' (Lu Shui). Made with the above spices, in whole form wrapped in a small square of cloth. See preparation, page 277.

Flour

Unleavened Wheat Flour (麥粉): finely ground, is used for making most steamed breads and some pastries. Additionally, the following are used in specific recipes.

High Gluten Flour (高筋粉): a special kind of 'strong' flour, which gives extreme elasticity, making it possible to roll out the dough to very fine layers. Used for wonton wrappers.

Rice Powder (粘米粉): a finely ground flour made from polished white rice and necessary to give a particular texture to certain pastries.

Tang Flour (筋粉): low-gluten content, finely-ground wheat flour which, when cooked becomes almost transparent. Used for making clear wrappers for 'dim sum'.

Cornstarch (Cornflour) (鷹粟粉): a finely-ground maize flour used as a thickening agent. It produces clear, viscose sauces.

Fried Beancurd Cubes: (see beancurd cubes, fried)

Fungi (see mushrooms)

Ginger （羌）
Fresh root ginger is a vital ingredient in Chinese cooking. (See also page 76). Powdered and preserved ginger are not satisfactory substitutes.

Ginger Juice （羌汁）
A flavouring agent and tenderiser made with fresh root ginger. See page 277.

Gingko Nuts （白果）
Small oval-shaped or round-shaped nuts. Tender and fleshy in texture. Used in stuffings, soups and stews. Sold canned in liquid, or dried.

Glutinous Rice （糯米）
Opaque, slightly long-grain rice of a particular type which, when cooked, turns almost transparent and very sticky. Used in puddings and as a sweet or savoury stuffing. Also known as 'Sticky Rice'.

Golden Fungus (see mushrooms)

Golden Needles (see lily flowers)

Hairy Gourd (see marrow, Chinese)

Hoisin Sauce （海鮮醬）
A seasoning sauce or condiment produced from red beans, soya beans, sugar and spices. Sweet-spicy and tangy in flavour. Many uses. Sold canned or in jars. Will keep indefinitely, after opening. Also known as Seafood Sauce and Barbecue Sauce.

Hot Bean Paste (see bean paste)

Jelly Fish, Dried （海蜇）
A gelatinous oceanic fish with a multi-tentacled inverted saucer-shaped body. Chewy in texture and bland in flavour. Used as a main ingredient. Sold (with tentacles removed) dried and 'squared' or dried and shredded. Occasionally available pre-soaked.

For method of preparation, see page 132.

Kale （芥蘭）
Leafy green vegetable, see photograph page 58. Also known as Chinese Broccoli.

Kaoliang Wine (Liquor) (see wines)

Leaf Mustard (see mustard greens)

Lily Flowers （金針菜）
The gold-coloured buds of the tiger-lily, musky in flavour. Used as a flavouring agent, especially in vegetarian dishes. Sold dried. Will keep indefinitely in dry conditions.

Lotus Leaf （蓮葉）
Fresh or dried leaves of the lotus plant are used to wrap foods prior to cooking, and impart a distinct flavour and fine aroma.

Lotus Root （蓮藕）
The root of the lotus plant. Crunchy in texture and delicately sweet in flavour. Used in soups and vegetarian dishes and when crystallized as a sweet meat. Sold fresh, canned in liquid, dried and sliced, and crystallized. Fresh lotus root will keep for two to three weeks, if refrigerated in a perforated plastic bag. Canned lotus root will keep for one week, after opening, if covered with fresh cold water in a screw-top jar. Dried and crystallized lotus root will keep indefinitely in dry conditions.

Lotus Seeds （蓮子）
The seeds of the lotus flower. Hard in texture and delicate in flavour. Used as a flavouring agent in soups and sweets and as a tit-bit.

Lotus Seed Paste （蓮蓉）
Sold canned or dried. A rich, sweet dryish paste made by cooking mashed lotus seeds with sugar and oil. It will keep for many months in a covered container in the refrigerator.

'Lu Shui' Sauce (in Cantonese 'Lu Soy') (滷水汁)

A 'master sauce' or more accurately, a stock made with soy sauce, sugar, five-spices and ginger. Used for simmering foods, particularly poultry. It gives a rich flavour and deep brown colour. For recipe see page 157.

Maltose (see sugar)

Marrow, Chinese (節瓜)

A green-skinned vegetable resembling a cucumber, but with a slightly hairy skin. Substitute: cucumber or zucchini. Also known as Chinese cucumber or Hairy Gourd.

Mao Tou Green Peas (毛豆)

Small peas, grown in the north, with dark-green, slightly hairy pods which should be removed. Substitute; lima beans.

Matrimony Vine (枸杞)

A shrub (Latin name: lycium barbarum), the leaves of which are used as a flavouring agent. Also known in the West as Box-thorn.

Melon, Winter (冬瓜)

A very large, light green skinned melon with soft, white flesh. Delicate in taste. Available cubed, canned in liquid. Substitute: cucumber or baby marrow.

Monosodium Glutamate (味精)

A white crystalline substance. Used as a meat tenderiser and as a flavouring agent in savoury dishes. Sold under various brand names: e.g. Ve Tsin, Aji No Moto. Also known as Taste Powder. It may be omitted, see note pages 76 and 101.

Mue Kwe Lo Wine (see wines)

Mulberry Paper (臘光紙)

A non-edible paper. Used as a wrapping during cooking. Not to be confused with the Paper Mulberry plant, the leaves of which may be eaten as a vegetable. Substitute: well-oiled tissue paper or greaseproof paper.

Mushrooms

Black Mushrooms, Dried (冬菇): greyish black mushrooms. Fragrant when cooked. Best are thick and firm, pale cream on the underside. Must be soaked to soften before use. Always remove the whole stem.

Brown Mushrooms, Dried (花菇): paler in colour than black mushrooms. More expensive.

Button Mushrooms (鈕粒白菌): canned champignons.

Cloud Ear Fungus, Dried (雲耳): dark brown fungus in wrinkled 'ear' shapes. Bland taste, musky aroma, crunchy texture. Used in vegetarian cooking and stews.

Golden Fungus, Dried (黃耳): pale golden mushroom-like fungus. Used mainly in vegetarian cooking. Expensive. Substitute: black mushrooms or cloud ear fungus.

Straw Mushrooms (鮮草菇): sold fresh or canned. Fresh, they can be kept in the refrigerator for only a few days. Canned, they will keep for at least a week after opening, if covered with fresh cold water and refrigerated (change water daily).

Mustard Greens (芥菜)

A green leaf vegetable. Crunchy in texture and slightly bitter in flavour. Used in soups and stir-fried dishes. Also known as Leaf Mustard.

Noodles

Bean Thread Vermicelli (粉絲): thin, transparent noodles produced from mung-bean flour (must be soaked before use).

Hand-made Noodles (拉麵): thick noodles produced from wheat flour dough by a process of stretching the dough by hand until the required diameter has been achieved.

Rice Sheet Noodles (河粉): wide, flat noodles produced by cutting sheets of steamed rice flour batter into strips. Also sold dried.

Rice Stick Noodles (米粉): thin noodles produced from rice flour (they expand when deep-fried to become very light and crisp). Also known as Rice Vermicelli.

Shanghai Noodles, Thin (上海麵): wheat flour based thin noodles of whitish colour, used most frequently in soups.

Shanghai Noodles, Thick (上海粗麵): spaghetti-like yellowish noodles made with wheat flour and egg. Sold in dried form or fresh. The latter can be kept in a plastic bag in the refrigerator for at least one week.

Oil, Cooked (Vegetable) (菜油)
Vegetable oil that has been used at least once for deep-frying. Used in preference to uncooked oil for stir-frying as it imparts a better flavour.

Okra, Chinese (see angled luffa)

Osmanthus Flowers (桂花)
Sweet scented small white flowers which grow profusely in the Kweilin area. Usually preserved in spirit with sugar, and are also added to certain wines to produce a liqueur favoured by women.

Oyster Sauce (蠔油)
A viscose dark-brown sauce produced from oysters and soy sauce through a process of fermentation. Used as a flavouring and/or colouring agent and as a condiment. Sold in bottles. Keeps for several months.

Parsley, Chinese (芫茜)
Fresh coriander, a herb of Near Eastern origin and properly called Mexican Cilantro (Chinese Parsley is a mismoner). So strong in flavour as to be an 'acquired taste'. Used as a flavouring agent and as a garnish.

Western parsley is not a substitute, except as a garnish.

Plum Sauce (梅醬)
A sweet/sour tasting thick sauce produced from Chinese sour plums and seasoning ingredients. Used as a condiment, a flavouring agent and as the base for other sauces. Sold canned or in jars.

Preserved Beancurd (see beancurd cubes, preserved)

Preserved Vegetables (see vegetables, preserved)

Red Beans (紅豆)
Small, hard dried red beans used to make sweet soups and fillings, the latter being known as Sweet Red Bean Paste (紅豆沙), see recipe page 278.

Red Vinegar (see vinegar)

Rice Crackers, Crispy (鍋巴)
'Cakes' of dried, puffed glutinous rice. If unavailable, see page 227 for method of preparation.

Rice Paper (米紙)
An edible paper, produced from the pith of a tree (Latin name: aralia papyrifera) and not from rice. Used as a wrapping during cooking and for sweetmeats.

Rice Powder (see flour)

Rice Sheet Noodles (see noodles)

Rice Stick Noodles (see noodles)

Rock Sugar (see sugar)

Rose Dew Wine (see wines)

Saltpetre (硝)
A crystalline substance. Used as a preservative for meats. Also known as niter or potassium nitrate.

Salted Fish (see fish, dried)

Samshu Wine (see wines)

Scallions (葱)
A vegetable of the onion family, having long deep-green stalks, bulbous white bases. Resembles a small leek. Known in some countries as the Spring Onion. Not to be confused with the small purple onion with a strong flavour, called the Shallot, which, in certain countries, may be known as the Scallion.

Sesame Oil (麻油)
An aromatic oil produced from sesame seeds through a process of extraction. Used as a seasoning, as a flavouring agent and as an ingredient in certain sauces. It is not used as a cooking oil. Sold in bottles.

Sesame Paste (芝麻醬)
A creamy paste produced from white sesame seeds through a process of grinding. The surface of better-quality sesame pastes carries a layer of oil that should be mixed in before use. Sold canned or in jars. Also known as tahin or tahina. Substitute: creamy peanut butter.

Sesame Seeds (Black) (黑芝麻)
Small black seeds from the sesame plant. Used to make a thick sweet soup of distinctive flavour, and occasionally as a garnish.

Sesame Seeds (White) (白芝麻)
White small seeds from the sesame plant. Used as a garnish, and in making sweets and fillings. Also used for making sesame paste.

Shanghai Crabs (上海毛蟹)
Small, 'hairy' crabs from the waters off the coast near Shanghai. The meat is delightfully sweet in flavour and the yellow 'yolk' is considered to be a particular delicacy.

Shanghai Salted Cabbage (see vegetables, preserved)

Shanghai Preserved Vegetables (see vegetables, preserved)

Shao Hsing Wine (see wines)

Shark's Fin (魚翅)
Edible gelatinous whole dried shark's fins. See also page 57.
For method of preparation, see page 188.

Shark's Fin 'Needles' (散魚翅)
The 'strands' comprising Shark's Fin — dried, cleaned and processed ready for use.

Shrimps, Dried (蝦米)
Very small shrimps — dried, cleaned and processed, ready for use. Strong in flavour. Used as a main ingredient and as a flavouring agent. Keep indefinitely in dry conditions.

Shrimp Paste (蝦醬)
A pungent paste produced from fresh shrimps through a process of fermentation, grinding and extraction. Strong and salty in flavour. Used as a flavouring agent. Sold in jars. Keeps for several months.

Silver Sprouts (see bean sprouts)

Slab Sugar (see sugar)

Snow Peas (雪豆)
Bright green crisp textured pea pods, eaten whole. Seasonal — winter crop. Also known as Mange Tout. Keep for at least a week in a perforated plastic bag in the refrigerator.

Soy Sauce (豉油)
Sauces extracted from the soya bean. See pages 77 and 78.

Soya Bean Paste (see bean paste)

Spinach, Water （甕菜）
A leafy green vegetable, with a delicate flavour similar to spinach which can be substituted.

Spring Roll Wrappers （春卷皮）
Paper thin wrappers produced by passing a ball of soft flour and water dough over a hotplate where it will dry into a white skin-like wrapper. Sold in packs of 25 or 50, frozen. Should not be exposed to the air for long or they will crack and become unusable. Store in the freezing compartment of the refrigerator, well wrapped in plastic. If unavailable, see page 226 for preparation method.

Squid (see cuttlefish)

Star Anise (see anise, star)

Straw Mushrooms (see mushrooms)

Sugar
Maltose （麥芽糖）: a molasses-like substance produced from germinating grains (particularly grains of barley), through a process similar to wine making. Also known as malt-sugar. Substitute: treacle, honey, golden syrup.

Rock Sugar （冰糖）: a crystallized sugar. Also known as rock candy. Substitute, a concentrate of granulated sugar.

Slab Sugar （片糖）: produced from dark-brown, semi-refined sugar through a process of compression. Substitute dark-brown sugar.

Sweet Bean Paste (see bean paste)

Sweet Vinegar (see vinegar)

Szechwan Pepper (see brown peppercorns)

Tang Flour (see flour)

Tangerine Peel, Dried （果皮）
Pieces of sun-dried tangerine peel. The best are several years old. Store in an airtight container. Used as a seasoning for stews. Expensive. Can be omitted from a recipe.

Tientsin Cabbage （天津白菜）
Creamy white, tightly packed cabbage, known also — confusingly — as Chinese cabbage. Leaves are thin and crinkled, with thick central stalks. Usually expensive. Substitute: Chinese white cabbage or Western cabbage.

Vegetables
See illustration, page 58 , for commonly used Chinese vegetables.

Vegetables, Preserved
There are innumerable types of preserved vegetables used in Chinese cooking and they are preserved by a variety of processes, including salting, sun drying, pickling in a brine solution, or pickling with vinegar and seasonings, including red chilli.

Most commonly used are **Preserved Mustard Greens** （咸酸菜）: preserved in a strong vinegar solution. They keep indefinitely without refrigeration.

Salted Cabbage （梅菜）: the Chinese white cabbage (pai ts'ai or pak choy) pickled in salt and partially dried. Sold by weight or in cans.

Preserved Shanghai Vegetable （雪菜）: the salt preserved tops of the giant white radish （蘿蔔）, the root of which is also pickled and served as an appetizer. Sold by weight and in cans.

Szechwan Preserved Vegetables （榨菜）: made from salted turnips, radish or even Tientsin cabbage, preserved in a brine solution. Used as a flavouring agent, main ingredient and appetizer. Available canned or in jars.

Radish, cucumber and cabbage pickled in salt, with chilli added to taste, can be prepared in advance and used as an effective substitute for any of the above preserved vegetables.

Vermicelli, Bean Thread (see noodles)

Vinegar
Chinese vinegars, of which there are four main types, are prepared from a distillation of fermented rice by a process similar to wine making.

Black Vinegar (黑米醋): deep-brown coloured strong flavoured vinegar used as a flavouring agent and occasionally as a condiment.

Red Vinegar (浙醋): bright amber coloured rice vinegar used as a condiment, particularly with seafood dishes. Also used in flavouring sauces.

Sweet Vinegar (甜醋): rich black vinegar, very sweet in taste, yet with a pronounced pungency. Used for braised and stewed dishes.

White Vinegar (白醋): clear, mild flavoured vinegar, Western distilled vinegar may be substituted, but is considerably stronger, so should be used in moderation in these recipes.

Water Chestnuts (see chestnuts, water)

Water Spinach (see spinach, water)

White Fungus, Dried (銀耳)
A crinkly off-white coloured fungus, which when soaked expands dramatically. Believed to ensure a clear, healthy complexion and is therefore sold primarily by Chinese Herbalists. A crunchy texture, but bland flavour. Expensive. Known also as Snow Fungus or Silver Fungus.

Wine
See illustration, page 298.
See also pages 297 and 300.

Wine Lees (紅糟)
The paste-like sediment of a type of red Chinese wine, stored in jars with red rice grains, which cause a further fermentation. Very difficult to obtain. May be found in some Shanghainese specialist grocery stores. Substitute: Japanese light Miso paste, or see page 278 for recipe.

Winter Melon (see melon, winter)

Wonton Wrappers (雲吞皮)
Opaque, pliable, dried 'skins'; produced from a dough made of special high-gluten flour and eggs. Sold fresh or frozen and can be kept in the freezer for several months (thaw before use) or in a plastic container in the refrigerator for up to a week. If unavailable, see page 226 for preparation method.

Yellow Bean Paste (see bean paste)

Yinh Hsieng Hua (香荽花)
Sweet smelling small white blossoms from a tendril-like plant of the Magnolia family (Latin name: magnolia pumila). Used as a decoration. May also be known as Chinese Mint.

Yunnan Ham (雲腿)
Produced through a process of salting and smoking. Substitute: best quality salted, smoked Western ham.

Index

Index to Recipes

Buns and Pastries

Special Occasions

Sauces and Dips

Index to Recipe Photographs

Measurement Conversion Chart

All measurements have been listed in Metric, with the Imperial equivalents in parenthesis. The following table of conversions has been used showing Metric, Imperial and the approximate Chinese measurements. American cooks can use this same table for solid weights, and may refer to the additional table below for volume measurements using the standard American Metric measuring cup, and American standard Metric measuring spoons.

Solid Measurements

Metric	Imperial	Chinese
15 g	½ oz	
30 g	1 oz	
60 g	2 oz	1½ taels
90 g	3 oz	
125 g	4 oz (¼ lb)	3½ taels
155 g	5 oz	
185 g	6 oz	
220 g	7 oz	
250 g	8 oz (½ lb)	7 taels
280 g	9 oz	
315 g	10 oz	
345 g	11 oz	
375 g	12 oz (¾ lb)	10 taels
410 g	13 oz	
440 g	14 oz	
470 g	15 oz	
500 g (½ kg)	16 oz (1 lb)	14 taels
625 g	1¼ lb	1 catty (16 taels)
750 g (¾ kg)	1½ lb	
1 kg	2 lb	
1¼ kg	2½ lb	
1½ kg	3 lb	
2 kg	4 lb	

Liquid Measurements

Metric	Imperial	American
30 ml	1 fl oz	
60 ml	2 fl oz	¼ cup
100 ml	3 fl oz	
125 ml	4 fl oz	½ cup
150 ml	5 fl oz (¼ pt)	
200 ml	6 fl oz	¾ cup
225 ml	7 fl oz	
250 ml	8 fl oz	1 cup
275 ml	9 fl oz	
315 ml	10 fl oz (½ pt)	1¼ cups
375 ml	12 fl oz	1½ cups
425 ml	14 fl oz	1¾ cups
500 ml	16 fl oz	2 cups
625 ml	20 fl oz (1 pt)	2½ cups
750 ml	24 fl oz	3 cups
1 lit	32 fl oz	4 cups
1¼ lit	40 fl oz	5 cups
1½ lit	48 fl oz	6 cups
1¾ lit	56 fl oz	7 cups
2 lit	64 fl oz	8 cups

Volume Measurements

Ingredient	Metric	Imperial	American
Flour	220 g	7 oz	2 cups
Sugar	220 g	7 oz	1 cup
Rice	220 g	7 oz	1 cup
Chopped Vegetables	220 g	7 oz	1 cup
Cornstarch	15 g	½ oz	1 level tablespoon
Sugar	30 g	1 oz	1 level tablespoon